A State of *Arrested Development*

A State of
Arrested Development

*Critical Essays on the
Innovative Television Comedy*

Edited by KRISTIN M. BARTON

Foreword by MITCHELL HURWITZ

McFarland & Company, Inc., Publishers
Jefferson, North Carolina

ALSO OF INTEREST

Fan CULTure: Essays on Participatory Fandom in the 21st Century. Edited by Kristin M. Barton and Jonathan Malcolm Lampley (McFarland, 2014)

LIBRARY OF CONGRESS CATALOGUING-IN-PUBLICATION DATA

A state of Arrested development : critical essays on the innovative
   television comedy / edited by Kristin M. Barton; foreword by
Mitchell Hurtwitz.
        p.   cm.
      Includes bibliographical references and index.

   ISBN 978-0-7864-7991-7 (softcover : acid free paper) ∞
   ISBN 978-1-4766-1938-5 (ebook)

    1. Arrested development (Television program)   I. Barton, Kristin
Michael, 1977–, editor.
   PN1992.77.A785S83 2015
   791.45'72—dc23   2014049668

BRITISH LIBRARY CATALOGUING DATA ARE AVAILABLE

Cover graphics © Dreamstime.com

Printed in the United States of America

McFarland & Company, Inc., Publishers
   Box 611, Jefferson, North Carolina 28640
   www.mcfarlandpub.com

For Wyatt—
You're the most important thing.

And for all of Wyatt's cousins,
both through blood and love,
none of whom will hopefully ever
use him to teach me a lesson:
Miranda, Daniel, Shelby, Anthony,
Jett, Billy, Lyla, Ryann, and Tyshon.

Acknowledgments

A book never comes to be as a solitary act, and as such there are always people who help in various ways that make an endeavor like this possible.

I'm thankful for my friends and colleagues who assisted by reading early drafts of chapters and offering their feedback in spite of their busy schedules: Dr. Joe Keener, Ms. Barbara Tucker, and Dr. Michael Graves. Also, Mr. Robert Lavache made himself available into the late hours of the night as a sounding board while I was working on the book's title.

My wife Gina spent more afternoons than I care to admit watching our son while I locked myself away in the office writing. This book couldn't exist without her patience and understanding.

But most importantly, I am forever indebted to Mitchell Hurwitz, not only for creating one of the best shows that's ever been on television, but for being a generous and magnanimous human being. Mitch indulged all of my calls, texts, and e-mails despite having obligations and deadlines of his own, and never once hesitated to offer his help in any way that he could. His success is not only well deserved, but also reaffirms my faith that good guys really can come out on top.

Table of Contents

Foreword: A Prebuttal

Mitchell Hurwitz

Arrested Development was designed to be about one thing above all else:

Hello. Thank you for your interest in this book—and by implication the show.

That's not the one thing *Arrested Development* was designed to be. I just realized I should have opened with that, and since I had your attention because of the colon I figured I should acknowledge the oversight, even if it did mean depriving myself of the most "attention-getting" of all the punctuation marks.

But don't worry, the seasoned writer has an arsenal of manipulations to refocus the reader to his desired reductivism. My favorite shame is the "promise of a tantalizing personal anecdote" that hits the reader halfway through the author's message—before even realizing no pledged titillation would ever materialize. I'll never forget who taught me this literary gambit ... and how it almost cost me my virginity.

Arrested Development was designed to be about getting laughs. That was really the *"pan aux raisin"* as one might say in France—if your whole *reason for being there* was to try the raisin bread. All the creative choices of the show were really in service of that.

And so the E.B. White apothegm (pronounced: [*coughing sound*]) must ineluctably be mentioned—how the analysis of humor is like the dissection of a frog, in that it *can* be done but the frog tends to die in the process. But as Lindsay herself might say after a day in the wetlands—"what are we trying to save this f**king frog for? Besides, it's *our* frog." And it is, Lindsay—good point (*he says, saying "good point" to himself because there is no "Lindsay"*). Besides, it's not like we're trying to cut up E.B. White. Although I'm certainly not the first to point out that carving up the author of *Charlotte's Web* is a little like forcing Bertrand Russell into an industrial juicer, in that it *can* be done, but it does strain the credible.

I actually think that as soon as you try to get an audience to laugh—*to actually make a noise*—in response to a creative work, you really can't complain about them continuing to discuss, criticize, make connections to, or find a way to relate to it as well. It's your frog now—it's been handed over to your brains—and I've always said the brain is the most important organ. Although, full disclosure—it's always been my brain's idea for me to say that.

Am I being too coy in saying all of this about a show that concerned itself with topics ranging from incest to entitlement? What if I sit over here on this porch glider and say it? You know, with a sort of sideways smile—kind of an "*I see you Mister!*" twinkle in my eye? Well ... maybe I am. *You guys know me too well!*

When I say the show was about comedy first ... I don't mean that's *all* it was about. *Arrested Development* chose to be funny through characters that struggled in ways that many of us do. And the show endeavored to place these characters in some simulacrum of the real world. And yes, that real world contains a lot of misinformed people. And sometimes depicting this runs the risk of "crossing a line," or dealing with issues of race, or sexual mores. But if there is truth in the storytelling, and if the themes are universal, a creator must trust that they're on the right side of the issue.

Who among us hasn't, for instance, tried to dupe some Asian developers into thinking a housing tract is nearly finished by harnessing the power of "forced perspective"? And how many of us have inadvertently cast aspersions on the cinematic history of a people by having a full size person trample this tiny town? Sure, maybe we're not actually dressed up like giant mole, and maybe a fight doesn't ensue with a boy in jet pack *at that exact* moment.... But we certainly have all struggled to understand the complicated video instructions that the Japanese jet pack people expect us to understand even though the video makes it *more* confusing!

But of course this is the great bulwark of the writer against the critics of his/her imputed social statements. Writing characters also allows one the chance to depict the problem without suggesting the answer. Fortunately it's not up to the creatives to deliver on a thesis statement, because the audience ends up feeling like "what do you need us for?" The Bluths provided a wonderful filter through which selfish behavior can be laughed at or viewed symbolically. What keeps them from being purely symbolic, however, are those moments when they behave unexpectedly. As Jeffrey Tambor once told me when I apologized for a George Sr. moment that had no precedent: "Are you kidding me? Character *is* inconsistency." It was a powerful lesson for me about a fundamental incongruity in the creative process—and then, almost as if to prove his point, he took a flower from a vase, affixed it to my lapel, and then rammed my head into a scissor lift.

And finally, I will say that at the heart of many of these stories there are two central themes: Fear, which is the great engine of misguided behavior and leads to so many of our mistakes as human beings, and the desire to be loved, which comprises all the rest of them. Fear is often about change—it's about hanging onto one's idealized self—no matter how miserable it has *consistently* proven to make us. And the desire to be loved for our actual self, which ... really ... we're mostly right in trying to cover up. And so there is this moment in our culture where we remain stuck like bacteria in an agar of arrested development. Our only hope is the sort of act three denouement wherein all inauthentic actions have failed and we are forced to stand before each other flaws and all. This is a fundamental law of the universe with one exception: That I'm probably wrong and just making all this shit up.

Mitchell Hurwitz is the Emmy award winning creator/writer/director/producer of *Arrested Development*. As a writer, he has worked on sitcoms such as *The Golden Girls*, *The John Larroquette Show*, and *The Ellen Show*, among others. He also created the Fox series *Running Wilde* and developed the animated series *Sit Down, Shut Up* based on the live-action Australian show of the same name. He can be found on Twitter by following the account @Mitch Hurwitz.

Introduction

Kristin M. Barton

I have two good friends that I've known since high school, and when we're able to get together we often find ourselves playing a game where we debate how we would respond to various hypothetical situations. *If you had to completely give up one food group and could never eat it again, what would it be?* (Meat.) *If someone was making a movie about your life, who would you want to play you?* (Harrison Ford.) And of course, the most difficult question of all: *If you could only watch one television show for the rest of your life, what would it be?*

Being a communication scholar and someone who watches a lot of TV, I naturally took the question seriously. On the one hand, I love Joss Whedon's short-lived series *Firefly* (2002), but at only fourteen episodes, even that might get repetitive quickly. On the other end of the spectrum is *The Simpsons* (1989–present), and while the more than five-hundred and fifty episodes would keep me out of reruns for a while, it's not nearly as fresh or subversive as it once was. The answer, I decided, was the one show that I could watch over and over again and still enjoy each time; a show with Gordian storylines, brilliant writing, and more entertainment-per-minute than anything that's ever been on television. To borrow a phrase from the show's opening credits: It's *Arrested Development*.

Since the show's debut on the Fox Network in 2003, *Arrested Development* has been hailed by critics as an innovative and groundbreaking comedy, and showered with a host of awards, including six Emmys, three Television Critics Association Awards, a Golden Globe, and a Writers Guild of America Award, among numerous other awards—and far more nominations on top of that. But for all its critical praise, the series struggled to find an audience, and episode orders diminished from 22 in its first season to 18 and 13 for seasons two and three. With the writing on the wall, Fox cancelled the series in 2006, and despite conjecture that the story could be continued as a feature film, the future of the Bluths seemed uncertain.

5

But then, like a phoenix (which seems apropos), the show was brought back to life for a fourth season on Netflix in 2013, giving viewers new Bluth antics to revel in, including Buster's homage to JFK Jr., Tobias' vanity license plate, and the realities of trying a case under maritime law. After 68 episodes across four seasons, these examples (along with too many others to list here) have created a litany of iconic quotes, scenes, images, and double entendres that have made the show revered within the pantheon of television comedies. Because of this, *Arrested Development* is, unquestionably, one of the most densely packed and content-rich television series of all time, making the task of selecting the topics for inclusion in this collection even more daunting. Given the sheer volume of jokes, puns, sight gags, callbacks to previous episodes, references to real-world events, and metatextuality present in the series, this book could have very easily contained twice as many essays (making further study of the series beyond the current volume essential). The contributors have each done an extraordinary job analyzing and exploring these aspects of the series, and have provided new and enlightening insight into *Arrested Development* from a multitude of backgrounds and academic viewpoints. With that in mind, the essays in this book have been split into four sections, examining the series from cultural, psychological, comparative, and televisual perspectives, respectively.

Section 1 explores the cultural and societal issues faced by the Bluths in their day-to-day lives and how they choose to engage with a host of contemporary topics. In "Living in Sudden Valley: The Bluth Family and the Fault Lines of Ideology," Edwin Demper looks at the role of money throughout the series and the ways it influences the Bluths. He argues that their financial issues serve as the ideological foundation on which their perspective of the world is based, a perspective that is warped because of the unstable and tenuous relationship the Bluths have with their money. Kristin M. Distel's essay titled "The Meaning of Charity: Depictions of Corruption and Altruism" explores the relationship between charitable endeavors and criminal activity on the show. Distel specifically examines how charity is used throughout *Arrested Development* as a means to extort money, flaunt social status, and exult in personal glory, but rarely (if ever) is it done for actual philanthropic purposes. In Elizabeth Lowry's essay, "Lindsay Bluth and the Politics of Sincerity: Environmental Rhetoric, Eco-Consciousness and Social Performance," the author's analysis of Lindsay's role as self-appointed conservationist provides a reflection of the current state of environmentalism in America. From her tree-saving exploits with Johnny Bark to her trip to the wetlands, Lindsay's superficial attempts to preserve the environment are little more than social performances that often do more harm than good. James Rocha deals with issues of race in "It Ain't

Easy Being Race-Sensitive: Things Whitey and African-Americany Aren't Ready to Hear," arguing that the show highlights the implicit (as compared to explicit) racism that is most prevalent in the United States today. His claim is that minority groups are objectified through established stereotypes, effectively making them caricatures of their cultures or nationalities, and that *Arrested Development* plays on these clichés as a way to raise awareness of the problem. Concluding Section 1 is Navid Sabet's "The Ways of the Secular Flesh: Destabilizing the Heteronormative and Negotiating Non-Monolithic Sexualities." Here, Sabet provides insight into the ways gender and sexuality play out in the series, specifically citing Tobias, George Michael, and Maeby as characters that eschew traditional media representations of expected sexual identities in favor of more complex portrayals, such as Tobias' ambiguous sexuality and George Michael's incestuous feelings towards his cousin.

Section 2 delves more deeply into the psychology of the Bluths in order to gain a clearer understanding of their excessive behaviors. This section opens with Jonah Ford's look at the confluence of horror and humor in "'I'm a monster!': The Monstrous and the Comedic." Ford uses the liminal space between the appalling and satire to explore how the monstrous—be it George Sr.'s fraudulent business practices or Buster's missing hand—elicit laughter from viewers. Dustin Freeley's essay, "Narrative and the Narrator in the Politics of Memory," argues that time and memory play significant roles in shaping the narrative of the series. For example, by appropriating cultural events such as the now-infamous "Mission Accomplished" banner or the capture of Saddam Hussein and incorporating skewed versions of them into the show, *Arrested Development* uses the past in the present to displace memories and provide revised versions of history. Co-authors Bethany Yates Poston and Crisman Richards examine parent/child role-reversal in their essay "Families with Low Self-Esteem: The Fünke Dynamic." The authors make the case that because of their habitual "un-parenting," Tobias and Lindsay fulfill the roles of aimless and lethargic adolescents who have unrealistic aspirations, while Maeby serves as the parental figure that maintains a successful career and possesses a more realistic perspective of the world. Section 2 closes with Joseph S. Walker's essay, "'Obviously this blue part here is the land': The Bluths, Decadence and Logic Adrift," which looks at the use of repetition and self-referentiality through the series as the primary means for progressing the story. Because the characters are trapped in a series of call-backs and references to previous events, Walker believes the Bluths have little control over their actions or behaviors.

Section 3 moves from the diegetic to the non-diegetic by examining *Arrested Development* as it relates to other famous narratives. This section begins with an interesting comparison between the series and Shakespeare in

Kristin N. Denslow's essay "*Hamlet*'s Ghost Meme: Accidental Shakespeare, Repetition Compulsion and Roofie Circles." Like contemporary Internet memes, Denslow examines how the Ghost meme from *Hamlet* has been replicated on numerous television series in the twenty-first century, and manifests within *Arrested Development* through the appearance of the "dead" father coming back to haunt his son(s). In "The Family Business: Bluths, Corleones and the American Dream," I compare the Bluths to another beloved multigenerational family involved in an illicit business: the Corleones from *The Godfather* films. In looking at the ways the characters mirror each other and how their stories play out, I propose that the representations of crime and family depicted in *Arrested Development* and *The Godfather* may be more reflective of reality than we care to think. Finally, Matthew Gannon's essay, "The Kafkaesque in the Trial of George Bluth," equates George Sr.'s arrest and imprisonment with that of Josef K. from Franz Kafka's 1925 novel *The Trial*. Gannon analyzes the ways in which both George Sr. and Josef K. are never explicitly told what crimes they are charged with and how their subsequent trials are put on more for show than discovering the truth.

Section 4 concludes the book with three essays that look at *Arrested Development* as a unique and innovative television event. In "'I swore I'd not go reality': The Bluths Through the Lens of Genre," Patrick Alasdair Gill cites the numerous genres that combine to create *Arrested Development*'s particular style of storytelling. Blending mockumentary and drama elements within a traditional sitcom format (and peppering in aspects of telenovelas, infomercials, and news programming), Gill maintains that *Arrested Development* has paved the way for new approaches to the comedy genre. For my second essay of the book, "Saving Our Bluths: Why the Smartest Comedy on Television Struggled to Find an Audience," I question what prevented the show from garnering the type of Nielsen ratings that would have allowed it to continue on Fox past its truncated third season. I make the case that the fans, the show itself, and Fox each had a hand in bringing about the series' premature cancellation. The final essay comes from Michael Graves, who focuses on the fourth season in his essay, "'Chalk one up for the Internet: It has killed *Arrested Development*': The Series' Revival, Binge Watching and Fan/Critic Antagonism." Graves finds that the decision to release the entirety of season four at the same time—and the binge watching that ensued—prompted serious discussions among fans and critics regarding how the season should be consumed and the ways this new content-deployment strategy is changing the way we watch television.

Section 1

Life in Newport Beach

Living in Sudden Valley

The Bluth Family and the Fault Lines of Ideology

Edwin Demper

In many ways, *Arrested Development* seems to be a show about money. At the very beginning of the show, the Bluth family is already teetering on the brink of financial collapse, and over the course of four seasons, the major plotlines, like the trial of George Sr. or the construction of the Sudden Valley housing development, primarily revolve around the family's financial situation. On a smaller scale, individual characters on the show are often driven by concerns about money: by anxiety about not having enough money, by hatching schemes to attain more money, or by knowingly spending money they do not have. However, while at first glance it seems that the Bluths are moments away from total ruination, the final blow is never struck. Instead, the Bluths are perpetually cast in a state of crisis, which never escalates to actual bankruptcy. They remain frozen in place, forever circling the drain, without ever quite washing down. Thus, their apparent financial descent is actually a state of stability, where crisis is the natural state. That is because for all its financial concerns, *Arrested Development* is not driven by the actual availability of money, but rather by the beliefs and attitudes the characters have *about* money. What the Bluths think about money never changes, and examining these beliefs and attitudes offers a much deeper insight into how to show works.

The difference between money and beliefs about money is not trivial. In a show as full of subterfuge, plot twists, and smokescreens as *Arrested Development*, it is hardly surprising that no clear picture of the family's finances emerges. There are glimpses of the family's self-inflicted financial decline, but it remains totally unclear how this actually changes the lives of those involved. For example, in the show's second episode "Top Banana" (1:2), one financial disaster follows the next. Maeby steals from the banana stand's cash register, and attempts to hide her crime by throwing away bananas from the inventory, effectively doubling the losses. Michael decides to burn down the banana stand for the insurance money, unaware that Gob has failed to mail the insurance check. In a final, painful twist, George Sr. reveals that there was $200,000 in cash lining the walls of the stand, which has now gone up in flames. Yet for all the consternation and stress these considerable financial losses cause, they have no noticeable impact on the Bluths' lives: Michael just ends up rebuilding the banana stand. The actual money lost is inconsequential in the context of the show, but the events do reveal a set of interesting and relevant beliefs about money.

Almost every character on the show seems to harbor misconceptions when it comes to money. The entire Bluth family appears prone to lavish impulse spending, and is accustomed to luxuries they can ill afford. Theirs is a lifestyle of luxury yachts, country club lunches, and charity auctions, funded from the dwindling company accounts. Although the family is extremely financially irresponsible as a whole, the attitudes differ significantly between the various characters. Some characters, like Maeby, are flat-out ignorant about even common sense economics, while characters like George Sr. seem driven by naked greed. While the show's economic conscience, Michael, appears as the lone voice of reason, his willingness to commit insurance fraud by burning down the banana stand shows an early glimpse of his real attitudes. In a reversal that's typical of *Arrested Development*, deceived and deceptive characters like Maeby or George Sr. find it much easier to come by (usually temporary) financial success than a relative straight shooter like Michael. While Maeby accidentally becomes a powerful Hollywood executive ("Switch Hitter" 2:7) and George Sr. launches a series of successful religious self-help videos ("Marta Complex" 1:12), Michael continues to struggle. In other words, it is clear that good behavior is not necessarily rewarded, while ignorance and deceit may reap rewards. The connection between attitudes about money and the ability to obtain money is often counterintuitive rather than straightforward.

The pattern that emerges is one of false expectations, cheating, miraculous windfalls, and self-inflicted ruin, and extends far beyond the limits of the Bluth family itself. The Bluths are not outliers in the society the show depicts: they seem to conform to what is the unofficial norm of behavior. The entire economy of *Arrested Development* is one where nothing is what it seems, and no one truly knows what they are doing. Everywhere the Bluths go they meet shysters and conmen, who are often just as clueless as the Bluths themselves. There is perhaps no better example of this than the incompetent family lawyer, Barry Zuckerkorn, whose only legal successes are purely accidental. Thus, the Bluths are not the bizarre outliers they appear at first glance. They are simply exponents of a society that seems to be founded on false assumptions. This society, on the one hand, praises and encourages certain ideals, but on the other hand issues rewards for behavior that directly contradicts it. The relatively upstanding character of Michael is presented as the central character, while George Sr. is under indictment—but in the end, the crooked father often triumphs over the sympathetic son. It is a society where no one practices what they preach and where success is not associated with hard work and honesty, but rather with chance and deceit.

As a result, the world of the show is an unstable one. It is not just the Bluths that are at risk, because the attitudes that get them in trouble are pervasive throughout their society. In a sense, the model home and the Sudden Valley housing development it is part of are emblematic of the show as a whole. At various points, the development threatens to fall apart due to shoddy construction ("Staff Infection" 1:15), plumbing disasters, or burrowing moles ("Mr. F" 3:5). The model home only looks luxurious, but is in reality a cheap imitation of a sumptuous villa. Even the name suggests instability: it reminds potential investor Stan Sitwell of a sinkhole, while George Michael more charitably associates it with a salad dressing ("Switch Hitter" 2:7). The foundations of the house (as well as the show as a whole) are unstable, and what passes for stability in *Arrested Development* may merely be a failure to grow. Yet, since these foundations are shared and accepted as the normal standard, it is impossible for any of the show's characters to understand or to alter the situation they are in. They deal with each crisis as it arises, but fail to see how their attitudes cause these crises to occur.

All the instability surrounding the Bluths, ranging from construction and organization to characters and events, forms a larger and remarkably coherent system, invisible to those participating in it while it shapes and alters their lives in significant ways. This system can be better understood by using the theories of the French philosopher Louis Althusser, whose concept of ideology is particularly useful in highlighting how the shaky underpinnings of the show are in fact part of a consistent outline. Althusser's idea of ideology describes "the imaginary relationship of individuals to their real conditions of existence" (168). In other words, it describes how the Bluths *think* their world works, and where, why, and how it differs from how their world actually works. The Bluths' attitudes about money provide a glimpse of the ideology at the foundation of *Arrested Development*. Just like the *attitudes* the Bluths have about money are more significant than the actual money, the Bluths' *beliefs* about their society are more significant than the actual facts of that society—ideology, rather than reality.

For Althusser, ideology is everywhere. While in everyday speech the word ideology is usually taken to mean a more or less coherent set of ideas and beliefs with a limited scope, Althusser's definition is more encompassing. It is not just a view on politics, law, or religion; instead it is all these at the same time and more. Ideology, to Althusser, encompasses the very foundation of society, on top of which rest the beliefs that are more commonly associated with the term. It consists not just of beliefs, but of the organization of society itself: its institutions, its culture, and its economic organization. Therefore, everything that happens in a society is mediated by ideology: ideology does not have an outside. It causes those inside it to perceive the world around them in a certain way, and to think and act along its lines. In other words, ideology is omnipresent and determines what people perceive, think, and do.

Paradoxically, ideology itself is difficult to perceive *because* it is so large and encompassing. Ideology is a little like the story of the three blind men finding an elephant: the first, holding the tail, thinks he has taken hold a rope; the second, holding a leg, thinks he is touching a tree; the third, holding the trunk, thinks he has found a garden hose. None of them has an inkling they are dealing with a larger whole. Similarly, the Bluths are unable to understand the predicament they continuously find themselves in because it is a symptom of a system that is larger than they can fathom, and which envelops them completely.

To make matters worse, Althusser explains that the experience of living within ideology entails the illusion that one is *not* caught in ideology, but simply living in the world. There is nothing about ideology that reveals itself as such: "one of the effects of ideology is the practical denial of the ideological character of ideology by ideology: ideology never says, 'I am ideological'" (Althusser 173). By that, Althusser means that ideology works unnoticed: its influence is usually not perceived, but rather mistaken for a normal or natural state of affairs. Like looking at an object through tinted glasses, ideology determines how reality is perceived—but unlike tinted glasses, the filter of ideology cannot easily be removed. Because the filter has always been there, those affected normally assume that there is no filter at all. If someone were born with rose-tinted glasses on, they might very well think that the world simply is rose-tinted—after all, it is what they perceive day after day. Even if the person were to come across a set of rose-tinted glasses, the color of their lenses would appear as neutral because of the set they were wearing. The difference between the way the world works and the way people *think* it works is almost, by definition, imperceptible because it is the perception itself that causes the mistake. Ideology deals with this perception, but also in other ways individuals relate to their world—relations between people, institutions, material objects, and society. Understanding this helps explain why it is impossible for the Bluths to resist the forces of ideology: they cannot see them at work. When the Bluths make the same mistakes over and over, hatching schemes and struggling to get ahead, they cannot understand that there might be other options or that their previous failures are guided by a certain ideology. The Bluths' understanding of themselves and their society rests on that ideology and they cannot escape it or even realize they are caught in it. Thus, their beliefs about money—how important it is, why it is important, what one is permitted to do in pursuit of it—are part of ideology.

One crucial feature of Althusser's understanding of ideology is the notion that individuals become unwitting accomplices to ideology. In other words, people participate in a system they do not fully understand, often to their own disadvantage. Many of the features of society that normally go unquestioned are in fact constructed and codified by ideology. What is more, there is often a system in place that is perceived as just or natural, but that in fact heavily privileges some while putting others at a significant disadvantage. One example can be found in the understanding of justice: ideally, everyone is equal in the eyes of the law, and presumed innocent unless found guilty beyond reasonable doubt. While that is the theory, in practice, people who enter the courtroom without the aid of a good (and expensive) lawyer find themselves at a significant disadvantage, irrespective of their guilt. Yet most people still believe that the system is fair and equitable, and serves the greater good. Althusser's concept of ideology explains why many people do not question the way society is organized, even if it runs against their best interest. It might even lead people to celebrate or defend a system that objectively works against their best interest.

Of course, the Bluths are—or were—the kind of people that can afford an expensive lawyer, or walk around in a $4,000 suit, or organize a charity benefit to show off their wealth. Although the Bluths are always on the brink of financial ruin, they nevertheless believe that they are somehow entitled to the level of wealth to which they are accustomed. The show's creator, Mitchell Hurwitz, explains how this sense of entitlement was a core concept in the show's creation: "[the show] was really about how money enables a lot of eccentricity" ("'Arrested' No More"). Because of their financial privilege, the Bluths were free to develop a wild range of idiosyncrasies. Yet when the veneer of wealth begins to crack, the Bluths still defy change: they maintain a lifestyle that is clearly unsustainable. What is more, they repeatedly try to regain their former wealth through the same methods they have employed in the past. Rather than question their attitudes and approaches, their belief in how to be successful, or rather, their idea of how society functions, never changes. After every failure, the Bluths redouble their commitment to essentially the same course of action, which predictably leads to another failure. Over the arc of the series, many of the Bluths' problems are caused by the fallout from a shady real estate project in Iraq. But instead of learning from the consequences (George Sr.'s imprisonment; being saddled with an inferior, substandard, and perpetually undeveloped Sudden Valley), the family's most level-headed member, Michael, puts all his efforts in a new and only slightly less shady real estate project (incurring major debt to deliver an inferior, substandard product, the now-finished Sudden Valley). The Bluths believe the world works a certain way and act accordingly—no matter how many times they fail.

The ideology that emerges for the viewers of the show is a system that seems deliberately unstable. While there is a nominal sense of more traditional values, primarily embodied in Michael and George Michael, the system ultimately encourages deceit, reckless spending, and backroom deals. Intelligence and hard work are not the driving factors for success, except when they serve to trick competitors or victims. The economy of the show is often predatory, where one person's gain directly comes from another's loss. Michael's perpetual car trouble is a prime example. For most of the series, Michael's only means of transportation is either his bicycle or the company stair car. In the face of his siblings' greed, he finally treats himself to a new sports car—but is forced to sign it over to Stan Sitwell in order to secure a date with Sitwell's daughter, Sally, at a bachelorette auction ("Burning Love" 2:9). The transaction goes awry when Tobias spends all of Michael's money bidding on his own wife. This zero-sum game approach leaves most of the characters on uncertain footing. Success usually emerges as a brief respite from a long string of failures, and an opportunity for competitors to set their crosshairs on their newly successful peer. The Bluths and their peers are buying into an ideology that does not afford them lasting success, but instead leaves them in a state of perpetual crisis. Yet occasional success and the almost perpetual urgency of crisis leave little room for introspection and routinely drive *Arrested Development*'s characters to launch themselves headlong into the next scheme.

Even if the Bluths appear blind to most of the trappings of the show's reigning ideology, there are ways in which they appear critical. Michael sees his father's crimes and deceit as a terrible example and is committed to doing things differently himself. Yet, while he vocally objects to the precedents set by the family patriarch, he ultimately fails to run the business any differently; either because George Sr. continues to run things from the prison or because Michael's hand is forced by circumstance, the Bluth Company conducts business as usual. More problematic still is the family's willingness to cheat. From "light treason" to theft, from prison breaks to sleeping with the enemy, there is hardly an indiscretion the family does not indulge in. Is this willingness to bend the rules an implicit form of critique of the system? After all, the show is not set in an amoral universe, and the characters obviously deal with ethics and justice. More often than not, the Bluths opt instead for deception and subterfuge in an effort to dupe the government, or clients, or debtors, or the courts. Their defiance could be read as a way of resisting a system they feel is unfair—or at least it would, were the rest of that system not just as willing to cheat as the Bluths are. Cheating, it appears, is part of the rules.

Dishonesty and foul play are rule rather than exception in the Bluth family. For some of the family members this is in keeping with their character. It is not a surprise to see Lucille attempt tax evasion by hiding her fur coats, or to see her manipulating her children to prevent an alliance against her interests with Machiavellian guile ("Charity Drive" 1:6). Similarly, George Sr.'s willingness to frame his twin brother for his own crimes becomes a running gag. However, even the more principled and moral family members slip up. George Michael, in a moment of frustration, tries to burn down the banana stand, and his father Michael lets him—in part as a gesture of understanding towards his son, but also in an ill-conceived attempt at insurance fraud ("Top Banana" 1:2). Yet, in each of these examples, the characters are covering up or reacting to some trick they were confronted with themselves, and are merely escalations in a chain of misleading and deceptive actions. But the Bluths are not alone in their willingness to deceive: no one plays by the rules. Everyone cheats, and the true measure of success is getting away with it. Cheating is institutionalized in *Arrested Development*, and defines even the very institutions whose ostensible mission it is to uphold justice and fairness. The show's ideology shows not only through its individual characters, but also through the foundations of its society and the institutions that shape and uphold it.

According to Althusser, one of the primary means by which ideology is spread and reproduced is by Ideological State Apparatuses (ISAs). ISAs include organizations and institutions like the law, organized religion, the educational system, and the political system. In one critic's words, these institutions represent ideology "in a material existence in the sense that it is embodied in all sorts of material practices" (Bertens 66). Bertens explains that it is not just the very foundations of society that constitute ideology, but that it also emerges in more tangible and concrete forms. Any one institution does not represent the whole of ideology, but it does play a part in shaping the way people view and understand the world. ISAs reproduce ideology and shape the fabric of society: the public as well as the private, the economic as well as the cultural, the religious as well as the secular (Althusser 145, 147–149). The ISAs that appear in *Arrested Development*, like the justice system or the media, are as willing to bend the rules as the Bluths themselves are, and as such are very revealing of the ideology of the show.

For instance, the justice system that is prosecuting George Sr. for an expansive list of offenses is corrupted by the same ideology as the Bluths. The attorneys and prosecutors working in the legal system vacillate between incompetence, intimidation, and iniquity. The family's own attorney Barry Zuckerkorn illustrates this point: He is an incompetent fraud whose greatest skill lies in his creative billing practices. When he squares off against prosecutor Wayne Jarvis in "Sad Sack" (2:5), it seems the contrast between the two legal professionals could not be greater. Jarvis is a consummate professional and a stickler for procedure, while Zuckerkorn's understanding of legal procedure is best described as tenuous. Yet in the episode, Jarvis proves to also be a manipulating bully, exploiting the privileges afforded to him by the Patriot Act to threaten Michael and to hack into the company email. Zuckerkorn unexpectedly ends up saving the day by correctly identifying a picture obtained from the Bluth Company email: It does not depict weapons of mass destruction as the prosecutor claims, but rather an accidental snapshot of Tobias' scrotum.

Meanwhile, in "Justice Is Blind" (1:18), Michael deals with the fallout of unintentionally having a one-night stand with his father's prosecutor, the blind Maggie Lizer. When Michael learns of her role in his father's trial, he struggles with the ethics of the situation but does not realize that in fact, Lizer has been manipulating him by plying him with false evidence. As it turns out, Lizer is not even blind—she used the guise of blindness to help her pass the LSAT exams, and found her fake disability garners so much sympathy in court that judges and juries let her win cases outright in spite of her actual performance in the courtroom. The courts, meant to uphold justice, are full of people willing to bend the rules. While they are in a legal position to punish the Bluths for their transgressions, they are cut from the same moral cloth: they are products of the same ideological system.

Even more telling than the court system is the school system seen in the episode "Shock and Aww" (1:14). The episode centers on ethical quandaries, but predictably, hardly anyone involved in the episode manages to make a morally justifiable decision. The show's two most straight-laced characters, George Michael and his father Michael, both fall in love with the former's high school ethics teacher, Ms. Baerly. Michael becomes romantically involved with Ms. Baerly after the two awkwardly swap jokes about Michael's deceased wife at parent teacher-night, and spends the rest of the episode spinning a web of lies to protect George Michael's feelings from getting hurt. George Michael defaces a rare book in order to impress Ms. Baerly, and Ms. Baerly herself has a fascination for Saddam Hussein that seems to cross over into fandom. Her puzzling predilection for dictators and her questionable judgment in pursuing a relationship with a student's parent are particularly troubling when coupled with the fact she is an ethics teacher. Through an ISA like an educational institution, the beliefs and values of a society are taught. In a sense, George Michael is learning the same things in school as he is in his own family. Society's values and the family's values turn out to be broadly similar, in spite of initial appearances.

The institutions within the show pursue goals in the same incompetent and duplicitous ways as the Bluths. Whether it is a court of law or a school, these ISAs seem as committed as the Bluths are to strategies that are short-sighted at best, and predatory and willfully fraudulent at worst. Other ISAs, like the prison George Sr. finds himself incarcerated in are no different. The prison regime is inconsistent, offering entertainment for the inmates on the one hand, but readily exposing them to violence on the other. The wardens of the prison appear as whimsical and petty, and more interested in their own hobbies and entertainment than in the regime of their prison and the wellbeing of their inmates. The first warden, James Buck, allows Gob into the prison as part of a bet ("Key Decisions" 1:4), while his replacement, Stefan Gentles, admits Tobias into prison to study for a character in exchange for the opportunity to have his screenplay read by seasoned actor Carl Weathers ("Staff Infection" 1:15). Similarly, when Buster enrolls in the army, it appears as a ramshackle and incompetent organization—evidenced not in the least by the fact that they admit Buster into their ranks ("The One Where They Build a House" 2:2).

In Althusser's theory, ISAs include not only the major institutions discussed above, but also more private entities like the family. While an organization like the family does not appear to be organized and constructed by large, anonymous entities like earlier examples, the idea of the family is in fact heavily influenced by other ISAs, like organized religion or political rhetoric.

The reality of the Bluth family is a disaster, featuring frequent betrayal, constant mistrust, and even recurring suggestions of incest. But when looking for ideology, ideas are more relevant than reality, and in the case of the Bluths, the individual members of the family exhibit certain beliefs and convictions (e.g., George Sr.'s greed, Lindsay's vanity, Maeby's dishonesty) that fit the picture of ideology that has emerged from the other ISAs. Going further, the notion of family itself and what values it entails also corresponds to this image. At a glance, the relationship and interaction between Michael and George Michael articulates a more positive notion of the family, one that is expressed in the very first episode of the show: "What comes before anything? What have we always said is the most important thing?," Michael asks his son. "Breakfast," George Michael replies ("Pilot" 1:1). Of course, his father's actual answer is "family," and thus, Michael appears to stand out with his wholesome family values. On closer inspection, those values are often indistinguishable from the family's other, less noble interests, and end up aiding and abetting the behavior that Michael vociferously condemns. Although Michael is very critical of the way he was raised by his father, he remains oblivious to the fact he is repeating the same behavior. In one flashback, we learn that George Sr. would shoot down Michael's business ideas as a management tool to keep Michael on his toes. "That was a hard one to shoot down," George Sr. sighs in "Switch Hitter" (2:7), leaving Michael desperate for his father's approval. The same structure of high expectations and no reward is in place with Michael's son George Michael, who is left working long, thankless hours in the banana stand, or, on one fateful afternoon, effectively running the Bluth Company by himself ("Staff Infection" 1:15). Michael is a good employee because he wants to be a good son, and he fails as a father because he cannot help but see his son as an employee. At the same time that Michael is attempting to escape the trappings of his demanding and manipulative family, he is teaching his son to stand by them.

Thus, even when characters in *Arrested Development* appear to be acting on a very personal level, and seem to be driven by nothing but their own fears and desires, ideology is still present. Ideology does not just constitute the whole of society, but structures even the most personal experience. As Althusser explained earlier, one of its defining features is that ideology works in ways that do not appear as ideological. According to the theory, our identity as individuals is illusory: every person merely fills a number of roles and functions that had already been made possible by the ideological structure, and those roles would have been filled by others had that given person not fulfilled them. Literary theorist Terry Eagleton offers a particularly lucid interpretation of how it is possible to simultaneously feel like an individual, and be a product of ideology:

> I do not feel myself to be a mere *function* of a social structure which could get along without me, true though this appears when I *analyze* the situation.... It is as though society were not just an impersonal structure to me, but a "subject" which addresses me personally— which I recognize, tells me that I am valued, and so makes me by that very act of recognition into a free, autonomous subject [149].

What Eagleton is arguing here is that within this understanding of ideology, any given person is utterly created by ideology in its various guises and instances. Yet one of the results of being thus created or enabled is the sensation or feeling of being an independent individual, equipped with free will and the possibility to shape his or her own destiny. In feeling like an individual, and thus feeling outside of ideology, the person is in fact becoming a part and an agent of that ideology. To understand the Bluths' failures to change or to realize their own situation, it is important to remember that they cannot exist outside of ideology. Individuals do not exist outside of ideology, but are always defined in relation to it. In Althusser's terms, ideology *interpellates* individuals as subjects (170–171). This means that a person is not defined by internal or inherent qualities, but rather by constructed relations around them. It is not possible to separate the individual from the ideologically constructed subject—existing, for example, as a member of a family, or having a certain job, or as a customer in a store. Rather than freely finding their own identity, the Bluths have to reinvent themselves within an already existing framework.

Ideology defines a person, but also guides the ways in which a person defines him- or herself. The clearest example of this in the Bluth family is Lucille. Although cold and capricious, Lucille often appears deeply insecure, and seeks constant affirmation from others to establish her self-worth. She cannot resist the adulation of either George Sr. or his brother Oscar for any serious amount of time, and is vulnerable to the flattery of sycophants like the family attorney Barry Zuckerkorn or her private investigator Gene Parmesan. Her chief outlet is her stunted son Buster, who she treats with a sickly mixture of constant reproach and doting affection.

Driven by insecurity and rivalry, Lucille strives to define herself in purely materialistic terms in "Charity Drive" (1:6). In a vain attempt to distinguish herself in the eyes of her long-time friend and rival, Lucille Austero, she decides to have herself auctioned off at a charity bachelorette auction. To make sure the auction will be a success and she will "sell" for more money than her rival, she decides set up a straw purchase: she instructs her own son Buster to buy her at the handsome sum of $10,000, which she herself provides. The scheme goes sadly awry when Buster, running late, accidentally bids on the wrong Lucille—incidentally kickstarting the budding relationship between Buster and Lucille Austero, and thus robbing Lucille Bluth of her dignity twice over.

Lucille Bluth's actions in the episode offer an insight in how important beliefs about money are to her sense of self-identity. In the run-up to the auction, the two Lucilles trade barbs about the Bluths' current financial predicament. Clearly, Lucille Bluth deeply resents being thought of as poor. Her self-worth is calculated in clear financial terms, but there is a twisted logic to the whole transaction. It involves a complicated interplay between wealth and beauty, self and other. The process starts with Lucille Bluth feeling financially insecure, and quite possibly unattractive as a result, compared to her peer Lucille Austero. She sees a chance to affirm her attractiveness at the bachelorette auction, where money will change hands to validate her desirability. Of course, Lucille is bidding with her own money (or possibly the Bluth Company's), so attractiveness also becomes a function of wealth. Interestingly, it is not enough to *have* money in order to be considered attractive; it has to be *spent*. Lucille feels it is important to be thought of as attractive. To her, to be attractive means to be worth money, and therefore, to be wealthy. However, to be wealthy is defined not in terms of possessing means, but in terms of distributing them. It is no wonder that a plan based on such complicated circular logic ultimately fails, but what is interesting is that the foundational aspects of Lucille Bluth's identity—wealth and beauty—are only realized when they are recognized for their exchange value. To return to an earlier theme, the role that *beliefs* about money play is far more relevant than the money itself: it justifies ugly behavior in the face of apparent beauty and there is never a second thought about the price tag attached to the idea of wealth.

Many of the economic issues shown in *Arrested Development* are funny because they are absurd. The successes and failures of characters like Gob or Maeby involve leaps of logic and bizarre coincidences. But simultaneously, many of the larger issues tackled are closely modeled on actual events. As one *Washington Post* article points out, "More than any other show, *Arrested Development* drew economics into its texture—harping on the corporate scandals of the day" (Queck and Sunkara). Much of *Arrested Development*'s ridiculous economy closely mirrors real-world examples. The original run of the show emerged in the wake of the Enron and Worldcom scandals, where unscrupulous executives embezzled millions and defrauded consumers as well as employees. It took on war profiteering in Iraq, and the erosion of civil rights in the wake of 9/11. In its fourth season, it dealt with the consequences of the real estate collapse, and the politics of the 2012 presidential election campaign.

Arrested Development takes place in society that is very different from the one we live in, yet there are enough parallels to invite speculation about whether any conclusions drawn about the show might have farther reaching implications.

In some cases, the show clearly takes liberties with real-life events and depicts scenarios that seem unlikely to ever occur in the real world. However, in other instances, the facts are barely exaggerated, yet fit seamlessly in the bizarre universe of *Arrested Development.* Tobias and Lindsay's loan to finance an extravagant mansion in "A New Start" (4:5) is not far removed from the practices that actually caused the 2007 real estate collapse: "NINJA loans, also called NINA loans ("No Income No Assets") weren't loans made to people who actually had no income or no assets, necessarily; they were loans where the lender didn't ask for asset and income information from the borrower" (Matthews). Rather than verifying that recipients had no means to pay back their loans, as is the case in the show, lenders supplying mortgages would simply not inquire about their means. Similarly, the risks of the real estate bubble had been described for well over a decade before the crisis occurred. The kind of willful ignorance that often propels the Bluths' most disastrous misadventures certainly appears to have its counterparts in the real-world economy.

The Bluths are often driven by their beliefs and attitudes about money, and stick to those same beliefs even when they are proven wrong time and again. They attempt to tackle the same problems using the same methods, hoping for a different solution, only to find themselves hilariously crashing once again. Yet the Bluths are not simply stubborn or stupid—although there is plenty of that, as well—but part of a larger system that encourages and reproduces these beliefs and attitudes. It is not possible for the Bluths to understand or alter their conditions, which is exactly what keeps them in their state of arrested development. The very structure of their world, perpetuated by the institutions that surround and shape them, is what prevents them from altering that same structure. It is by virtue of *not* being part of the same ideological structure that the role of ideology in the show becomes clear. Although the ideology of the show is not quite the same that shapes our own world, the Bluths' blindness to their predicaments might give us pause to wonder whether we are not living in our own version of Sudden Valley. The Bluths show us the disastrous consequences of not interrogating the almost imperceptible ideology that underpins their every action. It is worth wondering whether we might have similar blind spots of our own—to try and reach beyond the way we *think* the way world works and determine if it is as normal, fair, and beneficial as we assume it is.

Works Cited

Althusser, Louis. *"Lenin and Philosophy" and Other Essays*. London: New Left Books, 1977. Print.

"'Arrested' No More: Hurwitz on Why the Bluths Are Back." *Fresh Air*. NPR. WHYY. 5 June 2013. Radio.

Bertens, Hans. *Literary Theory: The Basics*. New York: Routledge, 2008. Print.

Eagleton, Terry. *Literary Theory: An Introduction*. Minneapolis: University of Minnesota Press, 2006. Print.

Matthews, Dylan. "How *Arrested Development* Explains the Housing Crisis (Among Other Things)." *Washington Post*. 27 May 2013. Web. 18 Dec. 2013. http://www.washingtonpost.com/blogs/wonkblog/wp/2013/05/27/how-arrested-development-explains-the-housing-crisis-among-other-things/.

Queck, Peter, and Bhaskar Sunkara. "*Arrested Development* Was a Communist Utopia and Season Four Ruined It." *Washington Post*. 28 May 2013. Web. 14 Mar. 2014 http://www.washingtonpost.com/blogs/wonkblog/wp/2013/05/28/arrested-development-was-a-communist-utopia-and-season-four-ruined-it/.

The Meaning of Charity
Depictions of Corruption and Altruism

Kristin M. Distel

Throughout the first three seasons of *Arrested Development*, the Bluth family both demands charity and disdains ethical behavior; a dichotomy that is at the center of many of the family's crises. In her 2004 article "Crimes and Banana Stands," Celia Wren noted, "Given the financial shenanigans of its characters, *Arrested Development* sometimes feels like a parable about the excesses of the 1990s and how that era's lax business ethics have come home to roost" (20). Indeed, the series illustrates a connection between immorality and the notion of family, requiring viewers to consider the role of charity in order to understand the show's statement on ethics. There is a consistent correlation between charitable actions and criminal behavior throughout the series, and indeed, this relationship is at the center of the series itself and serves as the premise of the show. That is to say, George Sr. performs a favor for the United States government when he builds model homes in Iraq; he is arrested in the pilot episode, eventually acknowledging that he may be charged with "light treason" ("Visiting Ours" 1:5). Without George, Sr.'s criminal activity—undertaken in the name of aiding the federal government—many of the troubles that befall Michael, Lucille, and the rest of the family may never have occurred. This direct link between helping others and involvement in criminal activity is fundamental to many of the struggles the characters face throughout the series. With *Arrested Development*'s four seasons, viewers will find the apparent incompatibility of charity and principles common for most characters, from the family's disdainful attitude toward those who even briefly demonstrate a strong work ethic (such as Gob working a short stint as a waiter) to those who attempt to be principled in personal affairs and business dealings (such as Michael). In examining the link between charity and crime, we are given a deeper understanding of the moral underpinnings of the show itself and the respective motivations of the main characters.

George Sr.'s Role in the Family's Downfall

Despite the fact that he is often operating under his wife's instructions, George Sr. propels many of the show's crises; this is particularly true of the problems that pertain to altruism and corruption. He is also frequently at the center of the family's demands for charity. As previously mentioned, events depicted throughout the series are set in motion as a result of George Sr.'s work for the federal government, which sets off a series of catastrophes for the Bluths collectively as well as the family members individually. Michael eventually realizes that his father is controlling the family's actions even as George Sr. is incarcerated, and much of this control revolves around the family's financial status and state of need. C.S. Fitzgerald's discussion of constructionism is essential to an understanding of crime and charity in George Sr.'s character and *Arrested Development* as a whole. Friedman (qtd. in Fitzgerald) explains that constructionism has its foundations in crimes committed by the elite and the desire of the wealthy to "maintain their privileged positions ... and to squelch the imposition of laws that are not conducive to their interests, such as those that prosecute white-collar crime or perceived immoral acts ... like extramarital affairs" (305). George Sr. embodies the principles of constructionism theory in that his demands for charity and favors help maintain his "privileged position" and excuse his unethical behavior.

This is particularly evident in the criminal activities George Sr. orchestrates from inside prison. Michael makes this observation early in the series, noting, "I think Dad is trying to run the business from prison" ("Top Banana" 1:2). A prime example of this is George Sr.'s association with fellow inmate, T-Bone. When Michael demands access to the family's flight records, George Sr. asks the recently released T-Bone to burn down the family's storage unit that contains the files Michael needs. As recompense, George Sr. provides T-Bone with employment at the family's frozen banana stand. Here, we can observe a distinct connection between the commission of a crime—namely, arson—and George Sr.'s request for assistance.

From prison, George Sr. also uses Gob's bachelor party as an elaborate means of entrapping the company's accountant, Ira Gilligan ("Best Man for the Gob" 1:19). This behavior reinforces an escalation in the family's entrenchment in crime committed in the name of kindness. Gob believes that George Sr. is generously throwing him a bachelor party, while in reality George Sr. is using the celebration as a way to frame the accountant for murder and to force him to leave the country. In essence, Gob naively trusts that George Sr. is acting out of fatherly love and selflessness, but George Sr.'s sole intent is to ensure that the accountant cannot testify against him, as George Sr. was the one who stole money the accountant noticed had gone missing. The honeymoon tickets that George Sr. gives Gob as a wedding gift are actually meant for the accountant to ensure he leaves the country. Again, it is significant that George Sr. orchestrates this ruse from within prison; it centralizes the family's locus of leadership in a criminal setting.

Under George Sr.'s ostensible leadership, the Bluth Company is a means by which the Bluth children become complicit in criminal activity. The company funds the children's financial ventures, some of which result in criminal investigations or legal action. For instance, the Bluth Company purchased Gob's Aztec Tomb, which Mr. Milford uses to escape from his retirement home. Subsequently, Gob is investigated for the disappearance, and news footage is edited to show him shouting, "I killed Earl Milford" ("Public Relations" 1:11). It is important to note that Gob was performing a magic show at the retirement home because the family's publicist instructs Gob to "start doing some charity work" ("Public Relations" 1:11). As a result, this incident establishes a distinct link between charity work and accusations of criminal conduct. Additionally, the pilot episode reveals Lindsay's involvement in charity and the problems her efforts cause. Lindsay boasts that her anti-circumcision movement raised $40,000, to which Tobias absentmindedly adds, "Most of that money was from the Bluth Company" ("Pilot" 1:1). This particular charitable endeavor results in Lindsay becoming embroiled in a conflict with the Jewish Defense League, which again draws a connection between George Sr. (specifically, the financial provision his company provides) and accusations of misconduct. As Will Leitch notes, this is "the story of possibly the most dysfunctional family ever produced by American wealth."

Leitch's statement illustrates the role of George Sr.'s financial support—namely, giving money to support his children's charitable endeavors—has played in the family's increasing involvement in litigious actions against them. Kathryn Reklis makes a similar case, observing, "This is a group of grown-up children whose parents went to elaborate lengths to teach them inconsequential lessons about leaving a note when the milk runs out but forgot to teach them not to lie, steal, or cheat" (43), which is to say that he has failed to teach them about financial responsibility or, at the most basic level, having morals. The result of this is that George Sr.'s unethical behavior and seeming generosity continue to have far-reaching effects on the family. Specifically, the Bluths sometimes act on George Sr.'s behalf and come to emulate his characteristics and even subtly imitate his behavior. As the narrator explains in "Top Banana" (1:2) after Michael abandons plans to spend time with George Michael in lieu of work, "Michael realized he had done to his son what his father had done to him." This similarity becomes more marked as the series progresses, to the point that Michael, who is perhaps least inclined to act unethically for personal gain, undergoes a character arc that results in him becoming increasingly like his father, exhibiting several of George Sr.'s unethical behaviors. This change in Michael's nature becomes most readily observable in the show's fourth season.

Charitable Actions, Accusations and Vengeance

"Charity Drive" (1:6) is particularly illustrative of altruistic behavior leading to criminal accusations. The episode includes several references to charitable giving, although the show's "labyrinthine complexity" (to use James Poniewozik's term) precludes a full discussion of each of the episode's examples. The main plot of the episode centers on a bachelorette auction intended to raise funds for the wetlands. Michael and Lindsay's argument about which of them is the most charitable leads Lindsay to volunteer in the wetlands for the day, a misadventure that reveals her essentially selfish and unethical nature (it also results in Lindsay spraying a crane with Mace and spearing a frog immediately after she boasts, "I've got some nature to save"). When Michael visits his father before the auction, George Sr. scolds Michael for refusing to give Gob a (free) frozen banana, stating, "That's not charitable" ("Charity Drive" 1:6). George Sr.'s comment subtly equates a demand for favors with charity. In turn, this leads to another instance of requesting help and committing a crime when Gob asks George Michael to break into the permit office and place a document in an incorrect file. While George, Sr. does not approve of Gob's decision to use George Michael in this way, the action *did* directly stem from George Sr.'s initial lie about filing the permits on time and his demand for his family's help. Most significantly, though, in a competition to prove that he is more charitable than Lindsay, Michael offers a ride to a woman he believes to be Lupe, his mother's housekeeper. While leaving the charity auction (and just after performing the ostensibly kind act of "bidding" on Lindsay), Michael is arrested for kidnapping.

What this all illustrates is that within the episode, there is a fine line between charitable and criminal acts which the Bluths routinely find themselves on the wrong side of. Indeed, some of the show's most notable comments on altruism and corruption include a significant physical location, such as the charity auction. At the end of "Charity Drive" (1:6), Michael is escorted into a police cruiser, where George Michael is also being held after having been arrested. George Michael's explanation for his arrest is that he was "Just trying to be a good guy" to which Michael responds, "Me too. Me too. Let's go see Pop Pop" ("Charity Drive" 1:6). This clearly implicates charitable deeds as harmful, a concept that becomes fundamental to the family's interactions and excessive greed.

The series revisits the theme of charity auctions in the second season, this time emphasizing the role of crime even more drastically. In "Burning Love" (2:9) and "Ready, Aim, Marry Me" (2:10), there are distinct correlations between charitable donations, favors, and misconduct. The bachelorette auction in "Burning Love" (2:9), which is conducted under the ostensible name of "charity," precipitates a series of unethical behaviors on the part of the Bluths. These episodes again condemn employment or obtaining money in any honest manner, instead showing the characters using one another to profit themselves, the family as a whole, and the Bluth Company. When Gob attempts to explain his romantic relationship with Lucille Austero, he admits, "I'm playing the part of the gigolo so she'll keep the company afloat" ("Ready, Aim, Marry Me" 2:10). While the family's reliance upon Lucille Austero has its roots in legitimate business dealings (she is the primary shareholder of the Bluth Company), their requests for charity from their Uncle Jack are comparatively more corrupt. Nearly all members of the family seem to believe that begging for charitable donations, whether from Uncle Jack or others, is preferable to performing actual work that will help save the company. Significantly, Michael arranges for Lindsay to go on a date with Uncle Jack, an act that George Sr. refers to as "pimping out" Lindsay for the benefit of the company ("Ready, Aim, Marry Me" 2:10). Multiple episodes have shown Lindsay as being unwilling to work to help the company or to provide for herself, with the exception of her short stint as a salesperson at a boutique ("Not Without My Daughter" 1:21). In "Ready, Aim, Marry Me" (2:10) she reveals that she went on the date to help convince Uncle Jack to save the Bluth Company, again drawing the link between charity (asking for money) and an act that, while not necessarily criminal, should certainly be seen as unethical (all-but prostituting herself for money). This is, perhaps, one of the most substantial implications of honest employment in the series: to Lindsay, agreeing to a date with Uncle Jack is preferable to holding an actual position at the company and earning money in an ethical manner.

"My Mother, the Car" (1:7) is another episode that illustrates many of the show's preoccupations with charity and criminal behavior, a relationship that becomes more prominent as the series progresses. Lucille's demand for a "surprise" birthday party is reminiscent of requests for favors and charity seen in other episodes. In this case, she insists that her children throw her "the most lavish party this town has ever seen for [her] birthday" ("My Mother, the Car" 1:7). Michael's attempts to coordinate the party result in marked instances of altruism juxtaposed with unlawful actions. Feeling bad after no one attends the second surprise party thrown for her, Michael cedes to Lucille's request to drive despite the fact that she has struck two pedestrians in the past; this immediately situates their conversation—and Lucille's request—within the contexts of both Michael doing his mother a favor while Lucille is (presumably) engaging in a criminal activity. When Michael allows Lucille to drive, she gets into an accident while trying to run down a man she believes to be Gob (she is attempting to punish him for failing to attend her party). Essentially, she decides to punish "Gob"—to commit a crime against him—because he did not acquiesce to her demands for special treatment. In the commission of this attempted crime, she commits another—framing Michael for their accident. After he has been knocked unconscious, and Lucille drags him to the driver's seat and lies to him about which of them had been driving. It is significant that, in this episode, Lucille and Michael both claim that the family does not "support" them; they comment on this mutual belief moments before Lucille attempts to run over "Gob" with the family car. Their demands for "support" actually reveal a desire for unfettered compliance with their demands. When said demands are not met, the Bluths—especially Lucille—respond with unethical and oftentimes criminal behavior. As the episode progresses, Lucille becomes further entrenched in misconduct in the name of altruism. She insists on caring for Michael at her home, refusing to allow him to use the telephone or have contact with the rest of the family. She also insists that the family doctor give Michael excessive amounts of an unnamed (though obviously strong) medication, which she refers to as "children's aspirin." In a particularly significant line, Lucille pleads with Michael in a simpering tone, "Let me take care of you" ("My Mother, the Car" 1:7). Of course, she is providing this apparent "care" in order to conceal her action of framing Michael and giving Gob "a scare." The episode clearly illustrates the extent to which Lucille takes advantage of others' charitable feelings and her unethical responses to kindness.

"Save Our Bluths" as a Thematic Archetype

While the connection between charity and crime has its origins in George Sr.'s actions on behalf of the United States government, this correlation culminates in the episode "S.O.B.s" (3:9). Fitzgerald's aforementioned discussion of constructionism is particularly applicable to this episode, as she explains, "According to the [constructionist] school of thought, those with power are privileged to define and, thus, to explain crime and delinquency" (309). The Bluths do indeed excuse their unethical behavior by blurring the line between charitable giving and deviance. Their requests for financial support are sometimes couched in criminality, a tendency that is most readily apparent in "S.O.B.s." Because of their once-affluent status, the Bluths are accustomed to using their power to influence others and excuse their unethical behavior. This attitude extends to their requests for charity, even long after the family has become financially unstable.

The premise of the episode centers on the family's decision to request charity from their friends to defend George Sr. against charges of treason. George Sr. acknowledges the relationship between crime and altruism when he informs the family, "We'll throw a legal defense fund dinner. Ask for donations" ("S.O.B.s" 3:9). The Bluths clearly see charity as a means of concealing their crimes, and the fact that requesting donations is a substitute for earning money is indicative of their sense of entitlement. The setting of the episode's charity dinner is also notable: the dinner must take place in the Bluths' penthouse, as George Sr. is on house arrest. This again provides a physical link between the family's crimes and their request for financial support.

The episode ultimately reveals the extent of the family's reliance upon charity as a means of concealing misconduct. Initially, the Bluths are reluctant to ask for monetary donations. Lucille notes, "We want them to think we'll take their help, but don't need it" ("S.O.B.s" 3:9). This changes drastically, though, by the end of the episode: with outright threats and references to poisoning, the family demands charity. Michael confesses, "I threaten people who I don't feel support me. He poisons them." (This is in reference to Michael's realization that George Sr. was the "Muffin Man," responsible for poisoning two teachers in the 1970s, an action that resulted in twenty-three "copycat" poisonings). The scene from the "next" episode of *Arrested Development* shows Lucille holding several checks, indicating that the charity dinner was a success and attributes this to Michael's speech, which clearly implicated both his father and himself in criminal activity. The family thus recognizes and accepts the relationship between crime and charity, which reveals their collective lack of ethics. Viewers will note, of course, that the donations likely stemmed from the threatening notes enclosed in the guests' "goody bags," which included messages such as, "I will come after you if you don't help me." The fact that these ultimatums resulted in financial dividends further implicates them in the use of charity as a means to hide criminal action. They request donations as a way to cover misdeeds, and they resort to threats when they fear that their guests will refuse to acquiesce.

The episode also reveals the Bluths' disdain for ethical behavior and employment. Gob jokingly poses as a waiter at the Balboa Country Club and "accidentally" works an entire shift. This develops into actual (albeit temporary) employment for Gob, who is ridiculed when the family learns of his work as a server. When Lucille learns of Gob's employment (after he accidently hits on her to get a bigger tip), she declares to everyone in the penthouse that she doesn't want Gob coming to the charity dinner. Clearly ethics (which, in this case, translates as earning an honest wage) and charity are incompatible; tellingly, Lucille and George Sr. openly acknowledge this. Similarly, Lindsay also briefly works as a salesperson in a clothing store and maintains, when asked about her new clothes, that she shoplifted them ("Not Without My Daughter" 1:21). In the Bluth family, theft is preferable to honest work, and licit behavior (that is, earning money legally) is in direct opposition to the family's criminal activity and their demands for charity.

Demanding and Accepting Charity

In myriad ways, several members of the Bluth family demand charity, or at least eagerly accept the largesse of others. For instance, Lucille, Gob, Lindsay, and Buster each receive paychecks from the Bluth Company, despite the fact that they do not perform any work for the business ("Staff Infection" 1:15). Perhaps the most significant example of these demands, though, is that of Maeby posing as "Surely Fünke" ("Altar Egos" 1:17), a student dying of a disease Maeby has termed "B.S." ("Justice Is Blind" 1:18). While the fundraising coordinator holds an enormous check over her head (which she subsequently presents to Surely), viewers are reminded of the extent of the family's corruption and their collective desperation for money. As Maeby sits in a wheelchair posing as Surely, she tells George Michael, "I figure I'll kill her off just before graduation just so everyone gets really sad before prom" ("Justice Is Blind" 1:18). The callousness of Maeby's attitude toward conning her classmates amplifies the unethical intent with which Maeby is capitalizing on others' charitable feelings: she is not only taking money under false pretenses, but she is also actively planning to send her schoolmates into mourning.

While Maeby's act of posing as Surely provides a distinct connection between charity and unethical behavior, the episode also includes an equally significant condemnation of honesty. As previously mentioned, the show has a tendency to punish characters who attempt to act in ethical ways, especially when that ethicality may prohibit others from realizing personal gain. "Justice Is Blind" (1:18) best exemplifies this through George Michael's involvement in Maeby's scheme. George Michael repeatedly warns Maeby that "someone's going to get hurt" through her act of deceiving their school and posing as a terminally ill student. His inherent moral code—specifically, his condemnation of her fraud—positions him as a character who is likely to be harmed or condemned by others in the near future, much in the same way the family ridicules and criticizes Gob for working as a waiter. Ultimately, George Michael is correct in that someone *is* hurt by Maeby's deception: in trying to help Surely up the bleachers, George Michael sprains his arm. Despite all this, George Michael eventually supports Maeby's deceptive behavior, though he only does so because Surely has announced that George Michael will "put an end to B.S." ("Justice Is Blind" 1:18), and he revels in the crowd's praise and attention.

It is perhaps important to note that Maeby's corrupt behavior *does* indeed have a positive effect: wheelchair ramps are installed in the local high school to accommodate Surely and others. However, Maeby is certainly uninterested in the ways in which others could benefit from charity. She overlooks the actual good that results from her greed and only focuses on her personal gain and the feelings of sadness she is able to incite in those who support Surely. The narrator notes that George Michael realizes Maeby is lying about attending a fundraiser because Maeby abstains from participating in charitable events as a way to rebel against Lindsay. This is similar to the aforementioned ways in which George Sr.'s unethical dealings have influenced the Bluth children: just as he supported and (indirectly) encouraged Lindsay to make a mockery of charitable causes (consider her oscillation between her campaigns for "No More Meat" and "More Meat and Fish" ["Storming the Castle" 1:9]), so too has Maeby learned this same lesson from her mother. It is noteworthy, then, that despite how much she does not want to be like Lindsay, Maeby does not seem to realize that she is, indeed, emulating her mother's behavior.

Such an attitude is also apparent in the family's collective fundraising efforts, particularly in the episode "Prison Break-In" (3:7), which features Tobias nearly dying from complications related to his hair plugs. The family takes advantage of Tobias's "disease"—Graft Versus Host (GVH)—in order to obtain charitable donations from attendees of the Bluth Family Foundation gala. Gob, in an effort to capitalize on the charitable feelings of the gala's patrons, films the event as a documentary featuring Tobias. Tobias is harmed multiple times during filming, but Gob and Lindsay, ironically, seem to be completely unconcerned with Tobias' wellbeing. When describing Graft Versus Host, Lindsay explains to Michael, "It's new. It's fatal. And guess who's got it?" ("Prison Break-In" 3:7), smiling broadly just before an image of a seriously ill Tobias appears on screen. In essence, Lindsay is pleased that Tobias is so sickly because his illness will be financially beneficial to her. The conversation between Tobias, his physician, and Lindsay is particularly telling in this regard:

> PHYSICIAN: Either you remove your hair graft or the host, you, will get sicker and eventually die.
> LINDSAY: Can you think of any benefits?
> PHYSICIAN: Benefits? No, he'll die.
> LINDSAY: Oh, yeah. No, I get that. But have there ever been any fundraisers? ["Prison Break-In" 3:7].

In explaining why she will not permit Tobias to have the grafts removed, Lindsay says, "No way. That horsehair is my ticket back into society. You cut it after those idiots at the gala accept me as one of their own" ("Prison Break-In" 3:7). Upon hearing her comments and learning that Tobias' fatal illness can be easily cured, the fundraiser attendees riot. In essence, a charity event has turned into an explosion of violence (inside the walls of a prison, no less). The donors' reactions may be interpreted as a larger comment on the misuse of charitable funds widely reported in contemporaneous national news. That is, *Arrested Development*'s preoccupation with charitable giving and misconduct can be read as a response to the spate of news reports on the subject of charity and crime that arose in the early twenty-first century. In a 2003 *New York Times* interview, Paul C. Light notes, "The questions raised about how the 9/11 charities were spending the money they received and how quickly they were disbursing it ... were followed by scandals in the Catholic Church and a steady drip, drip, drip of news stories raising questions about many aspects of nonprofit accountability" (Strom, "New Equation"). This sense of wariness is apparent in "Prison Break-In" (3:7), especially considering that the Bluths had previously misled donors' in their efforts to collect donations for "TBA." In discussing the rising concern over the allocation of charitable donations, Light also notes that, "Some 70 percent of respondents to a new survey among the general public thought charities wasted 'a great deal' or 'a fair amount.' Donors have already indicated ... that they don't have a great deal of faith in the way these groups handle money" (Strom, "Report"). In the sense that the episode demonstrates a disturbing element of verisimilitude, the family's unethical appeals for charitable funds are indicative of a larger national issue and originally aired at a particularly apposite time in the United States. In the wake of business ethics scandals and misuse of charitable donations still ubiquitous in the American consciousness, the Bluths' actions are particularly condemnable and, more significantly, they are worryingly realistic.

Requesting (or Demanding) Favors

Whether it is Lucille shouting, "Lupe, I need help with the groceries" ("Staff Infection" 1:15) or Gob couching his requests for money in compliments to Michael, the Bluths consistently ask others for favors. While not always thought of as "charity" in the more common use of the term, recent scholarship has established the proffering of favors as a type of charitable giving. Fred Feldman explains, "What we already know but may have forgotten about giving is that when we make a charitable donation, we are simply doing a favor. We certainly feel good about ourselves when we do a favor for family or friends. We should feel the same satisfaction when we give to a charitable cause." Likewise, Armin Falk and Urs Fischbacher's seminal study on reciprocity also reveals a link between receiving acts of kindness and the inclination to provide donations. With that said, the favors requested by the Bluths generally have corrupt consequences or tend to involve violence in some way (as do most other types of charity seen on the show). "Staff Infection" (1:15) and "Missing Kitty" (1:16) are illustrative of this point. At Tobias's request, Warden Gentles allows Tobias to research his upcoming role as "Frightened Inmate Number Two" at the prison, and almost immediately this favor is couched in an environment of violence; the favor Tobias asks is, in essence, to be imprisoned with violent criminals ("Staff Infection" 1:15). During Tobias' incarceration, George Sr. (a fellow inmate) sells Tobias "for a pack of cigarettes" to White Power Bill ("Missing Kitty" 1:16). While the act of "selling" Tobias is obviously unethical, Tobias uses his forced proximity to Bill as an opportunity to provide therapy. His intentions are clearly altruistic; Tobias wants to help his cellmate and he prompts Bill realize that he hates himself, rather than those he has long held responsible for his anger (his father and the government, for example). Tobias' attempts to help White Power Bill, however, prove disastrous: Bill kills himself as a result of Tobias' intervention. What is particularly enlightening about this example, though, is the way in which altruism and crime act as an equalizing force. Tobias, a graduate of M.I.T., and White Power

Bill, a racist criminal, become comparable characters when we view them in the context of a prison. As Fitzgerald notes, "It becomes increasingly difficult to define terms such as 'crime' and 'criminal' as it is recognized that these terms are not self-evident; rather, these terms are nested in a vast web of power relations that implicate all human behaviors and all people" (309). Bill, a powerful and fearsome presence in the prison, loses his authority in the presence of Tobias, whose "power" lies in his ability to bring Bill to a point of self-realization. Tobias' charitable intervention is ostensibly helpful, yet his presence in the prison blurs the line between therapist and criminal.

It is equally important to examine the character of Michael, as he provides useful examples of favors and altruism stemming from and resulting in questionable behavior. Since Michael has passing moments of naïveté about his family's true nature, he is sometimes unnecessarily generous toward them, which is apparent in his initial dealings with his uncle Oscar and Michael's buying his land, a lemon grove, as a favor. After signing the deal, though, George Sr. tells Michael that the land is worthless because of a government easement; Oscar has deceived him ("Whistler's Mother" 1:20). In selling Michael the useless land, Oscar perpetuates the family's cycle of using favors and others' sense of charity as a means for corrupt personal gain. Ultimately, Lucille resolves this situation on Michael's behalf, which prompts Michael to recall a similar situation from school (when a young Michael encounters difficulties with his teacher, Lucille ensures that the teacher loses his job and essentially disappears. Though her actions are never made fully clear, there is certainly an implication of violence and misconduct).

Buster's military training similarly provides a valuable example of the interchange between favors and violence. The army training officers are prohibited from intimidating or harming the recruits, and Buster is unable to climb the wall without such "motivation" ("Sad Sack" 2:5). In an incident that helps clarify his generally frightened, paranoid nature, he realizes that Gob—and physical violence—will help him meet the demands of his training. In the episode, we see a young Gob encouraging Buster to overcome his fear of going down a slide by punching him in the chest as he reaches the bottom. Buster considers the violence not only a form of motivation but also a charitable favor, even saying "Thanks, brother" in response to Gob's violent act. In dealing with his difficulties completing the army's obstacle course, Buster pleads with Gob, stating, "I need your help to get over the wall. Push me" ("Sad Sack" 2:5). Again, personal favors are couched in acts of violence, a relationship that is apparent for Buster in multiple episodes. "Beef Consommé" (1:13), for instance, shows Buster begging his brothers to include him in their brawl on the courthouse lawn. Specifically, he pleads, "Will someone please have the decency to punch me in the face?" ("Beef Consommé" 1:13). He sees the commission of violence as an act of charity toward him, as he believes it will help him mature and impress Marta, the woman with whom both Gob and Michael have been romantically involved. Buster equates charitable behavior and aggression, considering the infliction of physical pain as a means by which his brothers can demonstrate a sense of fraternity and kindness.

Conclusion

The Bluths' willingness to use charity as a means to increase their personal wealth, to cover their crimes, or even to commit violence is apparent in many episodes of *Arrested Development.* The Bluths pervert charitable acts as a means of exerting power, often in criminal ways, and the constructionist theory reinforces the idea that those in a position of power manipulate the definitions of crime in order to protect themselves (Fitzgerald 305). Even characters that pride themselves on their sense of honor, such as Michael, are remarkably fallible when faced with opportunities to seek personal gain through unethical means. In some ways, this simply makes the characters more believable. Even if we ourselves do not mimic the Bluths' egregious behavior, a brief glimpse of news headlines—both now and during the show's original airing—reveals myriad criminal misuses of charitable activities. In turn, this gives the world of *Arrested Development* a greater sense of realism, or, as Kathryn Reklis notes, "*Arrested Development* gives us plenty of fodder to laugh cathartically at human nature at its worst. But the small moments of actual connection between the characters pull us back from the edge of farce to see the real humanity of the stunted Bluths and maybe just a glimpse of ourselves" (43). Certainly, the Bluths tend toward the extreme in their abuses of one another, their greed, and their willingness to act unethically, yet these foibles ultimately cause the characters to feel lifelike. In essence, the series uncovers the occasionally unethical inclinations of average people in both their personal lives and business dealings. The connection between charity and corruption adds a degree of verisimilitude to the series in that these characters reflect the greed and misconduct so readily observable in modern culture.

Works Cited

Falk, Armin, and Urs Fischbacher. "A Theory of Reciprocity." *Games & Economic Behavior* 54.2 (2006): 293–315. Print.

Feldman, Fred. "Mindful Charitable Giving as a Pathway to Enlightenment." *The Huffington Post*. 5 Feb. 2013. Web. 13 Apr. 2014. http://www.huffingtonpost.com/fred-feldman/donating-charity_b_2616296.html

Fitzgerald, Charity Samantha. "Historical Theories of Crime and Delinquency." *Journal of Human Behavior in the Social Environment* 21.3 (2011): 297–311. Print.

Leitch, Will. "The Persistent Cult of *Arrested Development*." *New York Magazine* 46.16 (2013): 30–33. Print.

Poniewozik, James. "It's Not TV. It's Arrested Development." *Time*. 20 May 2013. Web. 1 Apr. 2014. http://content.time.com/time/magazine/article/0,9171,2143009,00.html

Reklis, Kathryn. "The Bluths' School for Virtue." *Christian Century* 130.12 (2013): 42–43. Print.

Strom, Stephanie. "New Equation for Charities: More Money, Less Oversight." *The New York Times*. 17 Nov. 2003. Web. 1 Apr. 2014. http://www.nytimes.com/2003/11/17/giving/accountability-new-equation-for-charities-more-money-less-oversight.html

_____. "Report Sketches Crime Costing Billions: Theft from Charities." *The New York Times*. 29 Mar. 2008. Web. 1 Apr. 2014. http://www.nytimes.com/2008/03/29/us/29fraud.html?pagewanted=all&_r=0

Wren, Celia. "Crimes & Banana Stands." *Commonweal* 131.6 (2004): 19–20. Print.

Lindsay Bluth and the Politics of Sincerity

Environmental Rhetoric, Eco-Consciousness and Social Performance

Elizabeth Lowry

Representations of environmentalism in *Arrested Development* imply that contemporary environmentalism is mired in insincerity and inconsistency and that it is based on mythology rather than fact. Lindsay Bluth's role as a laissez-faire activist reflects the sense that activism is little more than a social performance; Johnny Bark's ethos is called into question when he abandons "his" tree to court Lindsay, and Marky Bark's sense of logic is consummately skewed in that he is evidently more interested in blowing things up than in doing practical cultural work. Further, environmental theorists Killingsworth and Palmer suggest that the narratives we tell ourselves about the environment and how the media report on environmental issues are fraught with biases that cast the environmentalist as "other." Even when environmentalism is not merely performed as a bid for social identity, news stories inevitably turn environmental action into a social performance that serves only to foment existing socioeconomic boundaries. However, when examined more closely, portrayals of environmentalists on *Arrested Development* also imply a more complex interpretation of eco-consciousness as we know it; that is, an exploration of the politics of sincerity and the varying implications of an ironic approach to environmentalism. Based upon scholarship on environmental rhetoric as well as Aristotle's *Nichomachean Ethics*, it is evident that *Arrested Development* is castigating the relationship between sincerity (or a lack thereof) and the possibility of meaningful social change. However, before undertaking an examination of Lindsay's role as principal agent of faux-environmentalism on the show, it is first worth examining some of the other pseudo-environmentalists that populate her world.

The Romanticization/Colonization of Nature

Arrested Development presents two classic postcolonial viewpoints that originated in the early industrial age, yet are still endemic to the "mainstream" environmental movement. Despite the fact that George Sr. is framed as being unscrupulous, those who capitalize on natural resources are more typically represented in Western narratives of progress as being pragmatic entrepreneurs. On the other hand, environmentalists are frequently portrayed as being romantics who are out of touch with reality. In this regard, George Sr. and Oscar symbolize what appear to be opposing viewpoints on environmental debates. In contrast to George Sr., Oscar is a marijuana-smoking, trailer-dwelling dropout, with the dubious honor of having been named "the shallowest man in the world" ("Whistler's Mother"1:20). To some degree, Oscar is cast as a nature lover (although by no means an activist) whose essentialist views on nature frame wilderness areas as being sites of spiritual discovery. As Sturgeon and other environmental theorists point out, although a romanticized view of nature may lead to an increase in attempts at preservation, it will not lead to meaningful environmental initiatives because it does not address the problem of socioeconomic polarization. Social ecology, an environmental theory supported by Sturgeon and other environmental scholars, suggests that meaningful solutions to environmental problems cannot be found unless social inequality is first addressed. But neither Oscar nor George Sr. is particularly interested in equality. Instead, as George Sr. comes on the scene and charges large sums of money for executives to attend retreats at Oscar's sweat lodge ("Borderline Personalities" 4:2), nature and experiences of the natural world serve only to contribute toward a growing divide between the rich and the poor. Nature, in its most idealized form, becomes the exclusive province of the privileged.

Oscar's collaboration with George Sr. in organizing sweat lodge sessions and Native American vision quests foments the idea that their views are equally individualistic and therefore equally exploitative. While George, Sr.'s callous disregard for the natural world is of concern, Oscar's unbridled romanticism isn't much better. As Herndl and Brown note, "the individualism that lies at the center of this romantic vision considers knowledge and action as private affairs and sees nature as an aesthetic, even religious object" (6). Herndl and Brown theorize that this kind of romanticism which, perhaps as a response to industrialization and urbanization, began to manifest in the early nineteenth century was most likely "a nostalgic desire for an agrarian culture that was already lost or may never have existed" (6). Thus, although romanticizing and colonizing the natural world seem to represent two radically different points of view, romance and colonization (like Oscar and George Sr.) have similar origins. Oscar essentializes "nature" while George Sr. plunders it, but in the end, both are part of the same individualistic postcolonial venture. Herndl and Brown suggest that Americans need to think of themselves as a community, rather than as individuals. Meaningful political actions would be "those in which individuals act within social communities and the ethical values at play are often those of social responsibility rather than private pleasure and spiritual reverie" (7). As Herndl and Brown see it, we no longer have the luxury of simply sitting back and enjoying nature. We are part of the natural world and part of a web of life that includes others with whom we do not necessarily identify. In order to preserve the environment, we have to learn to identify with people whom we see as being unlike ourselves; to unite in social reform and meaningful cultural work.

Johnny Bark and the Enduring Myth of Progress

Arrested Development offers a portrait of twenty-first century environmentalism that reflects the movement's ineffective appeals, its unappealing ambassadors, its hypocrisy, and its outmoded narratives of progress and development. These issues resonate with those detailed by Killingsworth and Palmer in their landmark book, *Ecospeak: Rhetoric and Environmental Politics in America*. According to the authors, one of environmentalism's main issues is "the intractability of social problems like the environmental dilemma due to the inability of concerned discourse communities to form adequate identifications through effective appeals" (7). As far as Killingsworth and Palmer are concerned, care for the environment has become a "dilemma" because it has barely made any progress since the 1970s. Not only are genuinely "concerned discourse communities" few and far between, they are also impotent. Public spheres theorist Michael Warner asserts,

> Often one cannot imagine addressing a public capable of comprehension or action. This is especially true for people in minor or marginal positions or people

distributed across political systems. The result can be a kind of political depressiveness, a blockage in activity and optimism, a disintegration of politics toward isolation, frustration, anomie, forgetfulness [415].

In *Arrested Development*, we see both "political depressiveness" and oppression. There is a "blockage" in activity primarily because of apathy. The self-interest and insincerity of politicians engenders a sense of anomie—and all this drives the characters toward acts of increasing absurdity and hypocrisy.

Throughout the series, activism is always ineffective, in part because of the implied lack of sincerity of its adherents, but also because of the shrill tenor of their arguments, their rag-tag appearance, and their hostility. For instance, in season four Marky Bark reveals that his solution to social injustice is to "bomb" the podium at Herbert Love's campaign ("Red Hairing" 4:8). Strategies such as these cause the public to view activists at worst as terrorists and at best as pests. Essentially, this is a public relations problem: the activists do not effectively frame their appeals. As Killingsworth and Palmer so aptly state, environmental groups "have been unable to create strong communicative links with the mass public, links that would support a strong power base for reformative actions" (7). Here, Killingsworth and Palmer suggest that we are capable of "reformative actions," but when reading *Arrested Development* as social satire, it is questionable as to whether or not such reforms are possible. In *Arrested Development* no one is able to effectively communicate and, even if they could, it is uncertain as to whether they would care enough or whether they would even be capable of putting their self interests aside in order to create a meaningful agenda informing a "strong power base for reformative actions."

In season one, as Michael makes plans to develop the Bluth property after his father has been imprisoned, he decides that everything must be "bulldozed," including what appears to be an old California live oak (The tree's genus is never actually identified on the show, not even by Johnny Bark, the man who most wants to save it). As a result of Michael's decision to raze the property, environmental activist Johnny Bark takes residence in the tree to prevent its removal. When the local news station begins to report on Johnny Bark's mission to save the tree, we see how the news media typically reflect key issues with respect to contemporary environmental rhetoric. For instance, Killingsworth and Palmer point out that the media outlets present audiences with a "repetition of rhetorical situations whose narrative outlines contain similar plots and characters—the confrontation of environmental activists with land developers, for example" (8). The confrontation that Killingsworth and Palmer describe has become a well-worn narrative trope. Evoking the activists of the 1980s and 1990s who—largely framed as disrupting progress—chained themselves to old-growth Redwoods in Northern California and Oregon, the dour Bark, clad in a grimy flannel shirt and woolen hat, is cast as an environmental "everyman."

But Lindsay Bluth is as much a stereotype as Johnny Bark. In the 1980s and 1990s:

> Eager to discredit the environmentalists' assaults on their polluting practices, large corporations frequently employed conservative lobbyists to fashion an image in the mass media of the typical "pesty" environmentalist ... a white, wine-and-Brie upper-middle-class professional ... with no sympathy for the plight of the ordinary working man put out of work by the environmentalists' meddlesome "tree hugging" love of Nature [Luke 50].

Lindsay, of course, embodies the wine-and-Brie activist, and in this case the quintessential upper-middle-class activist's interest in the environment is cast as being purely selfish; her interests are motivated primarily by access to clean recreation areas for her personal use. Her discursive presence becomes a trope that, operating within the parameters of a privileged white environmentalism, is "used to contain real ecological concerns through the coercive cultural coding of environmentally minded individuals" (Luke 50). As such, allegations of "limousine liberalism" serve to immediately condemn the motives of almost any moneyed activist. However, in this scenario, sincerity itself is less of an issue than the revelation that Bark and Lindsay's carefully constructed self-identification as environmentalists has already been so negatively coded that they never had a chance of being taken seriously to begin with.

As Killingsworth and Palmer point out, "Familiarity breeds oversimplification, stereotyping, and pigeonholing—especially in the mass media, where telegraphic style mingles with the need to cultivate in the audience a quick recognition of issues and public figures" (8). These stock characters, scenarios, and stereotypes may indicate the predictability and inevitability of our cultural dysfunction, but they also become a means by which to perpetuate an unfortunate situation: an institutionalized disregard for the environment in the face of perpetual "development." The word "development" suggests inevitability. Throughout the show, development is framed as the answer to the Bluth's financial woes, and land development must go forward at whatever cost. As Sturgeon puts it: "Western ideology always presents those who are seen as more natural (including natural resources themselves) as ultimately destined to 'develop' to become part of a commercial, commodified system" (13). Colonial western ideologies tend to view marginalized people as being more "natural," and, throughout the show we see the Bluths make multiple assumptions about people of color—from Lucille's cracks about immigrants to Gob's use of African-American stereotypes via Franklin, to the Native American cultural appropriation marking the desert retreat and sweat lodge in season four.

Conflating development with civilization and intimating that the natural is somehow baser than the cultivated becomes a way to "obscure historical contingency and ongoing resistance—justifying power, inequality, and conquest by making those processes of 'development' seem inevitable, natural, and part of destined and unstoppable evolution" (Sturgeon 13). To this effect, Lupe and her family must find their place within the realm of late monopoly capitalism, Franklin is used to draw a wider audience for Gob's magic show, and stereotypical assumptions about a generalized form of "Native American culture" are the basis of George Sr. and Oscar's creation of an expensive spiritual "retreat." The Bluths interpret the appropriation of "other" cultures as being essential to their own (rightful) economic gain. What happens to others as a result of their development is not their concern—they are simply doing what they are expected to do. Further, in season four, we learn that Johnny Bark, who casts himself as being part of nature and a defender of the "natural"—the man who resists development—allegedly dies when he falls out of a tree. Bark is believed to have died because he would not accept "development." Thus, Western narratives of progress seek to trump the lone man who impedes progress by erroneously identifying with the "natural."

With respect to ineffective calls for preservation and conservation, Killingsworth and Palmer point to the language used by the media: language that reinscribes social boundaries and polarizes political agendas. Consequently:

> the environmentalist/developmentalist dichotomy has proved immensely attractive and durable, presumably because it provides busy reporters with a ready-made stock of plots and characters—it tends to conceal other sources of solidarity and conflict, which if closely examined, could provide hints toward the kind of social reorganization needed to cut through the environmental dilemma [10].

This "environmentalist/developmentalist dichotomy" is attractive not only because it offers a cache of recognizable plots and characters to draw from, but because it provides power-holders with an excuse to avoid social responsibility. Moreover, the notion of concealing other possibilities or approaches to environmental dilemmas is crucial to an understanding of how effective rhetorical appeals are stymied. Not only do effective appeals need to address easily identifiable aspects of a social problem and offer solutions for them, but they also need to address the sort of information that is being withheld from the public—that is, the implications of acting or not acting given a particular situation. Further, as long as the word "development" continues to retain its progressive connotations, reportage on stand-offs between environmentalists and developers will contribute to social polarization. When it is suggested that environmentalists' behavior is illogical, extreme, or unacceptable, we foment the idea that they are "other." Casting the environmentalist (rather than the developer) as the source of disruption naturalizes the idea of destroying nature. This means that Johnny Bark is immediately considered to be odd and subversive—or as Lindsay puts it: "gross" ("Key Decisions" 1:4). But beyond this, Bark's intentions are also questionable. Bark refers to the tree as "his" tree, thereby adopting the same sense of appropriation and entitlement that Michael assumes when he first plans on cutting the tree down. Bark is interested in the tree only when he is not distracted by the thought of a relationship with Lindsay, Lindsay is interested in the tree only as a bid for attention, and Maeby is interested in the tree only when Lindsay is not. The tree thus becomes symbolic of the sorts of power struggles emblematic of the environmental movement; power struggles that are more about petty personal agendas than conservation.

The Wetlands and the Problem of Sincerity

MICHAEL: You just do all this charity crap just to stroke your ego. You don't even know what the auction's for tonight.
LINDSAY: The wetlands.
MICHAEL: To do what with them?
LINDSAY: Dry them.
MICHAEL: Save them.
LINDSAY: From drying. Which is more than you would ever do. I mean you're like the least charitable person I know.
MICHAEL: I don't do anything for myself. Everything that I do is for this family.
LINDSAY: Oh, you don't do it for us, Michael. You do it because you love being the guy in charge ["Charity Drive" 1:6].

The truth is that Lindsay's self-serving attempts to sacrifice herself for the good of the wetlands are not much different from Michael's claim to sacrifice himself for the family. Neither are motivated by altruism because, in the diegetic world of *Arrested Development*, altruism simply does not exist. Later in the same episode, we learn that: "Lindsay, wanting to prove to Michael that she was a charitable person, joined a group of activists dedicated to preserving the wetlands" ("Charity Drive" 1:6). Aside from Lindsay's self-serving reason for going to the wetlands in the first place, her lack of ethos is underscored by her refusal to ride a bus with the other activists, instead opting to take a taxi.

The clean-up crew quietly climbs aboard a repurposed school-bus, casting curious glances at Lindsay who is on her cell phone. Later, at the wetlands, Lindsay is again on the phone, and the volunteers continue to stare, even looking a little shocked when she accidentally spears a frog with her poker. Since the wetlands clean-up crew's motives are not explored, we do not know that Lindsay's motives for being at the wetlands are really so different from theirs, but the way that they look at her suggests that they see her as being unlike themselves. Like the other volunteers, Lindsay wears an old (but flattering) T-shirt and a bandana; she chooses to don a "uniform" to join this particular discourse community in order to identify and be identified as an environmental activist. This signals that not only is Lindsay volunteering to prove a point to Michael, she is also volunteering with the intention of creating a sense of identity. As such, Lindsay's lack of sincerity in terms of the cause itself and her superficial moves toward creating a temporary (and unconvincing) environmentalist identity become the narrative force behind the wetlands episode.

Since much of Lindsay's comic appeal arises from her lack of sincerity, the issue of sincerity becomes an important component of Lindsay's work as an activist. In *Nichomachean Ethics*, Aristotle asserts that sincerity (which he refers to as "truthfulness") can be understood in the following terms: "With regard to truth ... the intermediate is a truthful sort of person and the mean may be called truthfulness, while the pretence which exaggerates is boastfulness and the person characterized by it a boaster, and that which understates is mock modesty and the person characterized by it mock-modest" (19). Here, Aristotle claims that when any virtue is over-emphasized or understated, it can become a vice. Therefore, keeping a virtue such as "truthfulness" in check is crucial to maintaining sincerity. Too much "truthfulness" may lead to ironic behaviors such as boastfulness or "mock-modesty." Irony and sincerity are inextricably intertwined. Irony threatens sincerity, or the balance of truth. Further, in order to be deemed "truthful" or sincere, one must have no ulterior motives, but in *Arrested Development* everyone is hiding something. The discrepancy between the characters' ulterior motives and the reasons they give for their behavior is essential to the comedic irony of the show. But in season one Michael and Lindsay both seem to want to be taken seriously as sincere people. They want to be more virtuous than they really are and their struggle is primarily with their own flawed human nature. However, over the course of the series, Michael and Lindsay's more or less positive intentions begin to erode. The desire to be a good person that seems to set Lindsay and Michael apart from their parents comes unraveled in season four when Lindsay takes up with both Marky Bark and Herbert Love, and Michael continues a relationship with a woman even after he discovers that she is dating his son. At this point, we see that Michael and Lindsay's own self-interests have taken over entirely. Despite themselves, they have become as unscrupulous as Lucille and George Sr.

Thus, the ethical climate depicted in *Arrested Development* is every bit as dire as the environmental climate. Being environmentally conscious is presented as an inconvenience rather than as a necessity. In this context, activism is sincere only to the degree that it serves individual self-interest. Even Johnny Bark, a man who has purportedly dedicated his life to environmental activism, is no more sincere than Lindsay. He leaves his post at the tree to declare his feelings for her, and because of the lack of attention he pays to his cause, the tree is felled. And it is precisely this problem that Killingsworth and Palmer point to in *Ecospeak*; that is, working to save the environment is seen as being something we do for self-aggrandizement, rather than because we are interested in preserving the ecosystem for future generations. The environment is treated as an inconvenient charity case—a sick relative for whom one feels obliged to care. As long as these narratives and beliefs are perpetuated, no meaningful environmental initiatives can be made. In the twenty-first century, environmentalism has become an umbrella term: "The variety of very different contexts in which we talk about the environment suggests that there is not one environmental discourse but many, a polyphony that makes it difficult to understand and resolve environmental disputes" (Herndl and Brown 4). What constitutes an environmental issue also varies in interpretation from context to context. What social ecologists define as an environmental issue, other more mainstream environmentalists may see as being an issue of social justice and therefore beyond their purview.

Although Killingsworth and Palmer don't believe that environmentalism ever really became "mainstream," Sturgeon claims that indeed there is such a thing as mainstream environmentalism, although it is largely ineffective. Mainstream environmentalists make problematic assumptions: for instance, they see nature and culture as being two entirely separate spheres, and they emphasize small localized solutions without considering the complex web of life. Further, "contemporary radical environmentalism differs from mainstream environmentalisms in that they argue ... that there is a relationship between social inequalities and environmental problems. Mainstream environmentalism does not make such arguments" (Sturgeon 8). This is perhaps one of the most significant ideological divisions among self-identified environmentalists: some believe that no progress can be made whatsoever without attending to social inequality (meaning that effective environmental initiatives are not possible within the context of late monopoly capitalism). However, others believe that environmentalism and capitalism do not have to be inimical. In suggesting that "mainstream" environmentalists do not acknowledge a relationship between social inequity and environmental degradation, Sturgeon's position becomes clear: mainstream environmentalism is not "real" environmentalism. Further, the *Arrested Development* diegesis demonstrates that those who see themselves as mainstream environmentalists treat environmental issues as if they were a form of charity—not unlike the fundraisers they might launch for starving children in developing countries. Tackling environmental problems within a mainstream (and privileged) milieu is equally problematic. For instance, at the bachelorette auction in aid of the wetlands, we have no idea where the money from the auction goes, how it is used, or indeed what percentage of the money goes to the wetlands at all ("Charity Drive" 1:6). Nor is the focus on the wetlands—it is on the bachelorettes. Small, relatively isolated activist groups, whether they are a group of volunteers on clean-up duty or bachelorettes at a country club auction, do not necessarily seem to do any good because their work is sporadic and decontextualized. These disjointed and superficial approaches toward environmentalism are reflective of what Luke refers to as "old school" attitudes, meaning that these ideologies pit economy against environment in touting "the necessity of real-estate development over protecting of the coastal wetlands in this or that corner of the nation" (116). The fact that *Arrested Development* presents this "old school" environmental discourse as being the norm suggests that, generally speaking, our culture has not moved away from binary thinking: nature versus culture, economy versus environment, and so on.

With Lindsay's foray into the wetlands, *Arrested Development* seems to be suggesting that social change can only happen (and indeed is only respectable) through acts of genuine altruism. Given the cynical and satirical nature of the show, a veiled insistence that social change should come from a position of authenticity initially seems to be oddly idealistic. Although it may be true that social progress—particularly in environmentalism—has stalled because people do not care enough to engage in sincere acts, can the case not be made that progress can still happen albeit for selfish reasons? At first, it seems as if the fact that Lindsay shows up to do the work is not valued, but when Lucille insults her daughter at the auction by telling her (with a smirk) that she is "not supposed to show up *as* the wetlands" followed by Michael's acknowledgement that he's impressed that his sister actually followed through with her plan, viewers are able to place Lindsay into the more sympathetic realm of a character who tries—who genuinely wants to care more, who wants to be "better" in some way ("Charity Drive" 1:6).

Social Performance and "Ironic Environmentalism"

In *Arrested Development*, environmental activism in and of itself is constructed as an intricate social performance. For the Bluths, charity and activism are conflated because, according to privileged white Americans, environmentalism is a charitable act rather than a social necessity. Moreover, the show's stance toward activism reflects the sense that people who act as ambassadors for social causes should be genuinely passionate about those causes. Eventually, this mindset makes it almost impossible for anyone to be an activist in good faith. An insistence on sincerity gives rise to a stymieing logic of purity that can undermine almost any engagement in socially conscious or civic-minded acts: unless our motives are pure, our work cannot be valued. A lack of sincerity therefore becomes an excuse to not do anything.

Szerszynski discusses this issue in his article "The Post-ecologist Condition: Irony as Symptom and Cure." Referencing Ingolfur Bluhdorn, Szerszynski claims that one of the reasons that the environmental movement is not more successful is because it has become largely symbolic; "a 'simulative politics' in which contemporary culture and the meanings through which it is reproduced have become self-referential, detached from any obligation to material referents or effects ... it is a pervasive syndrome in which even social movement activity is trapped" (338). Simulation and the layering of cultural meaning inherent to the digital age has left us disconnected from the material world. Without this sense of connection, it seems impossible to conceive of material problems as being "real" and as having real consequences. Lindsay's actions as an advocate for social change, particularly those she engages in as an environmentalist, are representative of this claim. Everything that Lindsay does in the name of a social cause ultimately deflects attention from the causes themselves and onto her self-styled image as an activist. The foray into the wetlands centers around Lindsay's communications with Michael. Indeed we know nothing about the other activists or even the wetlands itself, and Lindsay's involvement with the wetlands ends with Michael bidding on her at a charity auction. The folly of adopting the trappings of activism in the hope that going through the motions of acting for a cause will allow one to proclaim an identity as an activist is reflected strongly here. However, Szerszynski does not lay the blame for such behavior entirely on individuals such as Lindsay, or even on "the logic of the capitalist system," but suggests that the problem is more deeply rooted and systemic than that: environmental initiatives are staged, and the reason for their existence is nebulous, often pertaining to competing agendas that have nothing to do with environmentalism at all. This means that it is virtually impossible for anyone to act in good faith within a late monopoly capitalist system. It is, Szerszynski says, a "crisis in political meaning in which we are all implicated" (338). Without proper monitoring, without real definition and a strong set of directives, the environmental movement seems to be quite ineffective: "any meaningful aspiration to robust monitoring and regulation has been replaced by systems of self-regulation and environmental management that are frequently little more than forms of what Goffman refers to as 'impression management'" (Szerszynski 344). Szerszynski's reference to Goffman underscores the performative aspects of activism: the drama of appearing to be engaged. Lindsay, for instance, is not joining the group of activists because she actually cares about the wetlands, she is joining the activists to prove a point to her brother and arguably—in skewering a frog—does more harm than good while she is there. This implies that we want to solve problems, or at least to be recognized for solving problems without ever really engaging with them. Worse still, this scenario is disturbingly transparent to audiences who alternately revel in and cringe at its irony.

When Aristotle describes the most important social virtues, "truthfulness" or sincerity is cast as manifesting in relationships between oneself and others—and therefore could be construed as a kind of social performance. Sincerity, Aristotle says, lands somewhere on the spectrum between boastfulness and "mock-modesty" (19). Boastfulness is simply offensive, Aristotle suggests, but mock-modesty is in some ways more insidious because it can be perceived as irony. In this manner, Aristotle pits irony and sincerity against one another suggesting that they are binary opposites. While irony can no doubt be amusing, sincerity is more valuable to social progress. However, within the context of the Bluth family, when what is said never quite means what is understood (and often means the exact opposite), irony usually precludes sincerity altogether. Nonetheless, it is precisely this lack of ethos that makes the show's characters so endearing.

Lindsay's actions as an environmentalist and later her efforts to engage with Southland politics are deeply ironic—but when it comes to Lindsay, the kind of dramatic irony customarily deployed in *Arrested Development* is taken a step further in that there is irony within the irony; "an 'irony of self betrayal,'" which is to say, a scene in which the characters within a drama "are made unconsciously to expose their lack of moral reflexivity" (Szerszynski 347). With the exception of George Michael (and perhaps the charmingly clueless Tobias), virtually every character on *Arrested Development* displays a "lack of moral reflexivity," but they almost always display this lack consciously and unapologetically. However, Lindsay sincerely believes herself to be beyond reproach, which makes her character's ironic moments all the more pronounced. The element of unconscious self-betrayal is underscored in season four when Lindsay, apparently intending to champion social justice, ends up doing the exact opposite in encouraging the construction of a wall between Mexico and the United States.

When Szerszynski speaks of an "ironic environmentalism," then, he means taking a stance of moral reflexivity. He is essentially advocating a form of environmentalism that can account for the many contradictory practices that we find ourselves engaged in simply by virtue of living in a late monopoly capitalist society. Szerszynski speaks of being able to accept:

> what Muecke calls "general irony," a metaphysical position in which the human condition is understood as riven with fundamental contradictions, such as those between freedom and determinism, intention and outcome, the infinite universe and finite existence. Unlike verbal irony, here there are no separate groups of perpetrators and victims [348].

This kind of "general irony," and the adoption of this particular stance toward the environmental movement is useful, Szerszynski suggests, because it frees us from the paralysis we feel when we know that we are enacting contradictory behaviors—for instance, when otherwise environmentally conscious people claim to be against drilling in Alaska, yet drive gas-guzzling vehicles. These contradictions are not to be encouraged, but to some degree they are inevitable. Therefore, insisting on total authenticity (an absolute purity of intention and a complete absence of hypocrisy within the environmental movement) is not likely to move us forward. As Szerszynski points out, "no one can know political truths perfectly or live blamelessly, especially under current circumstances" (352). Instead of pointing to the endless foibles and contradictory aspects of the environmental movement, we should take more personal responsibility and attempt to be more aware of our own individual stances toward environmental initiatives in order to consider how we might more effectively act upon our core beliefs.

We do not need to reject environmental initiatives simply because they are not based on the kind of sincerity that we "should" be seeing in the world. We can enter, depart from, and re-enter the world of activism, reshaping it through increased self-reflection and awareness, and we do not have to negate it altogether because we cannot enact it in the "right" way. As Szerszynski emphasizes, to adopt a productive stance of "thoroughgoing ironic environmentalism" we need to understand the human condition as being "intrinsically paradoxical and aporetic" so that the "most clear-sighted antidote to the condition of unsustainability will be found" (351). Lindsay Bluth may be incapable of moral reflexivity, but that does not mean that we are. For most, "ironic environmentalism" could mean something quite different from Lindsay's uninspired trip to the wetlands in a taxi.

Conclusion

Sturgeon argues that exploring environmental themes in popular culture is important because popular culture so often reveals ways in which we "explain ourselves to ourselves" (7). *Arrested Development* does this by questioning the logic and efficacy of the stories we tell ourselves to justify what we do and who we are within the context of Millennial America. The diegetic world of *Arrested Development* reveals that our history of colonization and development in the name of progress has in fact created a culture whose values are largely contradictory and that we spend a great deal of time and energy justifying our actions and attempting to convince others of the purity of our motives. Killingsworth and Palmer essentially blame the "environmental dilemma" on a failure of rhetoric; no sense of identification, heavily biased reporting, and weak ethical and logical appeals. *Arrested Development* blames rhetoric too, but it also suggests that the problem is not entirely about making meaningful connections with the public—it is about the inherent selfishness of human nature. However, Szerszynski urges us to consider accepting hypocrisy and contradiction within the environmental movement. In doing so, we may break down some of the existing ideologies surrounding environmental activism and use irony in a more positive and productive way: "An ironic ecology ... rather than either dominating or venerating nature, would instead be more likely to value and proliferate 'impure' and vernacular mixings of nature and culture, new shared meanings and practices" (351). This binary between domination and veneration is represented by George Sr. and Oscar; one the "capitalist developer" and the other a self-styled visionary who holds a romanticized view of nature. Both agendas are exploitative in their own way, and eventually we see how they are conflated. For instance, in season four, George Sr.'s plan to charge dehydrated retreat attendees extortionate amounts of money is disguised by appeals to spiritual transformation and self-improvement ("Borderline Personalities" 4:2). In this regard, we see how spiritual capital and the naturalization of capitalism have come to signify the same experience. The uncontained "natural" and "spiritual" place where people go to find themselves must be tamed and contained before the industrialists and developers can go there for spiritual succor. Nature cannot be taken on its own terms because nature is wild and so often deceptive. The "natural" realm of spirituality and naturalized industrialization have become one and the same, with George Sr. and Oscar's interchangeability emphasizing this point. However, these ostensive attempts at "spiritual growth" and the desire to break free from cultural strictures are illusory. The boundaries between the unenlightened and enlightened are revealed to be unstable: Oscar's vision of a Native American spirit turns out to be spurious when we discover that the befeathered figure he sees is in fact, Marky Bark ("Red Hairing" 4:8). Further, we also discover that the land that George Sr. believes has been marked for the wall between the U.S. and Mexico is in the wrong place. These arbitrary divisions, the reinscription of boundaries, the parceling and compartmentalizing of countries and cultures, is part of the capitalist project and also becomes the boundary at which capitalists go to attempt to be more sincerely "themselves."

The creators of *Arrested Development* suggest that most of us practice environmentalism in a similar manner to the Bluths and that, as it stands, it's possible that the environmental movement actually does more harm than good. Most of the environmental initiatives in which we involve ourselves are superficial and distract us from the social transformation that we would need to effect in order to make a tangible difference. Our superficial moves are more about us; about how we appear to others and about how we want to be perceived. In reality, we are unwilling to participate in the kinds of self-reflection and sacrifice that we would have to in order to effect real change. We feign concern and perform a backhanded sincerity that has been replaced by an ironic stance not simply toward the environmental movement, but toward the environment itself in that we are no longer capable of interpreting in good faith even the most superficial moves toward conservation and preservation. However, Szerszynski believes that change is still possible. That is, we need develop a more positive kind of irony that will allow us to take action in spite of ourselves, to act in spite of the painful recognition that we are all subsumed in an intricate and embarrassing social performance.

Works Cited

Aristotle. *Nichomachean Ethics*. Acheron Press. 2012. Kindle Edition.

Herndl, Carl George and Stuart C. Brown. *Green Culture: Environmental Rhetoric in Contemporary America*. Madison: University of Wisconsin Press, 1996. Print.

Killingsworth, M. Jimmie, and Jacqueline S. Palmer. *Ecospeak: Rhetoric and Environmental Politics in America*. Carbondale: Southern Illinois University Press, 1992. Print.

Luke, Timothy W. *Ecocritique: Contesting the Politics of Nature, Economy, and Culture*. Minneapolis: University of Minnesota Press, 1997. Print.

Sturgeon, Noël. *Environmentalism in Popular Culture: Gender, Race, Sexuality, and the Politics of the Natural.* Tucson: University of Arizona Press, 2009. Print.

Szerszynski, Bronislaw. "The Post-ecologist Condition: Irony as Symptom and Cure." *Environmental Politics* 16.2 (2007): 337–355. Print.

Warner, Michael. "Publics and Counterpublics (abbreviated version)." *Quarterly Journal of Speech* 88.4 (2002): 413–425. Print.

It Ain't Easy
Being Race-Sensitive

Things Whitey and African-Americany Aren't Ready to Hear

JAMES ROCHA

Is *Arrested Development* ~~a racist show~~? Marta Estrella, Lupe, and Perfecto Telles are each objectified in distinct ways (Marta is sexually objectified as a trophy in a sibling rivalry; Lucille Bluth makes a point of attempting to replace Lupe with a Roomba; and Lucille Austero adopts Perfecto to gain sympathy with Latino voters). Annyong is so invisible that no one uses his actual name (Hel-loh), and Carl Weathers is the cheapest person you've ever seen. Almost every character of an underrepresented racial identity fits quite snugly into a racial stereotype: the Latina maid, the invisible Asian, the cheap black man, etc. Does this mean that the show is racist?

While overall *Arrested Development* is not a racist show, there is a nagging feeling of discomfort with all the racial jokes. Though the show supplants racial ideas into the Bluths that are both uncomfortable to watch and politically incorrect, *Arrested Development* does not support the racialized views of its main characters; in fact, it uses these views to undermine its audience's own racial comfort zones. That leads to a second question: Are the Bluths racist? The Bluths certainly are not racist in the same sense as Nazis and Klansmen. To judge the racism of the Bluths, it is necessary to distinguish different kinds of racism to see how even people who would never join supremacist organizations can be still be racist. Once it is established that the Bluths are racist in ways that call for universal self-examination, it will establish that *Arrested Develop-*

ment has used an over-the-top quirky and amoral family to subvert the every-day contentment that most people have when they believe they are not racist.

Two sets of distinctions will be useful for judging the show. The first is the distinction between implicit and explicit racism. The second is Kwame Anthony Appiah's three-part distinction between racialism, extrinsic racism, and intrinsic racism. The first distinction shows why racism is easy to overlook as it can lie under the surface in a manner that is unknown even to the person harboring the racist beliefs or attitudes. The second distinction establishes how certain kinds of racism can seem innocuous and even natural, but they remain irrational and morally problematic nonetheless. Examining these dis-tinctions will illustrate how the Bluths embody the complexity of everyday racism and will shed light on the challenges everyone faces in attempting to avoid it.

Making a Huge Distinction, or Two

The Bluths are racist, but their particular brand of racism is more implicit than explicit. "Implicit racism" refers to the expression or harboring of an atti-tude or belief that carries an implication that some racial group is inferior, even where the person is unaware of this implication. By contrast, an agent is explicitly racist if he or she openly expresses or knowingly harbors an attitude or belief that some racial group is inferior in some fashion. An explicit racist will act on, express, or hold to a view that one racial group is inferior in some fashion. An implicit racist will say, do, or believe something that implies, but doesn't outright express, that some racial group is inferior.

When George Bluth, Sr. assumes it is wrong to tip African Americans ("Flight of the Phoenix" 4:1), his belief is implicitly racist: something he believes about African Americans implies the wrongness of tipping them. George Sr. assumes something is *wrong* with African Americans (perhaps they are too proud to take tips) such that it makes sense not to tip them. At the same time, George Sr. may not know exactly what he thinks is wrong with them. He may have given little thought to his reasons for not tipping them; his assumption lies implicitly underneath his overt action (of refusing to tip). Thus, his belief is implicitly racist.

White Power Bill, on the other hand, is explicitly racist. Of course, where someone like George Sr. has racism underlying his seemingly innocuous beliefs, White Power Bill has a deep self-hatred underlying his explicit racism, as seen when Tobias confronts him in jail:

TOBIAS: Yes, but where does the hate come from, Bill? What causes it?
WHITE POWER BILL: The Jews, I guess.
TOBIAS: Well sure, but I think you need to look deeper. I think these are issues
    of self-esteem ... I'm gonna take a shot at something and say that I think you
    hate White Power Bill ["Missing Kitty" 1:16].

Though White Power Bill attempts to ascribe his hatred to different causes (Tobias, the government, his father), he eventually responds to Tobias' request to look deeper by seeing that he truly hates himself. Although White Power Bill is willing to openly express his explicit racism, such as in his attempt to blame his problems on "the Jews," White Power Bill eventually has to admit that his problems derive from his own self-hatred.

In addition to implicit and explicit racism, philosopher Kwame Anthony Appiah distinguishes between racialism, extrinsic racism, and intrinsic racism. For Appiah, racialism is the view that there are natural and distinguishable differences between people of different races (4–5). A racialist need not believe that some races are better than others—they are simply different for naturally entrenched reasons. Almost every one of the Bluths (with the possible exception of George Michael) shows evidence of racialist thinking. Consider the episode "¡Amigos!" (2:3) where Buster thinks he has run away to Mexico, though, as the narrator explains, "In fact, he was in Santa Ana, a town six minutes inland from his own." Buster comes to love living and working among Mexicans:

BUSTER (TO LUPE): Oh, I love this way of life. This is where I belong. I love
    being Mexican.
LUPE'S RELATIVE: We must work now, Amigo. Adios.
BUSTER: Oh, no, no, no. I'm going with you. (Switching to a Mexican accent) I
    am one of you now. Si? ["¡Amigos!" 2:3].

Buster is assuming there is a distinctly Mexican way of living and working, and that he can simply step into that way of being. The idea that there is something distinctly Mexican about a way of life suggests there is something about Mexicans that differs from Americans or Canadians—which the show is critiquing since Buster has not gone to Mexico at all. Of course, Buster does not think there's anything inferior or lesser about this Mexican way of being—he *loves* it and wants to *be* a Mexican. While this is racialist thinking (it treats Mexican as a distinct way of being), it is not necessarily racist.

It isn't surprising to find so much racialist thinking among the Bluths since such thinking is an unquestioned part of almost all racial discussion. Almost any racial statement ("Black people like hip hop" or "White people are scared of ghettos") will be racialist because it implies an attribute belongs to a person because of their race. It may seem so ubiquitous that one might wonder whether racialism is wrong at all. There are two primary reasons why racialism is worrisome: first, it is false and thus irrational to accept, and, second, it is interlinked with racism.

The general consensus among biologists is that there are no biological races among human beings. As evolutionary biologist Joseph Graves says, "The traditional concept of race as a biological fact is a myth" (xxv). "Race" has a specific connotation in biology, though this connotation is similar to what is meant in common usage. A race is a sub-group among a species that is genetically distinct enough from other members of the species so as to require a different classification. Biologists have two requirements for races, and humans fall far short of each requirement. The first requirement is that the groups have distinct genetic lineages, indicating they evolved in isolation from one another and had little inter-group mating over a significant period of time (Graves 5). Humans travel to such a wide extent and have offspring with so many people from a variety of lands that it does not make sense to think of human groups as having isolated genetic lineages (Graves 12). Humans do not meet the genetic lineage requirement.

The second requirement for at least two groups to count as races is for the genetic distance between those two groups to be significantly greater than the genetic variability between individuals (Graves 5). "Genetic variability" refers to the amount of difference between two individuals' DNA codes (Graves 6–7). Though differences between individuals of different races may stand out (skin color, nose shape, eye color, etc.), the DNA coding for any two randomly selected humans overlaps quite a bit: it comes to about 95.38 percent identical (Graves 7). So, the genetic variability between individuals is just over 4 percent. As Graves explains, "There is greater genetic variability found within one tribe of western African chimpanzees than exists in the entire human species" (Graves 10). "Genetic distance" is a term that tracks the amount of difference across two groups' DNA codes (Graves 8), and when genetic distance is measured for non-human animals, the animal groups that count as races have a genetic distance of approximately 20 percent (Graves 9–10). The genetic difference across different groups of humans is only 2 percent.

This second requirement can only be met if genetic distance is significantly greater than genetic variability. In other words, the difference between two races (such as blacks and whites) would have to be much greater than the variability between any two individuals (such as two black individuals). However, the genetic difference for human races is roughly 2 percent while genetic variability is roughly 4 percent. Since 2 percent is clearly not significantly greater than 4 percent, there are no human races, biologically speaking.

In spite of this biological claim, medical professionals appear to use racial categories. However, racial claims in medicine are often shortcuts for social or geographical claims. For example, sickle cell anemia is related to living in tropical climates, as sickle cells help to combat malaria (Graves 8). Since black people (using the social grouping) are the predominant inhabitants of tropical climates, it is easy to associate the disease with black patients. However, individuals from tropical Middle Eastern countries are more likely to have sickle cell anemia than individuals from non-tropical African countries, such as Kenya. As the disease is patterned on geography, race is merely a shorthand substitute.

Racialism is not only false but also dangerous because it provides the impetus for racism. Like those people who accept racialism, extrinsic racists not only believe that races have different attributes, but also imbue the attributes in question with moral status, holding to the perception that certain races are more courageous, artistic, intelligent, etc. (Appiah 5). The mere difference in attributes that is suggested by racialism becomes racist as soon as those attributes imply some people are superior to others simply because of their race.

The Bluths have their own share of extrinsic racism. Consider Lucille's refusal to allow Lupe's family to meet in the Balboa Towers parking lot ("Staff Infection" 1:15):

> LUCILLE: They've got a bus and they want to use the parking lot to this building as a meeting place. I mean for God's sake, it's not a hardware store. We can't have them hanging around like a bunch of freeloaders looking for an easy buck.
> MICHAEL: What's the emergency, Mom?
> LUCILLE: I need money.

Clearly, Lucille believes that Lupe's Latino family members are freeloaders who would embarrass her merely through association. Yet the scene ends by pointing out the obvious fact that Lucille and her children are unapologetic freeloaders. Of course, in Lucille's mind, there's a clear difference between the two cases: Lucille is an extrinsic racist precisely because she thinks the freeloader mentality is connected to Latinos in a fundamental fashion, while for her and her family, the same attribute is a mere coincidental fact of no real import.

According to Appiah, intrinsic racists believe that there are moral differences between races that have nothing to do with their attributes (5–6). Unlike extrinsic racists, intrinsic racists do not feel some races are better than others because they happen to have better attributes; they simply believe some races are better regardless of their attributes. The racism is intrinsic in that it does not require reasons for giving racial preference, but instead simply asserts that some races just are intrinsically superior. Thus, White Power Bill is an intrinsic racist since he merely believes being white is superior to being a member of any other race.

Racist Objectification: El Premio Desi para la Rivalidad de Hermanos

One way in which *Arrested Development* criticizes society's racial beliefs and behaviors is through the consistent illustration of how social attitudes towards Latinos in the United States have an objectifying quality to them. As previously mentioned, Latinos on the show are regularly objectified, but this fictional objectification highlights a routine social objectification that sees Latinos as sexual objects, laborers, and voting blocks. Thus, in its portrayal of Latinos, *Arrested Development* provides a depiction of a racial problem that runs quite deep, and yet is often overlooked in contemporary society.

Philosopher Martha C. Nussbaum says of objectification, "I suggest in all cases of objectification what is at issue is a question of treating one thing as another: One is treating as an object what is really not an object, what is, in fact, a human being" (256–257). Objectification then consists of treating a human as if he or she lacks some of the characteristics that distinguish humans from mere objects. Nussbaum lists seven key methods of objectifying a person: using the person as an instrument or tool (instrumentality), denial of the person's autonomy as if they should not make their own decisions (denial of autonomy), treating the person as if they lack the ability to act as an agent (inertness), denying a person's individuality by treating the person as interchangeable with any other person or object (fungibility), ignoring the person's boundary-integrity as if it were acceptable to break or harm the person (violability), treating the person as an owned item (ownership), and not caring about the person's emotional states or feelings (denial of subjectivity) (257).

Nussbaum notes that while objectification tends to be immoral, this may not always be the case: objectification can be morally benign when it "is symmetrical and mutual ... in a context of mutual respect and rough social equality" (275). Sexual relations, for example, can be objectifying: one individual is using another's body for sexual pleasure—it is specifically the body, not the person as an individual or their mind, which provides the sexual pleasure. Yet, when sexual objectification is mutual and carried out in a way that is consistent with the partners having complete respect for each other as individuals with rational minds, then it is morally permissible. Objectifying a person indicates a lack of respect for the person's humanity and individuality, but it can be permissible if that respect is already established.

The wrongness of objectification is more inescapable when an entire group of people is objectified. Though stereotypes do not always objectify, they can do so if a group is depicted in a fashion that diminishes or disrespects the humanity of the group members. To use a clear example, in the first century of U.S. history, blacks were routinely objectified and stripped of their humanity through the practice of slavery. Though that case is extreme, in any case of racial objectification, it is difficult to see how there can be any mutual respect when an entire race is objectified with respect to certain stereotypes.

Consider the fight the Bluth brothers have over Marta Estrella, who fits into the stereotype of the overly-sexualized Latina woman—a stereotype that portrays Latinas as exotic, sexual objects instead of as full individuals with identities beyond their bodies. Gob's objectification of Marta is clear well before he learns Michael is also interested in her. Consider this exchange between Gob and Lucille in the episode "Bringing Up Buster" (1:3):

LUCILLE: What, did that Mexican throw you out?
GOB: She's not "that Mexican," Mom. She's my Mexican. And she's Colombian or something. Anyway, it's over.
LUCILLE: You've got three days.
GOB: Hey, if I can't find a horny immigrant by then, I don't deserve to stay here.

This exchange begins with Lucille's clear racialism: she refers to Marta not by name, but by her assumed nationality, which implicitly (though not explicitly) hints at the racial difference between Gob and Marta. Lucille's use of the word "that" also exhibits objectification: "that" is a word for objects, not humans. Even Gob notes that his mother's use of "that" is problematic, and corrects her with a more personalizing "my." Yet Gob's response is problematic as well. Not only is he not sure of her nationality (she is indeed Columbian, but Gob adds "or something"), his modifier ("my") contains another instance of objectification: Marta is not her own individual, but is instead, *Gob's* Mexican (or Columbian). Gob's phrasing references the ownership element of objectification: Marta is sexually objectified as a conquest, to be seized and owned by Gob.

Gob's ownership is questioned through a brotherly rivalry that appears to be more about each brother's attempt to obtain Marta as a sexualized trophy than about getting to know her as a person. It is Marta's sexuality, more than her individuality, which inspires the brotherly rivalry, which then becomes its own motivation for objectifying Marta. This point is trivial since Gob makes it clear that he has little interest in Marta as a person and tries to break up with her until he learns he has competition for her affection. For Gob, the competition, especially with respect to his rivalry with Michael, increases his interest because the competition raises Marta's worth as an owned item: to win her is to establish his worth in defeating his challengers.

For Buster the point is also trivial because he knows nothing about Marta. Buster's putative love for Marta is based only on seeing her and watching her on a television show, thus emphasizing sexual objectification since he does not know anything beyond the superficial televised depiction of her. Since Buster's alleged love is based on a fictional representation, which he surely appreciates more on a visual level since he is just starting to learn Spanish, it establishes objectification features such as denial of autonomy, denial of subjectivity, and even inertness since his love is for a character, and not a living, breathing woman who has the right to autonomously determine her own values and actions, to subjectively experience her own emotional life, and can act in the real world (and not just on a television screen).

The only character that almost moves beyond objectifying Marta is Michael, but even his relationship with her is problematic. Despite the fact that Michael gets to know Marta as a person when he takes her to Los Premios Desi, when Marta tells Michael that they cannot be together because they live by a moral code to honor family, Michael still objectifies her by responding, "Yes, that's one of the things that attracted me to you—your sense of right and wrong. I also like your hair, your face, and your breasts" ("Beef Consommé" 1:13). As Nussbaum points out, it is possible to objectify someone in a morally permissible way as long as there is a clear sense of mutual respect (it is debatable whether Michael shows such respect when he openly objectifies her). After all, once Marta, upon catching the brothers fighting, says she is interested in neither Gob nor Michael (and she doesn't even know who Buster is), Michael says that he will not throw away his bond with his brother "over some woman" ("Beef Consommé" 1:13). When Gob responds, "Especially not my woman," Michael finds offense not at the idea that Marta, a person, should be considered owned as Gob's objectifying response implies, but that she would be owned by Gob, not Michael: "I don't know how you call her your woman when she clearly prefers me" ("Beef Consommé" 1:13). Marta immediately returns to trophy status in the sibling rivalry instead of being valued as a full human.

Labored Objectification: Roombas and Aliens

Just as the Bluths fall into the racialized behavior of thinking of Latina women as overly sexual, they likewise objectify Latinos as mere workers—as if they were machines whose production and ability to service their employers were more important than their personhood. This objectifying treatment can be seen even in the name used for Latinos who cross the border without proper documentation: "illegal aliens" suggests a strange and complex objectification. First, their personhood is undercut by the term, "alien," which denotes one who is unnatural or does not belong. Second, these persons are treated as if their very being were illegal, as opposed to their activities. Murderers are not *illegal killers*, but rather it is the act of murder that is illegal. Similarly, with all other criminal activity, the "illegal" adjective modifies an action, not a person. Thus, to use that adjective to modify undocumented immigrants subtly implies that they are somehow not fully persons: the wrongful application of the adjective "illegal" lowers their status.

The United States economy makes a great deal of use of the work of undocumented immigrants. Undocumented immigrants often take difficult, demeaning, and dangerous jobs—including manufacturing, agriculture, and service sector jobs that are vital to the country's economy—for little pay, almost no governmental support, and a major lack of respect from most members of society for their contributions (Chomsky). Gob provides a clear example of this mistreatment when he attempts to hire some (presumably) undocumented workers outside of the Dr. House Improvement Center (a clear reference to undocumented workers waiting for work outside of major home improvement stores). When Gob asks them, "Who wants to help me build a wall..." many raise their hands before he finishes, "...to keep Mexicans out of America?" After noting the workers' angry reactions, Gob attempts a new inquiry: "all right, who wants to help me build a wall for no reason?" ("A New Attitude" 4:11). Gob clearly sees these workers as possible contributors to his project—he requires their labor to complete the wall—but he does not recognize that they have their own attitudes, views, and rational abilities. Gob objectifies these workers since his attempt to get them to work without any concern for their feelings about the nature of the project denies their autonomy and subjectivity.

In addition to the objectification, the treatment of undocumented immigrants also has aspects of extrinsic racism. The extrinsic racism can be seen in the way in which Latinos in general are thought of primarily as people who are good at menial tasks and are properly placed in subservient roles. Lucille

Bluth best personifies these perspectives in *Arrested Development*. Lucille repeatedly shows enough disrespect for the work of her maids that it rises to the level of objectification and extrinsic racism. In a direct example of objectification, Lucille tells Gob and Buster that she has replaced Lupe with a Roomba ("The Immaculate Election" 2:14). This objectification is seen at numerous points throughout the series, as, for example, in a flashback when Michael brings home a Latina woman that he's dating, and Lucille immediately hands her gloves and cleaning supplies ("Forget-Me-Now" 3:3). Similarly, when Lucille yells at Lupe for not having an exit strategy (meaning that she doubts Lupe has figured out how she will walk out of the room without dirtying the floor after cleaning it), Michael scolds his mother, to which she responds, "Oh, please. They didn't sneak into this country to be your friends" ("Charity Drive" 1:6). Not only does she yell at her maid without knowing whether Lupe has made any mistake, but her inability to see the possibility of a friendship with a worker suggests the objectification in question: Lucille sees Lupe, who she believes to be undocumented, as a mere worker, and not as a person who happens to work for her.

Lucille's attitude infects her children as well, such as when Lindsay assumes a group of Latinos (who are actually Lupe's family) are day laborers who would find working to be "fun" ("Staff Infection" 1:15). The empirical fact that many Latinos often find themselves performing menial labor in this society translates into an extrinsic racist view that Latinos are inherently meant for menial labor. Thus, Lindsay assumes this group of Latinos would not only do the work needed for building houses, but also would enjoy it. But Lupe's family is certainly more diverse than the stereotypical laborers Lindsay assumes them to be, best highlighted when one of them turns out to be a professor of American Studies. In the Bluths' treatment of Latino workers, we see how extrinsic racism and objectification intersect.

Political Objectification: The Perfected Voting Block

In addition to the sexual objectification and the objectification as laborers, *Arrested Development* provides a glimpse into the political objectification of Latinos as a voting bloc. Within American politics, there has developed a regular pattern of tacos-and-sombreros-politics, where politicians running for office pander to minority groups by wearing cultural attire, consuming ethnic cuisine, or stumbling through a few lines of a speech in a foreign language. For example, consider when then Vice President George Bush famously donned a Sombrero at a taco stand in 1988 (Harrison). In such cases, the politician treats Latino voters not as rational individuals who vote based on their own distinct considerations of issues, but as a voting bloc that can be swayed by a visual stunt that merely amounts to appropriating some form of Latino cultural identity. These types of politicians objectify Latinos in that they do not look at them as unique individuals or as informed citizens with distinct values, but rather, through extrinsically racist thinking, they see Latinos as being easily swayed by minor acts of cultural appropriation.

Lucille Austero's act of cultural appropriation, of course, is not minor. She actually adopts Perfecto Telles to attract Latino votes, an act that is clearly objectifying in that it treats Perfecto as a means to her end. This act meets multiple objectification requirements: instrumentality insofar as Perfecto is a political tool; denial of autonomy—both of Perfecto and of Latinos who are being emotionally manipulated; ownership since in adopting him, she comes to own him, which would not be problematic if it were done in a respectful and loving manner; and fungibility because Perfecto could be replaced with any Latino child.

Though there are other clear cases of objectification in the show that do not involve Latinos (Lucille Bluth using Annyong as a purse, for example), it is important that these attitudes about minorities—the sexualization of Marta, the objectification of Latinos as mere workers, and the use of Perfecto to attract Latino votes—provide clear examples of racism that reflect current social attitudes. These cases represent systematic social treatments in contemporary U.S. society that objectify Latinos in extrinsically racist ways that assume that there are inherent features of Latinos that make them different.

Words of Racism: The Hello Loophole

While explicit racism may often be easy to spot, implicit racism often lies underneath the subtleties of language: phrases, words, and even certain pronunciations may expose an implicitly racist belief or attitude that the speaker may not be fully cognizant of. *Arrested Development* consistently uses the turn of the phrase, a particular word, or the mocking of a certain dialect to establish a character's racism without the character necessarily saying something explicitly racist.

Many of the interactions between the Bluths and Asian characters highlight the connection between racism and language. The Bluths' mocking of the difficulties some Asians have in pronouncing certain English words is surely explicitly racist, almost certainly best exemplified in the episode "Mr. F" (3:5) when several members of the family yell "Godzirra!" in fake Japanese accents. Similarly, when Lucille speaks about the women of the Jade Dragon Triad ("Their bark is louder than the dogs they eat back home"), her language is explicitly racist ("Queen B." 4:10).

The use of Annyong's name is much more difficult to analyze. On the one hand, no one knows that they are using his name incorrectly. No character, in calling him "Annyong," intends to convey any disregard for him in any racist fashion. This behavior does not even qualify as racialist since the characters are neither making racial comments nor acting from any racial beliefs. Nonetheless, there is something implicitly racist about the characters' inability to *learn* that they are getting his name wrong. The evidence is both available and regularly repeated: it makes no sense that he would repeat his own name as often as he does. Additionally, it should be incumbent on his new family to learn enough Korean to engage in simple conversations with him, which would include "hello" as one of the first words one would expect to learn. While no one is being explicitly racist in failing to learn Annyong's real name, the fact that they never figure it out indicates implicit racism.

This point is important because language can be implicitly racist in obscure ways. Language barriers may appear to present insurmountable obstacles to effective communication, but this position can sometimes be a convenient crutch for an unwarranted assumption that the difference is not worth surmounting. The notable oddity in the repetition of the word "annyong" should have raised flags for the Bluths if they were sincere in attempting to better know the newly adopted member of their family. Yet their failure to care about his name represents the failure to see past linguistic and racial differences, and highlights the selfish and ethnocentric attitudes held by the Bluths.

Undermining Stereotypes: A Tobias Fünke Type

While much of *Arrested Development* undermines racial stereotypes, the depiction of black characters contains a certain amount of indulging in these stereotypes. Carl Weathers is an incredibly cheap man. Herbert Love has a host of problems: he is an adulterer, greedy, and not very intelligent. In these cases, the black characters are not setting up the racism of the Bluths, as seen in previous examples. Instead, the black characters themselves fit racial stereotypes in a fashion that suggests the show is providing a racist depiction for the sake of cheap laughs. While this stereotypical depiction is definitely worthy of criticism, it is important that other black characters, at the same time, are being used to undermine racial stereotypes.

One character that challenges black stereotypes is the bounty hunter, Ice. In many ways, Ice fits into the stereotypes that Carl Weathers and Herbert Love perpetuate: he is a large, possibly scary black man whose life is intricately connected to a love of money. Just as Carl Weathers is cheap and Herbert Love is greedy, Ice works two jobs, one of which involves hunting down people for payment. Yet, it is Ice's second job—his first love, really—that tears down the stereotypical expectations concerning him: party planning ("Good Grief" 2:4). Unlike Weathers and Love, whose love of money is never fully explored, in Ice's case, it is clear why he hunts down people for money: to support his party planning career. If there were any doubt about which aspect of Ice's character is more dominant (the stereotypical tough black man or the enthusiastic party planner), he alleviates any doubts when describes his location as, "20 minutes from Legoland" ("¡Amigos!" 2:3). Though it is a small moment, there is nothing stereotypical about it: Ice is a complex character that subverts racial stereotypes.

Although this example may be controversial, another black character who consistently defies racial stereotypes is Tobias Fünke. First, it is important to make the case that Tobias is represented as black on the show, after which an analysis of Tobias' racial identity will be possible. To begin, there are many instances within the show where Tobias' racial identity as a black man is (sometimes subtly) alluded to. When Lindsay flirts with Ice, Tobias tells Maeby, "I am surprised, though, that she's going after somebody so similar to my own type" ("Good Grief" 2:4). Similarly, as the narrator informs us, Herbert Love reminds Lindsay "so much of Tobias when they first started dating" ("Red Hairing" 4:8). Further, when Lindsay says, "People hear the name Tobias, they think big black guy," Tobias responds, "Well, obviously, I'm not a big guy. I'm not a Carl Weathers, *par example*" ("Afternoon Delight" 2:6). The way he drops the word "black" and simply says he is not a "big guy" implies quite clearly that Tobias is a black man, though not a big one. Tobias is thus compared to all three of the main black male characters on the show in order to establish his racial identity.

If Tobias is a black man, then he certainly undermines racial stereotypes in the strongest fashion possible. First and most importantly, Tobias defies the visual expectation by not having black skin. Human race is not a biological grouping, but a social categorization. There is no scientific reason to assume that people of the same race share any properties, including skin color. Just as there can be people socially categorized as white with dark skin, there can be people socially categorized as black with light skin. It is not contradictory for a black person to have lighter skin than a white person. If Tobias is black, then he stands as a great example not only to the limit of racial stereotypes, but also to the limit of racialized thinking in general. Further, Tobias is not obsessed with money since he gives up a lucrative career as an analyst and therapist to pursue an acting career where he makes almost no money. He is not cheap since he is willing to buy a mansion he cannot afford. He is also most certainly not large and scary looking.

While some black characters (Carl Weathers and Herbert Love) fit racial stereotypes too closely and other black characters (Ice and Tobias) clearly defy stereotypes, one character meets stereotypes but in a completely unproblematic fashion: Gob's puppet, Franklin. Franklin is a black puppet who embraces racial stereotypes in an openly extrinsic racist fashion. Consider the song that Gob and Franklin sing together in "Righteous Brothers" (2:18):

> GOB: It ain't easy bein' white,
> FRANKLIN: It ain't easy bein' brown.
> GOB: All this pressure to be bright,
> FRANKLIN: I got childrens all over town.

Through this song, both Gob and Franklin are endorsing extrinsic racist views: that white people live under a pressure to live up to high intelligence expectations while black and brown men have uncontrollable sexual appetites that result in numerous children with different mothers. Franklin would be a very worrisome character if not for the fact that he is a puppet. Franklin does not present an image of black people, but instead presents an image of how a particular white man, Gob, sees black people. *Arrested Development* makes it quite clear that Franklin is not merely the projection of Gob's own racism onto a black puppet; instead, Gob's projection is generalized when the police pull their guns on Franklin just because they see his blackness as clear evidence that he is a kidnapping suspect ("Meat the Veals" 2:16). Through Franklin, we see how *Arrested Development* uses race to show how stereotypes are in fact nothing more than false projections.

A Conclusion That Won't Kidnap and Kill You

In depicting the problems of the racism of the Bluth family, *Arrested Development* is able to highlight several elements of race theory that shine a light on racism in contemporary society. While there is little explicit racism on the show, implicit racism tends to be more problematic in societies where people are taught not to say racist things out loud. Similarly, there is not as much intrinsic racism on the show, but intrinsic racism is perhaps less common in the 21st century. Yet the show provides numerous examples of racialized thinking, which is merely the belief that there is something real (that is to say, biological) about race. For example, when Lucille asks questions that imply that the Guatemalan painters would steal from her, she is engaging in explicit, extrinsic racism since she is obviously suggesting that Latinos are more likely to be thieves. This, by comparison, suggests that people of other races do not steal, or at least are not as likely to ("Making a Stand" 3:8). Similarly, when Michael responds to her, "If you're going to speak to these guys like this, you might want to sleep with one eye open," he is likewise engaging in extrinsic racism since he is implying "these guys" are inherently violent, though, knowing Michael, his racism is more likely implicit since he may not realize he is drawing out this implication ("Making a Stand" 3:8).

Given these distinctions, the show makes interesting points about racism. The Latino characters on the show can be used to establish how racist it can be to objectify an entire group, such as when women of certain races are sexually objectified, when laborers are objectified for their work product, or voters are objectified for their votes. From the show's depiction of Asian characters, it is clear how important the use of language can be to finding and analyzing racism. Finally, the show's various black characters both exhibit worrisome stereotypes, and separately undermine stereotypes, especially when Tobias and Franklin are included in the analysis. *Arrested Development* may have racially troubling aspects to it, but it is not a racist show. In fact, it subverts racist tendencies that are spread throughout the modern world. Thus, *Arrested Development* can be used to help with reflection over these various issues related to race, especially with respect to the intricate distinctions of racism as in contemporary society.

Works Cited

Appiah, Kwame Anthony. "Racisms." In *Anatomy of Racism*. Ed. David Theo Goldberg. Minneapolis: University of Minnesota Press, 1990. 3–17. Print

Chomsky, Aviva. *"They Take Our Jobs!": And 20 Other Myths About Immigration.* Boston: Beacon Press, 2007. Print.

Graves, Joseph. *The Race Myth: Why We Pretend Race Exists in America.* New York: Dutton, 2004. Print.

Harrison, Scott. "Vice President George Bush Tries on a Sombrero." *Los Angeles Times.* 26 Oct. 2012. Web. 24 Jan. 2014. http://framework.latimes.com/2012/10/26/vice-president-george-bush-tries-on-a-sombrero/

Nussbaum, Martha C. "Objectification." *Philosophy and Public Affairs* 24.4 (1995): 249–291. Print.

The Ways of
the Secular Flesh

Destabilizing the
Heteronormative and Negotiating
Non-Monolithic Sexualities

Navid Sabet

Postmodernism has created new spaces for ideas of sexuality to evolve in the social consciousness, including the waning of the homo/heterosexual binary, the deconstruction of gender, and the challenging of normative sexual behaviors formerly embedded in heterosexual marriage (Roseneil). Media representations have worked with and against—or perhaps more accurately inside and around—these social and cultural shifts. In this sense, television may be considered a medium that does not necessarily "present firm ideological conclusions—despite its formal conclusions—so much as it comments on ideological problems" (Newcomb and Hirsch 565–566). This chapter will examine the ways in which sexuality is represented in *Arrested Development*, both creatively and discursively, with a particular focus on the characters Tobias Fünke, George Michael Bluth, and Maeby Fünke, in order to contextualize and demonstrate broader issues regarding sexuality in the series. In order to do so, it is important to more specifically explore the intersections of sexuality and gender in the show's narrative, characterization, and dialogue, as well as the instances of representation that go beyond the boundaries of the heteronormative. Ultimately, this will serve to demonstrate that in some ways, *Arrested Development* disturbs heteronormative constructions of sexuality and gender, as well as the social and cultural assumptions that perpetuate them.

The turn of the century has brought on a new wave of representations of sexuality on television, somewhat characterized by the increased visibility of non-heteronormative sexualities (Tomsen and Markwell 202). However, we should not assume that the Western media has been entirely "liberated" from the impact of heteronormative hegemony and gender-based essentialism. A quick investigation of contemporary popular programming will demonstrate that these issues still exist, however they are articulated in different ways than in the past. In some respects, *Arrested Development* is unique in its approach to representation, and in other ways it toys with patterns of representation that were popularized in Western media during the 20th and 21st centuries. This meeting of old, re-imagined, and innovative approaches is partially what makes the series an interesting case study for critical analysis, supporting claims that television is "an ambiguous medium that is able to both consent to and contest normative assumptions about sexuality" (Dhaenens 304). *Arrested Development* features a number of representations and scripts (narratives for understanding social interactions) relating to romance, attraction, sexual behaviors, and sexual dynamics that are not common to the average sitcom. However, they are also not entirely groundbreaking—they are still, as all representations and scripts are, interconnected with the normative discourses from which they grow, and the comedic passages through which they speak.

Freedman describes *farce* as a space characterized by the "discontinuous and dysfunctional," where "aggression and regression are not in the service of the ego but directly opposed to ego mastery" (*Staging the Gaze* 105). Thus, the fact that *Arrested Development* is a 21st century television series, fuelled by dysfunction and ridicule, is also significant. In particular, it is important to note that representations of sexuality and gender in the series occur through the lens of farce, and thus the implications of the genre, as well as the nature of humor more generally, should also be considered when examining the discourses they evoke. Freud believed that humor serves to temporarily free an individual from inhibition, enabling them to relieve aggression and sexual tension that conflict with social norms (Lynch 33–34). However, more recent scholarship tends to focus on the dynamic cultural implications of humor. For example, Palmer suggests that while comedy generates moral, political, and rhetorical dilemmas (11), it also holds an intrinsic value that rests on political and moral ambivalence, and thus never fully commits to any particular position (213). Other scholars have identified the socially progressive potential of comedy, and its power to "prod a reluctant society into recognizing shared values" (Christiansen and Hanson 162).

Struken and Cartwright propose that meaning is constructed in the moment of viewing, rather than embedded in media itself. Furthermore, it is through exploring the collaborative, meaning-making space between the viewers and signifiers that we are able to understand their broader implications (O'Donnell 149). Narratives and representations of sexuality are often referred to as *sexual scripts*, and Markle argues that through sharing and engagement with sexual scripts, "individuals develop strategies for realizing their particular sexual desires" (47). The visual and aural signifiers that facilitate meaning-making (Fiske 56) are perhaps particularly important when exploring representations of sexuality, as television has a significant bearing on sexual socialization (Golanty and Edlin 168). In the case of non-heteronormative sexualities however, this is more difficult, as there are fewer representations available for critical analysis. While this chapter will focus predominantly on the three cases mentioned earlier, Tobias, George Michael, and Maeby, it may be important to note that rarely does a character in *Arrested Development* fully embody the "desirable" qualities that the heteronormative paradigm reinforces—and when it seems like they do, it is so exaggerated, contradictory, and disjunctive, that it mocks the idea that these expectations ever exist. Thus, *Arrested Development*'s response to heteronormative sexualities and gender-based essentialism can be seen in its refusal to fill the gaps that normative representations often seal with resolution.

"In the dark, it all looks the same..."

On *Arrested Development*, themes relating to homosexuality, gender, and queerness are often expressed through Tobias Fünke, who is arguably one of the most sexually "prominent" characters of the series. This is not to imply that Tobias engages in sexual acts with other characters. Rather, issues of sexuality (and in particular—implied homosexuality) are prominent in the way his character is portrayed and used for the sake of narrative and farce. Some scholars suggest that comedy is often used to desexualize and contain homosexuals, thus "reducing the "threat" they pose to the patriarchal order" (Griffin 355). However, parody has also been linked to the destabilizing of social assumptions about gender identity (Butler 175–177). Thus, while it seems that comedy, parody, and farce can be useful in challenging social expectations about identity, even revealing the ways in which gender is falsely naturalized, they certainly do not function *outside* power relations, and thus can never be fully liberating. Consequently, it should be made clear that Tobias' sexuality is not immune to heteronormative hegemony, and in many ways, his anxieties and insecurities are quite vividly products of it. However, what emerges from the tension between his intrinsic inclinations and the hegemonic social expectations that try to regulate him is a dramatic expression of resistance.

In the media, representations of non-heteronormative sexuality often draw on what Dyer calls "signs of gayness," which may involve "gestures, expressions, stances, clothing, and even environments that bespeak gayness" (19), and serve as culturally recognized signifiers that flag what isn't otherwise evident to viewers. Furthermore, while representations of gay men on television became more frequent during the 1990s and 2000s, most still drew on stereotypical signifiers that allowed little diversity for gay characters, particularly regarding ethnicity, physical appearance, and social class (Avila-Saavedra 19). Consequently, it is becoming increasingly important for research to explore the hegemonic complexities of gay representations (Avila-Saavedra 8).

Many sociologists and cultural theorists have explored the ways in which sexualities have developed in the social consciousness over time. For example, Foucault traced the history of sexuality to social construction, governance, and institutional practices that operate through discourse and exercises of power, and thus his work has played a significant role in queer theory (Hodges, 9–12). Sedgwick argues that "queer" may signify "the open mesh of possibilities, gaps, overlaps, dissonances and resonances, lapses and excesses of meaning when the constituent elements of anyone's gender, or anyone's sexuality aren't made (or can't be made) to signify monolithically" (8). In this sense, queerness opposes the binaries perpetuated by heteronormative discourses relating to both gender and sexuality. In some ways, the constant interrogation of Tobias' sexuality could be seen as precursor to "coming out," yet this never actually occurs. Thus, Tobias retains his ability to traverse the boundaries of heteronormative expectations, but without categorizing himself as a gay man in order to justify and *normalize* his behavior.

Many hints to Tobias' sexuality result from moments of unwitting "gayness" when Tobias says or does something that he does not seem to recognize as sexually suggestive. Verbal, material, and gender-based signifiers, or "signs of gayness" (Dyer 19) are used to construct Tobias as a character self-evidently confused by issues of sexuality and gender. Interestingly, the question of Tobias' sexuality, while perpetually forced to the forefront of the narrative, is never actually resolved; it is merely used as a "running joke in the family" ("A New Start" 4:5). Furthermore, through and concurrently with the many signifiers that question Tobias' ambiguous sexuality, the viewer is also presented with a series of performances that are complexly gendered. Thus, as representations of sexuality are frequent sites for the reinforcement of gender roles (Gunter

105), Tobias' diverse interaction with gender could be seen as a form of rene-gotiation and disruption of the heteronormative. Ultimately, while Tobias' homosexuality is never fully resolved, neither is his gender confusion.

At the forefront of queer visibility at the turn of the century were TV series like *Will & Grace* (1998–2006), *Queer as Folk* (2000–2005), and *Queer Eye for the Straight Guy* (2003–2007), the latter perpetuating the idea that homosexual men were inherently gifted with cultural and domestic expertise (Clarkson 235). Interestingly, Tobias' masquerade as a female housekeeper, Mrs. Featherbottom ("The Immaculate Election" 2:14), could be read as a loose parody of these discourses, particularly when Maeby calls him "Mr. Fin-gerbottom," which links the performance to both gender and sexuality. The TV series *Queer as Folk*, which was "the first show to provide gays and lesbians with individually nuanced identities" (Silverman 264), is often credited as a step forward in the diversification of queer representations on television. However, some scholars still argue that *Queer as Folk* relied on stereotypical represen-tations that involved heavy drug use, constant partying, and promiscuity (Evans). Again, some of Tobias' comments and experiences are relevant as a reflection of essentialist representations of gay lifestyles, such as when he explains that he was, "jacked up on amyl and disco music" ("Family Ties" 3:11), or when he visits clichéd gay bars like The Gothic Asshole by mistake. Regarding the latter, the meaning-making process is called to action, and the viewer is left pondering the appropriateness of such a "mistake." In other words, if Tobias is already queered by the viewer, this mistake might be reimagined as a destined moment of queerness—an appropriate step in the forging of his sexual identity.

On *Will & Grace*, homosexuality is represented through the juxtaposition of stereotypical and flamboyant queerness against a straight-acting gay char-acter who embodied many characteristics that viewers associate with hetero-normativity, especially when seen in contrast to a more striking, self-evident queerness. While Jack is used as "caricature representing America's image of the gay man" (Poole), straight-acting Will is closer to the homosexual embod-iment of heteronormative masculinity, which was perhaps used to establish a subtextual "what if" tension with Grace, the female lead. Furthermore, through the interplay of flamboyantly queer and not-quite-straight characters, the show created a platform for constant comparison by the audience member, where neither Jack nor Will were "fully masculine as measured against the dominant construction of what masculine is" (Poole). Tobias, in a sense, is an embodi-ment of this binary, as he awkwardly tries to assert his masculinity while failing to contain himself within the boundaries of heteronormative expectations. For example, when Tobias refers to himself as "The big manly man. The big strong Daddy" to his nephew, he simultaneously unpacks various pairs of tight denim shorts from his suitcase ("Marta Complex" 1:12). Here his performance almost parodies the idea of the ideal masculine father through the collusion between his clothing and the gendered ideals to which his comments refer.

Several verbal signifiers throughout the series draw on stereotypically gay terms, or symbolize stereotypical behaviors associated with mainstream gay culture. For example, when visiting his father-in-law in prison, Tobias is referred to as "Dorothy," a reference to the "Friend of Dorothy" slang term relating to homosexual men ("Missing Kitty" 1:16). Tobias also uses the term "butch" to describe working as a security guard ("Not Without My Daughter" 1:21), a queer descriptive term, and when sharing a bed with his wife again, Tobias says, "nice to be back in a queen" ("The One Where Michael Leaves" 2:1). In a way, these three examples relate to the circular effect of linguistic practices that govern the mainstream identification of homosexuals. Cameron and Kulick argue that "gay language was assumed to be instantiated in the speech of people who were homosexual" and thus "anything a gay or lesbian person said or did was taken to be characteristic of gay and lesbian language" (93). From these "circular assumptions" (ibid) came frameworks that determined the way gay and lesbian people were expected to act. Interestingly, while Tobias does indeed toy with "gay language," he often does so without linking it (knowingly) to any gay significance, and perhaps by doing so he challenges its authenticity as an inherently gay vernacular. This reflects the assertions of Struken and Cartwright who propose that meaning is constructed by the recipient. Furthermore, it embodies the notion that the interpretation of signifiers is influenced by cultural practices (O'Donnell). Thus, the viewer may construct Tobias as gay simply by drawing on the cultural practice of "gay speech." In other words, when Tobias doesn't make the queer connection himself, it is the viewer who forges the link.

Other instances of Tobias' use of verbal signifiers refer more specifically to sexual acts, including the double entendre-laden "I can just taste those meaty leading man parts in my mouth" ("For British Eyes Only" 3:2), "banger in the mouth" ("Meat the Veals" 2:16), and, during an exchange with Buster, "even if it means me taking a chubby, I will suck it up" ("Queen for a Day" 2:8). Similarly, when Michael is organizing a romantic getaway for Tobias and Lindsay, Tobias remarks, "I tell you, you can zing your arrow into my buttocks anytime" ("Ready, Aim, Marry Me" 2:10). These not-quite-subtle innuendos continue in season four, when, for example, Tobias remarks, "I've got a bit of a stick up my bunghole about what I've now found is a running joke about me" ("A New Start" 4:5). Even his nonverbal expressions offer suggestions about his sexuality, as when, working at a restaurant, his name tag reads "Tobias Swallows" ("The One Where

Michael Leaves" 2:1). Interestingly, the frequency of these action-focused signifiers could be read as a reference to the cultural perceptions that have historically constructed the gay man as "promiscuous, predatory, and obsessed
with sex" (Fajer 538, discussing how gays are marginalized through essentialist
narratives). Again however, Tobias is rarely implicated through physical actions,
other than (arguably) the occasional slap of Michael's buttocks. In a sense, this
challenges the viewer to sexually categorize Tobias, to conceptualize him as the
sexually obsessed gay subject, to visualize him as an eager participant in various
sexual acts, and ultimately to use these images in order to fill the gaps in his
non-monolithic identity. However, this occurs entirely in the minds of the
viewers through their own desire to find meaningful resolutions to these con-
flicting signs, signs that are never actually confirmed or acted upon by Tobias.

On certain occasions, the use of language to imply Tobias' homosexuality
is much more confronting and unrestrained than gentle signifiers. For example,
in the episode "Forget-Me-Now" (3:3), Tobias condenses his *analyst* and *therapist* titles to "analrapist," which leads to loaded comments like "if I may take
off my acting pants for a moment and pull my analrapist stocking over my
head" ("S.O.B.s" 3:9). Similar tactics are used in season four, when Tobias gets
a license plate that reads "ANUSTART," which he intends to be read as "A New
Start," but is ultimately interpreted by everyone else as "Anus Tart" ("A New
Start" 4:5). Again, what makes these representations unique is that they are
negotiated using signs and language through an unwitting, non-participating,
and sexually unconfirmed subject, rather than performed through sexual
actions that may be associated with deviance and promiscuity. In a way, this
is a departure from more action-focused representations of sexuality, which
Cramer suggests, "are significant for the attitudes, morals, and standards they
portray or implicitly endorse" (409). While Tobias' ignorance may be typical
of the medium of farce, where "the more the characters seek gratification, the
more severely the plot punishes them for it" (Freedman, "Reading Errantly"
286), his lack of tangible participation (aside from making uncomfortable comments) serves as an effective instrument in the mockery of discourses that link
homosexuality to deviant behaviors (for examples see Goode). Furthermore, this
potentially gives the viewer the opportunity to explore and negotiate the significance of "deviant" discourses without the forceful coercion of physical acts.

Concurrently with the many reminders of Tobias' ambiguous sexuality,
the viewer is also fed verbal signifiers relating more specifically to Tobias' gender. The way Tobias simultaneously toys with, resists, and longs to be realized
as a gendered subject plays an interesting role throughout the series, embodying
the instability of gender norms. This is representative of Judith Butler's theory

of gender performativity, the "stylized repetition of acts" that are "internally discontinuous," and responsible for constructing the normative gendered subject (179). Interestingly, Tobias' gendered enactments could be interpreted as subversive performances that illuminate the "the imitative structure of gender itself" (Butler 175). For example, a key component in the social construction of gender is the use of linguistic binaries (Brady and Schirato 38). Thus, a performed resistance can be observed when Tobias refers to Steve Holt as "fair lady" after recasting the roles in the school play ("Bringing Up Buster" 1:3) or when he refers to Stan Sitwell as "Miss" ("Ready, Aim, Marry Me" 2:10). Similar instances relating to language are self-directed, including when Tobias compares himself to female actresses Katharine Hepburn ("Out on a Limb" 2:11) and Jada Pinkett-Smith ("Public Relations" 1:11), or when he refers to himself as a cocktail waitress ("The Cabin Show" 3:1) and a "non-traditional mother" ("S.O.B.s" 3:9). Bolich (17) argues that pronouns are value-laden and work to preserve gender schemes. In this sense, Tobias disrupts the heteronormative status quo by chaotically drawing to the surface the ways in which we, as social agents, link ideas to gender even when we are discussing something else (Eckert and McConnell-Ginet 62). Furthermore, it is through the intersections of the queer and the gendered performance (both of which contribute to an environment where Tobias cannot be read monolithically), that the Bluth family (and the viewers) are challenged to reduce or withstand Tobias' ambiguous identity, and to construct him, or resist constructing him, as a subject that fits within a framework of normative expectations.

Through the use of clothing, we can see quite clearly how Tobias' sexuality is linked to gender and identity negotiation, allowing his character to challenge the limitations of gender and sexuality concurrently, in the way he also does through language. In the episode "Visiting Ours" (1:5), Lindsay and Tobias are in the bedroom, arguing about an upcoming therapy session. Shirtless and wearing a towel around his waist, Tobias asks his wife "How am I not addressing your needs?" Frustrated by her husband's cluelessness, Lindsay rips off the towel, revealing the cut-off denim shorts that Tobias wears at all times to hide his genitals, due to a crippling fear of being fully naked. Embarrassed and distressed, Tobias runs away from his wife and into the bedroom closet. Tobias' fear of being naked, which mirrors the medical condition gymnophobia (Parmelee 64), is soothed by wearing a pair of tight-fitting denim shorts. In this scene, the viewer observes a connection between the troubled marriage and Tobias' taste (and *need*) for non-heteronormative clothing, and the implications of this tension are further emphasized through his physical movement into the closet.

Several other episodes use clothing to negotiate Tobias' ambiguous identity. As discussed earlier, an example can be seen when Tobias tests his acting skills by becoming Mrs. Featherbottom, a character inspired by *Mrs. Doubtfire* (1993), in order to get close to the family ("The Immaculate Election" 2:14). The performance attracts a sexual commentary when Maeby calls him Mr. Fingerbottom, although interestingly, Tobias merely corrects the pronoun. A second incident occurs when Tobias dresses up as Lucille in order to help Buster deal with his dependence ("Forget-Me-Now" 3:3). In both instances, Tobias' performances could be seen as subversive. This is partially due to the nature of the practice that Tobias engages in; quite literally, Tobias *acts* as Lucille and Mrs. Featherbottom. His actions, gestures, and behaviors form a *performed* gendered identity, and while Tobias' performances are in a sense noble and intend to serve the family's interests, the viewer is still challenged to associate his performances, despite their good intentions, with gender confusion or closeted homosexuality, due to the numerous loaded signifiers that precede them.

When Tobias confesses to Michael, "I just need to prove to my wife that I can act like a man" ("Whistler's Mother" 1:20), the words "act like a man" stand out. Rather than simply say "*be* a man," Tobias' choice of words relates directly to imitation and performance, which draws attention to the way gender is realized—through a "stylized repetition of acts" (Butler 179). Furthermore, while traversing (generally unwittingly) the boundaries of socially acceptable norms relating to gender and sexuality, Tobias also persistently mocks them through moments of exaggerated insecurity coupled with profound ignorance. When he describes having sex with his wife as "heterosexual intercourse" ("Family Ties" 3:11), some viewers may interpret this as solely a reflection of Tobias' discomfort at the thought of sleeping with a woman. However, when Michael replies, "you can just say intercourse," our attention is drawn again to the linguistic binaries that perpetuate the performativity of both gender and sexuality. Tobias' performances are, in a sense, an embodiment of the tensions that flow through the intersections of sexuality and gender; and through their perpetual lack of resolution, Tobias works as an antagonist to the construction of a monolithic gendered and sexualized subject.

"And the thought of loving you is getting so exciting..."

Incestuous relationships, with the exception of those clearly linked to abuse, are not commonly depicted on television, and thus academic scholarship in this area is relatively rare. Narratives that focus on familial romances are more common in literary fiction, where critical analysis tends to focus on classic works. For example, Glenda A. Hudson discusses familial romances in the work of Jane Austin, in the context of the social and political changes of the 18th and 19th centuries, while Kathleen Rae Bryan explores similar themes in William Faulkner's novels. In American culture, normative social behaviors have historically been regulated by representations of the nuclear family, and inter-cousin couples are certainly not widely acknowledged as part of this framework (Khan). However, *Arrested Development*, in some respects, diverges from this idealism by perpetually failing to reach any clear resolution regarding non-normative familial behaviors, despite Michael's often-noble efforts to "keep them all together." Furthermore, the show often validates the notion that the heteronormative family ideal is an illusion, by demonstrating the many surprises and deviations that occur well outside of its control, and the many feelings and desires that cannot be (and more controversially, *should not have to be*) contained by heteronormative hegemony.

The idea that the family is inherently incestuous is not only acknowledged by the series, but it is almost exploited as a central comedic device. This is evident in the cartoonish Oedipus complex of Buster Bluth, whose inability to free himself from maternal dependency leads him to date (and possibly murder) his mother's best friend. Furthermore, Héritier's re-reading of Oedipus, and re-theorizing of the incest taboo as "the contact between identical bodily fluids" (11), implicates indirect sexual contact as an incestuous act. This includes sharing a partner with a blood relative, a common theme in *Arrested Development*. For example, Michael and George Michael both sleep with the same woman ("Blockheads" 4:15); Gob is involved with George Michael's ex-girlfriend Ann ("Development Arrested" 3:13); Michael pursues Gob's girlfriend Marta ("Marta Complex" 1:12); Gob seduces Buster's ex-girlfriend Lucille Austero ("Storming the Castle" 2:9); Lindsay flirts with her daughter's love interest, Steve Holt ("Sad Sack" 2:5); George Sr. and Gob both sleep with Kitty ("Charity Drive" 1:6); and Lucille sleeps with her brother in-law Oscar ("Switch Hitter" 2:7). Furthermore, the assertion that the incest taboo serves to avoid sexual rivalries in the family (Mitterauer) is also explored through George Michael's sexual narrative, as he crosses sexual paths with both his father ("Blockheads" 4:15) and uncle ("Development Arrested" 3:13) through a common romantic interest. In both instances, their "sexual rivalries" lead to acts of physical violence.

George Michael experiences the most frequent and sustained issues relating to incestuous attraction, sexuality, and love. His case may be particularly important as he goes through a considerable amount of adolescent growth during the series, a period that involves "learning to reconcile sexual feelings with social demands" (Smith 322). His journey in this regard is more heavily emphasized by the narrative, particularly compared to the character he pursues romantically—his cousin Maeby. While Maeby's attraction to George Michael is certainly represented (to a lesser extent) throughout the series, it offers fewer clues and signifiers relating to the negotiation of non-heteronormative sexuality. George Michael, on the other hand, struggles to negotiate the moral connotations of his secret love through a process of ongoing reconciliation, where he anxiously avoids being found out, and even fears being arrested for kissing his cousin ("Pilot" 1:1). When Maeby kisses George Michael for the first time in an attempt to teach their family a lesson (which proves unsuccessful), the incident serves as a trigger for George Michael's love and lust for his cousin. As the series progresses, he continues to search for ways to be close to her, including suggesting they "kiss again" to once again try to teach the family a lesson ("Pilot" 1:1), auditioning for a role in the school play that would also allow him to kiss her ("Bringing Up Buster" 1:3), blindly supporting her ventures to rebel against her mother ("Key Decisions" 1:4), trying to get fake IDs so that he and Maeby can see a movie about inter-cousin love ("My Mother, the Car" 1:7), and launching an investigation to uncover if Maeby is his real biological cousin ("Beef Consummé" 1:13). When Lucille reveals that Maeby was "made in a cup" ("Beef Consummé" 1:13), George Michael is excited to tell her the good news, but resists doing so when Maeby expresses how much she appreciates having a cousin. This could be read as a sign of self-regulation, or "a means of self-defense, not against an incestuous desire, but against the expansion and the implications of this deployment of sexuality which ... among its many benefits, had the disadvantage of ignoring the laws and juridical forms of alliance" (Foucault 109). Thus, while Maeby's comment, "I have a cousin here, so even if my parents do get divorced, I have you, right?" ("Beef Consummé" 1:13) does not reduce his attraction to her, it questions (and thus regulates) his commitment to the preservation of their familial relationship.

George Michael also competes with stereotypically masculine football star Steve Holt (who later turns out to be another Bluth cousin) for Maeby's affections, which begins with both of them auditioning for the same role in the school play ("Bringing Up Buster" 1:3). Not long after, George Michael wants to quit the play when he learns that Maeby is only participating in order to kiss Steve Holt, who lands the role of the male lead. However, he signs back on after learning that Steve will be missing several rehearsals, which would allow him to kiss Maeby as the understudy. When Tobias takes over as director, Maeby gets frustrated and quits the play, and Steve Holt is cast as the female lead. This is perhaps the most vivid example of an intersection of the issues of sexuality and gender raised by multiple characters. While Tobias' choice to cast two males together may be interpreted by audiences as an implication of his sexuality, stereotypically macho Steve Holt is more than happy to play a female role, which creates an interesting inversion that challenges the viewer's expectations regarding normative masculinity.

Romantic feelings are evident again when George Michael and Maeby share a kiss in the episode "Righteous Brothers" (2:18). However, they are interrupted when the model home collapses, and in the following episode George Michael sleeps in the car as the two awkwardly try to avoid each other ("The Cabin Show" 3:1). The narrative of season three also touches on the issue of inter-cousin marriage. For example, in the episode "Fakin' It" (3:10), George Michael talks Maeby into participating in a fake wedding (which inadvertently becomes a real wedding) for Alzheimer's patients at the hospital. Remarkably, this incident could be read as a parody of the performativity of marriage, where artificial performances lead to the real recognition of their union. In the episode "Exit Strategy" (3:12), George Michael is the only one in the family who remembers Maeby's birthday, which leads to the two reaching "second base." In the following episode ("Development Arrested" 3:13), Tobias shows Maeby and George Michael some photos of Lindsay giving birth to Maeby, debunking the idea that Maeby was "made in a cup," as Lucille once implied. Interestingly, the situation is not used to flatten and normalize their attraction, nor is it used to internalize a normative lesson, as the two still find it difficult to stop kissing each other, despite the new developments. George Michael eventually tells his father about his feelings for Maeby in the episode "Development Arrested" (3:13), explaining, "I know it's wrong, you know, but my feelings are real, even if it was a mistake." To this, Michael replies, "well obviously, acting on those feelings is not an option. She's a blood relative." Later in the episode however, Michael reveals to his son that Maeby is not his cousin after all, as her mother Lindsay was adopted, and thus Maeby isn't related to anyone in the Bluth family. Despite this, Michael makes it clear that being with Maeby is not an option because the relationship wouldn't last due to their age, and also because "she might not be a blood relative, but she is still family, and that's a bond that lasts forever" ("Development Arrested" 3:13). Foucault's assertion that the prohibition of incest resists the breakdown of familial alliances (109) is quite clearly demonstrated in this scene, and more broadly in Michael's attempts to "keep them all together." Thus, Michael, while being the "good guy" in the series, also acts as an embodiment of heteronor-mative hegemony.

Somewhat similar to Tobias' struggle, George Michael's ongoing attempts to concurrently pursue and justify a romance with his cousin is illustrative of a non-heteronormative and non-monolithic sexuality trying to actualize in a world of established sexual norms. His attraction doesn't simply exist in the abstract, unspoken, and repressed, nor is it momentary and fleeting, which is more common in representations of taboo sexualities, but rather it articulates in a series of calculated, strategic plans to win Maeby's affection. In this way, Michael's efforts to police his son's desires and feelings in order to preserve the family structure are clearly unsuccessful, as seen when George Michael, while attending college, decides to ignore his father's advice by attempting to initiate a relationship with Maeby ("It Gets Better" 4:13). However, what is often most intriguing about George Michael's attempts to pursue his cousin, which in some ways challenges the expectations and norms of the heteronor-mative, is that he often does so through the simulation of heteronormative behaviors that clearly don't come naturally. In order to make himself more desirable, he tries to assert his masculinity through ridiculous acts and per-formances that generally require misinformation, sacrifice, and going against his own ethical code. For example, he tries to create the impression that he's a seasoned visitor of prison, despite being afraid ("Visiting Ours" 1:5); he buys a leather jacket and talks about getting a motorcycle ("Storming the Castle" 1:9); he breaks into the permit office ("Charity Drive" 1:6); he keeps wearing the muscle suit from the Living Classics Pageant after Maeby remarks on his "kickin' bod" ("In God We Trust" 1:8); and when he's reunited with Maeby in college ("It Gets Better" 4:13), he attempts to come off as a confident, suave, risk-taking, and overtly sexual entrepreneur. He does all this despite being evi-dently more comfortable as a studious, honest, hairless, "boring old nice guy" ("Storming the Castle" 1:9). In this way, George Michael's sexual script is an expression of multiple hegemonic tensions, and a site for the negotiation of various issues relating to both sexuality and gender.

"I think I will do better once I get a little Mexican in me..."

While the lack of emphasis on female sexual scripts reflects the overall dominance of male characters in the series, the narrative avoids conforming to gendered stereotypes when it comes to female characters. Maeby Fünke cer-tainly isn't "associated with passivity and dependence," as is common in representations of women (Moore 78), nor does she fit into the dichotomized tropes of female sexuality, where female characters are depicted as either "passive and innocent or as hypersexual aggressors" (Bindig and Bergstrom 191). While George Michael is clearly attracted to her, she is not highly sexualized by the narrative in order to establish a tension between them. Ultimately, this gives Maeby much more agency and depth than many representations of female sexuality on mainstream television allow. Furthermore, although Maeby's boldness doesn't always generate perfect outcomes, she consistently avoids normative gender representations, including the ways in which her sexual script is realized, which are neither passive nor hypersexual. For example, while the narrative depicts George Michael's conflicted feelings and desires through visible anxiety, gestures, and disastrous plans to win her affection, Maeby's journey is more commonly demonstrated through gutsy (yet not overtly or essentially sexual) actions. Early incidents include kissing George Michael in the pilot episode and, later in the season, kissing Annyong to make George Michael jealous ("Let 'Em Eat Cake" 1:22). Her interest is also implied through dialogue about physical acts. For example, when Maeby becomes intrigued by the potential success of the Fakeblock software, she jokes with George Michael, "when you become an Internet billionaire, you could do whatever you want with me in bed" ("It Gets Better" 4:13). Interestingly, while this comment implies passivity, Maeby is generally depicted as the dominant initiator of physical contact between the two. For example, when they engage in a passionate kiss in the episode "Righteous Brothers" (2:18), Maeby is clearly in the dominant physical position, while George Michael is hunched back awkwardly on the sofa. Ultimately, while George Michael is portrayed as the most invested in their unlikely romance, Maeby, despite being given much less screen time in that regard, is certainly more assertive and confident.

In the episode "Señoritis" (4:12), Maeby is still attending high school at the age of 23 when she starts dating fellow student Perfecto Telles, who is 17. Under the impression that Perfecto is an undercover cop, Maeby seduces him for blackmailing leverage. However, the plan backfires and Maeby is arrested for being a sexual predator. The gendered implications of this example can be seen in contrast to another age-based sexual offence—the relationship between Gob and Ann. In the latter case, Gob is never legally reprimanded for being involved with a teenager, and thus the audience is forced to adjust to the relationship, which continues into the fourth season ("A New Attitude" 4:11). The varying ways in which these offences are handled by the narrative could be read as a response to the gendering of age-based sexual offences in Western societies. For example, Cocca argues that the "gender-neutrality of

the laws does not appear to erase the idea of young women as victims of predatory older men," a phenomenon that can also be observed in the media. The
handling of these two examples is made even more outrageous by the differences in age gaps. In Maeby's situation, the gap is only six years, while Gob
and Ann are separated by decades. Thus, the striking contrast between these
two relationships and the inconsistency between the "severity" of their age
gaps and legal outcomes generates an interesting gender inversion that effectively brings to our attention the discourses that usually surround incidents
of this nature.

Conclusion

While the intent of this analysis was not to focus on male experiences
depicted on *Arrested Development*, the research found enduring and non-
normative sexual scripts were more common among male characters. However,
while female characters have historically been (and in many ways, still are)
represented as "submissive, weak, dependent and affiliation-oriented," and
male characters are more commonly "dominant, powerful, independent and
achievement-oriented" (Gunter 31), *Arrested Development* certainly does not
appear to function according to such essentialist binaries. Maeby, for example,
despite being stuck with two fairly narcissistic, absent, and superficial parents,
manages to thrive in a role as a movie executive, while the rest of the family
festers in the aftermath of various company scandals. She is, in many ways,
despite all obstacles and lack of strong role models, the strongest, most capable
and determined character in the series.

Khan argues that the visibility and acceptability of inter-cousin intimacy
is rare in the global North, and thus "the small amount of representation available takes on heightened significance" (272). Khan also uses the film *Kissing
Cousins* (2008) as an example of the struggle for the negotiation of inter-
cousin relationships, a struggle that eventually leads the protagonist "onto the
path of cultural-sexual normativity" (292). In the case of George Michael,
however, the conversation with his father in the episode "Development
Arrested" (3:13) almost promises to mark the end of his attraction to Maeby,
the point where George Michael is supposed to internalize a lesson about normative sexuality. However, the fact that George Michael's feelings aren't
resolved after hearing his father's advice indicates that his feelings for Maeby,
whatever form they may take (sexual, romantic, familial, or mixed), haven't
been neatly, seamlessly, and unrealistically swept under the rug. Some critics

might argue that the series, in some respects, filters and naturalizes their intimacy through the story of Lindsay's adoption, and "retroactively cleanses their physical interaction of its taboo features" (Khan 287). However, George Michael and Maeby's feelings were still strong (and in some ways, acted upon) when they thought they were biological cousins. Thus, at the very least, the series manages to explore the ways in which less acceptable sexualities struggle to actualize against hegemonic social norms and familial expectations.

Returning now to Sedgwick's notion of queer, which refers to the ways in which "anyone's gender, or anyone's sexuality aren't made (or can't be made) to signify monolithically" (8), we can see how the term might be extended to many themes of sexuality in *Arrested Development*, not simply the more obvious examples that relate to same-sex intimacy. In the case of Tobias, the show does not offer a clear-cut response to the issues of sexuality or gender negotiation that his character raises. The audience ultimately has the power to construct a complete (if subjective) picture of Tobias based on various signifiers that imply meaning, including what Dyer calls "signs of gayness" (19). Whether they should construct that picture, however, is another question entirely. In this way, watching the series may resemble an exercise of resistance in itself; repelling the urge to categorize Tobias using the heteronormative criteria embedded in our social consciousness. In the end, what makes Tobias an interesting case study is that he does not quite perform as a homosexual, and in this sense, the very crucial meaning-making process that occurs at the moment of viewing is made even more crucial and even more powerful (Struken and Cartwright).

Finally, the "subversive laughter" (Butler 186) that stems from the practice of parody, which has the potential to illuminate the binaries and hegemonies that operate in relation to sexuality and gender, is certainly present in several performances throughout the series. Interestingly, by running these narratives alongside each other, and by resisting the resolution-focused outcomes that are common in popular television, particularly in relation to non-heteronormative characters, the series creates the space for multiple and negotiable identities to form. In other words, Tobias does not hop out of the closet, challenging a society where confession is "the general standard governing the production of true discourse on sex" (Foucault 63), and thus retains the mobility he draws on so frequently, whether consciously or not, to traverse heteronormative boundaries. In the case of George Michael, his attraction to his cousin does not reach a miraculous resolve, nor does he outgrow it—the show simply goes on, and his life continues. Perhaps it is due to unresolved issues like these that we may observe *Arrested Development*'s progressiveness within its outrageousness. Perhaps it is here, where the queered subjects are not resolved or "unqueered," that the show challenges the heteronormative status quo rather than reinforces it.

Works Cited

Avila-Saavedra, Guillermo. "Nothing Queer About Queer Television: Televized Construction of Gay Masculinities." *Media, Culture & Society* 31.1 (2009): 5–21. Print.

Bindig, Lori, and Andrea M. Bergstrom. *The O.C.: A Critical Understanding*. Lanham: Lexington, 2013. Print.

Bolich, G. G. *Conversing on Gender*. Raleigh: Psyche's Press, 2007. Print.

Brady, Anita, and Tony Schirato. *Understanding Judith Butler*. London: Sage, 2011. Print.

Bryan, Kathleen Rae. *The Theme of Incest in William Faulkner's Novels*. Diss. University of California, San Diego, 1987. Print.

Butler, Judith. *Gender Trouble: Feminism and the Subversion of Identity*. New York: Routledge, 1990. Print.

Cameron, Deborah, and Don Kulick. *Language and Sexuality*. Cambridge: Cambridge University Press, 2003. Print.

Christiansen, Adrienne E., and Jeremy J. Hanson. "Comedy as Cure for Tragedy: ACT University Press and the Rhetoric of Aids." *Quarterly Journal of Speech* 82.2 (1996): 157–170. Print.

Clarkson, Jay. "Contesting Masculinity's Makeover: Queer Eye, Consumer Masculinity, and "Straight-Acting" Gays." *Journal Of Communication Inquiry* 29.3 (2005): 235–255. Print.

Cocca, Carolyn E. " Prosecuting Mrs. Robinson? Gender, Sexuality, and Statutory Rape Laws." *Michigan Feminist Studies* 16 (2002): n. pag. Web. 03 Apr. 2014. http://quod.lib. umich.edu/cgi/t/text/text-idx?cc=mfsfront;c=mfs;c=mfsfront;idno=ark5583.0016. 003;g=mfsg;rgn=main;view=text;xc=1

Cramer, Janet M. "Discourses of Sexual Morality in *Sex and the City* and *Queer as Folk*." *Journal of Popular Culture* 40.3 (2007): 409–432. Print.

Dhaenens, Frederik. "Teenage Queerness: Negotiating Heteronormativity in the Representation of Gay Teenagers in *Glee*." *Journal of Youth Studies* 16.3 (2013): 304–317. Print.

Dyer, Richard. *The Matter of Images: Essays on Representation*. 2nd ed. London: Routledge, 2002. Print.

Eckert, Penelope, and Sally McConnell-Ginet. *Language and Gender*. 2nd ed. Cambridge: Cambridge University Press, 2013. Print.

Evans, Victor D. *"Curved TV*: The Impact of Televisual Images on Gay Youth." *American Communication Journal* 9.3 (2007): n. pag. Web. 03 Apr. 2014. http://ac-journal.org/ journal/2007/Fall/5CurvedTV.pdf

Fajer, Marc A. "Can Two Real Men Eat Quiche Together? Storytelling, Gender-Role Stereotypes, and Legal Protection for Lesbians and Gay Men." *University of Miami Law Review* 46 (1992): 511–651. Print.

Fiske, John. "Moments of Television: Neither the Text nor the Audience." *Remote Control: Television, Audiences and Cultural Power*. eds. Ellen Seiter, Hans Borchers, Gabriele Kreutzner, and Eva-Maria Warth. London: Routledge, 1989. 56–78. Print.

Foucault, Michel. *The History of Sexuality*. New York: Pantheon, 1978. Print.

Freedman, Barbara. "Reading Errantly: Misrecognition and the Uncanny in *The Comedy of Errors* (1991)." *The Comedy of Errors: Critical Essays*. Ed. Robert S. Miola. New York: Garland, 1997. 261–298. Print.

Freedman, Barbara. *Staging the Gaze: Postmodernism, Psychoanalysis, and Shakespearean Comedy*. Ithaca: Cornell University Press, 1991. Print.

Golanty, Eric, and Gordon Edlin. *Human Sexuality: The Basics.* Sadbury: Jones & Bartlet, 2011. Print.

Goode, Erich. *Deviant Behavior.* Englewood Cliffs: Prentice-Hall, 1984. Print.

Griffin, Hollis. "Queerness, the Quality Audience, and Comedy Central's *Reno 911!*" *Television & New Media* 9.5 (2008): 355–370. Print.

Gunter, Barrie. *Television and Gender Representation.* London: John Libbey, 1995. Print.

Héritier, Françoise. *Two Sisters and Their Mother: The Anthropology of Incest.* New York: Zone, 1999. Print.

Hodges, Ian. "Queer Dilemmas: The Problem of Power in Psychotherapeutic and Counselling Practice." *Feeling Queer or Queer Feelings?: Radical Approaches to Counselling Sex, Sexualities and Genders.* Ed. Lyndsey Moon. London: Routledge, 2008. 7–22. Print.

Hudson, Glenda A. *Sibling Love and Incest in Jane Austen's Fiction.* London: Macmillan, 1999. Print.

Khan, Ummni. "Kissing Cousins: Racism, Homophobia and Compulsory Able-bodiedness in the Controversy over Inter-Cousin Marriage." *Jindal Global Law Review* 4.2 (2013): 268–295. Print.

Lynch, Gerald. *Stephen Leacock: Humour and Humanity.* Kingston: McGill-Queen's University Press, 1988. Print.

Markle, Gail. ""Can Women Have Sex Like a Man?": Sexual Scripts in *Sex and the City.*" *Sexuality & Culture* 12.1 (2008): 45–57. Print.

Mitterauer, Michael. "The Customs of the Magians: The Problem of Incest in Historical Societies." *Sexual Knowledge, Sexual Science: The History of Attitudes to Sexuality.* Ed. Roy Porter and Mikuláš Teich. Cambridge: Cambridge University Press, 1994. 231–250. Print.

Moore, Henrietta L. *The Subject of Anthropology: Gender, Symbolism and Psychoanalysis.* Cambridge: Polity, 2007. Print.

Newcomb, Horace, and Paul M. Hirsch. "Television as a Cultural Forum." *Television: The Critical View.* Ed. Horace Newcomb. Oxford: Oxford University Press, 2000. 561–573. Print.

O'Donnell, Victoria. *Television Criticism.* Thousand Oaks: Sage, 2007. Print.

Palmer, Jerry. *The Logic of the Absurd: On Film and Television Comedy.* London: BFI, 1987. Print.

Parmelee, Maurice. *The Play Function of Sex.* New York: Vantage, 1966. Print.

Poole, Jay. "Queer Representations of Gay Males and Masculinities in the Media." *Sexuality & Culture* 18.2 (2014): 279–290. Print.

Roseneil, Sasha. "Queer Frameworks and Queer Tendencies: Towards an Understanding of Postmodern Transformations of Sexuality." *Sociological Research Online* 5.3 (2000): n. pag. Web. 5 Apr. 2014. http://www.socresonline.org.uk/5/3/roseneil.html

Sedgwick, Eve Kosofsky. *Tendencies.* Durham: Duke University Press, 1993. Print.

Silverman, Rachel. "Comedy as Correction: Humor as Perspective by Incongruity on *Will & Grace* and *Queer as Folk.*" *Sexuality & Culture* 17.2 (2013): 260–274. Print.

Smith, Sarah H. "Scripting Sexual Desire: Cultural Scenarios of Teen Girls' Sexual Desire in Popular Films, 2000–2009." *Sexuality & Culture* 16.3 (2012): 321–341. Print.

Struken, Marita, and Lisa Cartwright. "Introduction to Practices of Looking." *Visual Culture: Critical Concepts in Media and Cultural Studies.* Eds. Joanne Morra and Marquard Smith. London: Routledge, 2006. 27–33. Print.

Tomsen, Stephen, and Kevin Markwell. "Violence, Cultural Display and the Suspension of Sexual Prejudice." *Sexuality & Culture* 13.4 (2009): 201–217. Print.

Deconstructing the Bluths

"I'm a monster!"
The Monstrous and the Comedic

Jonah Ford

"Delores, listen to me. Empty the account. Why are you crying? Why are *you* crying?" George Sr. shouts into his cell phone during the climactic scene in *Arrested Development*'s pilot episode as police sirens wail in the background and his grandiose retirement party erupts into a scene of panic and confusion. In a frantic attempt to cover his tracks, as the Securities and Exchange Commission prepares to board his yacht, he hastily deliberates with his secretary, "Shredder. No. Save it. Save it. Shredder" ("Pilot" 1:1). In November of 2003, when *Arrested Development* first aired, the infamous Enron scandal had been uncovered two years prior, a scandal that made white-collar fraud front page news and had disastrous consequences for the investors victimized by Enron's duplicitousness. The first few years of the new century saw various other corporate scandals as well, making many questionable business practices public. Many of these scandals played important roles in setting the stage for the cultural tensions brought to the surface by the Great Recession of 2008, as they added to a growing ambivalence within America toward white-collar, pseudo-aristocracy. As with any television show, the pilot episode of *Arrested Development* affixes the frame within which we read the rest of the show's humor and plot, and it is not coincidental that the narrative frame this pilot establishes is one of corporate fraud. As one laughs at George Sr.'s hurried conference with his secretary, one cannot help but hear echoes of the notorious document shredding and evidence tampering that surfaced in the wake of Enron's investigation. So, why does one laugh? After all, this is a pilot for a sitcom, not the newest franchise of *Law & Order* (1990–2010). Telling a story of corporate malfeasance through comedy elicits decidedly different responses than that of drama or suspense. Something, then, seems to be happening in the telling of the Bluths' story. Somehow, within the thirty-minute scripted space of an evening sitcom, the real life horrors of business bamboozling are transformed into comedic buffoonery.

Just like our jocund response to George Sr.'s fraudulence, Buster's horrific deformity is also framed as comedy. Buster's signature refrain, "I'm a monster!," comes after he loses his hand to the monstrous appetite of a loose seal in "Out on a Limb" (2:11), and this lament becomes the situational punch-line in numerous scenes thereafter. The description of this subplot sounds more like the nefarious intrigue of a hilariously terrible B movie Creature Feature than it does a situational comedy. Having acquired a taste for mammal blood, by feeding first on small cats, this once-tame show animal is released into the wild "from whence it came" by a jilted Gob who can no longer contain it. He returns to feed on an unsuspecting Buster Bluth, who apparently thought it safe to go in the water ("Hand to God" 2:12). But Buster's cry of abjection also reveals a bewildering phenomenon which this chapter will attempt to explore: the unholy union of comedy and monstrosity.

Buster first utters his lament when he tries to show affection to his uncle-father, Oscar, the only way he knows how: with a warmhearted shoulder rub. Tragically, he is confronted with the Frankensteinian reality of his unnatural deformity—his attempts to show affection and compassion elicit only pain and reproach. Looking down at his gleaming hook-of-a-hand, Buster's warm, childlike "Hey, brother!" becomes a gothic refrain of self-loathing: "I'm a monster!" Unleashing a bestial fury, Buster tears through Lucile's condominium, thrashing curtains and destroying bric-a-brac, as a bloodied Oscar runs to escape his path. The screen confronts the audience with visages of monstrosity, and yet they are intended to laugh, instead of clutch their pearls. Audience members are not provoked to grab torches and pitchforks, but why not? What is it about this particular context that instead provokes laughter? Why are these scenes of horror, like the fraudulence of George Sr., not threatening?

The comedic frame of the sitcom genre seems to transform the terrible into something else. A great deal of the humor of the Bluths involves absurd exaggerations of various points of cultural unease within contemporary America. Race and gender, for example, are the basis of a wide variety of characters, subplots, and punch-lines within *Arrested Development*, perhaps most memorably seen in Gob and Franklin's attempts at race relations and Tobias' slippery sexuality. However, these parodies also bear close resemblance to matters of substantial cultural anxiety and unease. One laughs at Gob and Franklin singing about the difficulties of social expectations ascribed to whites and blacks ("It ain't easy bein' white/It ain't easy bein' brown/All this pressure to be bright/I got childrens all over town!" ["Righteous Brothers" 2:18]) or Tobias's ambiguous and innuendo-laden statements ("Oh, I can just taste those meaty leading-man parts in my mouth." ["For British Eyes Only" 3:2]). Yet even recent history can bear witness to various moments when the discrimination of non-whites (most recently middle-easterners, presumed to be terrorists) and LGBTQ persons has had decidedly unfunny consequences. Philosophy and cultural studies have time and again illustrated how these same cultural categories of race and gender are sutured and contorted in the construction of all manner of terrible beasts, oddities, and nightmares.

Class is also a very conspicuous element in *Arrested Development*. Lucille Bluth's elitist sardonicism and callousness toward "the help" is a constant theme throughout all four seasons ("Luz, that coat costs more than your house! Oh, that's how we joke. She doesn't even have a house!" ["Top Banana" 1:2]), and Lindsay Bluth is regularly lampooned as a representation of unapologetic self-indulgence, superficiality, and manufactured, store-bought beauty ("Great. So now we don't have a car *or* a jet? Why don't we just take an ad out in *I'm Poor* magazine?" ["Key Decisions" 1:4]). And yet social class and the dehumanization so frequently embedded in rigid systems of social stratification are also found in a variety of modern monsters (McNally). Count Dracula, particularly in his iconic Universal Studios manifestation, is perhaps the most well-known expression of monstrous elites. With his combination of fatal attraction and demonic repulsion, he is laden with unmistakable symbols of aristocracy and capitalist enterprise. Perhaps then it is not coincidental that this 1931 box-office hit came only two years into the start of the Great Depression, when free-market capitalism had shown its darker side, and the continued struggles for workers rights and unionization threw the opulence of the 1920s into strong relief. And eerily, the same categories and anxieties about race, gender, and class lampooned by the Bluths are the same ones that coalesce like the fog that haunts the moors and the marshlands, and the other perennial places of monstrous provenance.

Monstrosity and comedy. They seem, at first glance, to come from opposite ends of the emotional spectrum, and yet, upon further inspection, appear to reveal something of a Jekyll and Hyde relationship. Like the conjoined twins so often heralded as freaks and oddities, monstrosity and comedy are joined by a common origin. The field of anthropology has called it the *liminal*—that strange place "betwixt and between" the categories and schemas humans devise to make sense of the world they inhabit (Turner). The assertion that those things which make us laugh and those which make us recoil are in fact more closely related than we might think is not just the stuff of lofty, ivory-tower chin scratching. Even a cursory glance at television and movies reveals this same union between the horrific and the hilarious. For the slapstick trio par excellence, *The Three Stooges* (1925–1966), bodily harm and personal torture are the stock from which their buffoonery precipitates. Much more recently, the *Scary Movie* franchise has made a killing off of stitching together characters and plot lines from successful horror movies, and reanimating them to create, to date, five blockbuster comedies. Even 2013's *This Is the End* recapitulates the horror and monstrosity of western culture's canonical apocalypse, The Book of Revelation, to produce the kind of comedy that Seth Rogen and Jonah Hill have become known for.

Historical Context

Arrested Development begins its story by evoking well known episodes from the Enron scandal exposed in 2001, which was followed by the company's rapid downfall in the months to come. Other episodes from season one also focus on the ongoing investigation and initial prosecution of the Bluth Company. Michael Bluth goes to great lengths to cooperate by locating important flight records requested by the courts ("Top Banana" 1:2), and with the introduction of Kitty, George Sr.'s scandalous secretary, Michael and Gob try unsuccessfully to obtain information regarding questionable international business accounts ("Charity Drive" 1:6). Although a host of other subplots are introduced throughout the subsequent three seasons, underlying themes of corporate intrigue are revisited and alluded to throughout the series. With the addition of season four in 2013, the economic critique of the show's comedy becomes even more prominent. A number of crises leading up to, and developing out of, the Great Recession of 2008 become interwoven into the story of the Bluths, such as the inflation and eventual collapse of the real estate market ("Indian Takers" 4:3), as well as high unemployment rates and job insecurity ("Flight of the Phoenix" 4:1). Given the primacy of these themes about corporate misconduct and economic uncertainties, the comedy of *Arrested Development* must be read within the context of growing tensions and ambivalence, percolating in the early 2000s and continuing throughout the decade, regarding the ills and spoils of the free market and its impact on the stability of the American economy.

Enron was certainly a potent symbol of such ambivalence and mistrust in the early 2000s, especially since Enron itself had long touted that communication and integrity were pillars of its business ethics (Cruver 42–43). However, before October of 2001 when the Enron mirage (or, in the words of Gob, "illusion") came quickly crumbling down, it was seen as a paragon of American corporate innovation and success. Brian Cruver, a young, ambitious Enron employee in the months leading up to the company's collapse, offers the following perspective: "Highly respected, bitterly admired—if you were craving the fast track, you dreamed of working at Enron" (1).

The American capitalist culture of the 1990s and early 2000s can perhaps be summed up in two words: arrogance and greed. And Enron was in many ways a corporate embodiment of this cultural zeitgeist. From 1996 to 2001, Enron was named "America's most innovative company" by *Fortune* magazine—a title that they flaunted proudly. The evolution of what would later become Enron grew out of the merger of Houston Natural Gas and Northern Natural Gas in 1985, creating an expansive matrix of gas pipelines that spread throughout much of the continental United States. Under the leadership of CEO Ken Lay, whose name and face would later become synonymous with corporate fraud, Enron began looking to the future and spread internationally, setting up locations on almost every continent. However, as diversification seems to be part and parcel of modern business—even George Sr. had to move his sights beyond the sweaty, chocolaty confines of the banana stand to build his empire—innovation would be Enron's guiding principle (Cruver; McLean and Elkind). A *Fortune* magazine article from one year before the scandal broke praised Enron's innovation:

> No company illustrates the transformative power of innovation more dramatically than Enron. Over the past decade Enron's commitment to the invention—and later domination—of new business categories has taken it from a $200 million old-economy pipeline operator to a $40 billion new-economy trading powerhouse [Stein].

Enron's profits seemed to only increase year after year, and shortly before its implosion the company had claimed profits in excess of $100 billion (McLean and Elkind). Although many seemed enamored with the mind-bogglingly persistent Enron gains, there were some who were skeptical about just how it was that a company could experience such aggressive, unchecked growth.

Bethany McLean, a journalist with *Fortune* magazine at the time of the Enron collapse, became the first to outspokenly question Enron in her article,

"Is Enron Overpriced?" Posing what should have been a simple question, McLean opened the floodgates of inquiry into the house of mirrors that Enron had become. "How exactly does Enron make its money?," McLean asked plainly, "Details are hard to come by because Enron keeps many of the specifics confidential for what it terms 'competitive reasons.' And the numbers that Enron does present are often extremely complicated." As more and more important people began trying to find the answer to such a basic question, it was quickly revealed that Enron was actually hemorrhaging money on a myriad of very risky deals that had been made in the name of "innovation," but this debt had been hidden from investors, and the public, by some "creative" book-keeping (McLean and Elkind; Feder, Barnaby, and Brick). Hence, the notorious document shredding parodied by George Sr.'s conference with his secretary. In January of 2002, the *New York Times* wrote that Enron had been covering its tracks for some time, shredding countless documents that might expose its deception (Feder, Barnaby, and Brick). So much shredding, it seems, that Cruver describes witnessing "a steady stream of people using [the shredder], each with stacks of unstapled and un-paper-clipped documents ... I thought if we stopped supplying it, [the shredder] might just sprout legs and race madly across the trading floor, sucking down every scrap of paper in his path" (Cruver 143).

Enron's department of Risk Assessment and Control (RAC) was supposed to monitor the level of risk involved in each business deal. However, the reality was that the RAC was unable to keep up with the amount of deals coming in because Enron was trading at such astronomical levels. Consequently, inflated and overvalued deals were getting through. And with the level of carelessness, naivety, or both, displayed by the founders of Gobias Industries ("Whistler's Mother" 1:20), "The [company's] strategy was less about booking profitable deals or controlling the risk of deals— and more about backing as many of the biggest deals as possible" (Cruver 80). But if Enron was operating on the maxim that "greed is good," even before Enron's very public dissolution various developments throughout the 1990s would show that perhaps the story of Enron was a symptom of a much larger problem—a problem that would ultimately contribute to the catastrophe of 2008.

Paul Krugman, in his first edition of *The Return of Depression Economics*, takes a close look at economic crises in Asia and Latin America throughout the 1990s and argues that these crises should have been seen as a warning sign that the economic growth experienced by his American reading audience was not as untouchable as many presumed. Krugman's argument, in a nutshell, was that the economic crises these areas experienced exposed important glitches in the global economic matrix that would have important consequences for the United States economy. The United States had come to view itself as invulnerable to such market uncertainties because it had held the privileged role of arbiter in global economic affairs since the conclusion of World War II (Krugman; Kuttner). Krugman's admonition of American hubris seemed justified in 2008, with the hit of the Great Recession, prompting him to reprint an updated edition of the book in 2009, *The Return of Depression Economics and the Crisis of 2008*. In this updated edition his message was clear: The United States had taken the wrong lessons from these crises, namely the arrogant presumption that the economic turbulence experienced in Argentina, Mexico, China, and Japan was limited to only those national economies. Moreover, these economic crises appeared easily "fixed" by international intervention, wherein the United States could see itself as, once again, playing the heroic role. This, according to Krugman, only bolstered the sense of American exceptionalism which in turn stoked the coals of economic hubris and short-sightedness that led to playing fast and loose with the free market, and forgetting many of the lessons hard learned from the Great Depression.

Looking ahead, to the "financial whoopsie daisy: aka the single greatest global financial disaster since the Great Depression" (Colbert 91), this arrogance had developed an entire banking industry which operated in much the same fashion as the greedily short-sighted brokers at Enron (Krugman; McLean and Nocera). As comedian and satirist Stephen Colbert sums up the catastrophe, "[T]he poor set up a roadside shop labeled 'The American Dream.' Then they lured Wall Street rubes into handing over low interest-rate mortgages, no questions asked, and duped those same bankers into repackaging those mortgages into insanely overvalued tradable securities.... Oldest trick in the book" (Colbert 91). In "Indian Takers" (4:3) Lindsay and Tobias are made to look like the rubes when, attempting to buy a modest house, they get roped in to buying instead a comically huge, ostentatious mansion, as the real estate broker tantalizes them with more and more expensive houses in order to make a larger commission. As an out of work actor and a fallen Bluth heiress, it does not take long for Tobias and Lindsay to default on a loan they could never afford. And such was the situation of the countless mortgages that undergirded vast amounts of the economic matrix.

Huge financial institutions, such as Merrill Lynch, were no longer concerned about the immense risk involved in trading securities that were backed by subprime mortgages, and instead saw these highly profitable deals as a golden goose that would never stop producing (McLean and Nocera). "I bet you didn't know," writes Stephen Colbert, "that Wall Streeters earn their bonuses with 18-hour stress-filled days, where the smallest mistake can mean a multi-billion dollar loss, and the banker is personally on the hook for as much as none of it" (88). In the aftermath of 2008, these mortgage securities and derivatives, which also added to the inflation of the housing market, had become a substantial part of the larger economic machine and were crucial pieces to the overall economic unraveling.

As the dominoes fell and more and more homeowners defaulted, the entire economic organism began to unravel. And it would be the thousands of ordinary individuals who would bear the consequences of such unscrupulous greed. Stories of families left homeless became a regular theme in newspapers, online forums, and evening news shows, and as the recession of 2008 got underway, unemployment rates would approach those not seen since the Great Depression. In her book, *Down the Up Escalator: How the 99 Percent Live in the Great Recession* (2013), Barbara Garson provides journalistic, narrative snap-shots of both families and individuals left to pick up the pieces for themselves in the aftermath of 2008. Long-term unemployment forced many to burn through their savings just to stay afloat, and even question their own self-worth after being passed over for job after job due to the vast numbers of individuals flooding the job market (Garson).

Much of the humor within *Arrested Development* purposefully evokes such real-world monsters—corporate monsters, and ethical monsters; monsters of markets, and monsters of fraudulence. Metaphorical monsters though they may be, the threat is the same. Thus, when read against the backdrop of Wall Street scandals and economic uncertainties, the fraudulence of George Sr. and the ongoing investigation into the Bluth Company echoes the villainy exposed in the Enron scandal. Enron's monstrous greed affected many thousands who lost massively when their stock plummeted, cost thousands of jobs in and around the Houston area (Pace), and caused a ripple effect throughout the economic matrix of the early 2000s. One laughs at the deception of George Sr. and his continued attempts to evade justice, while real white-collar monsters threaten the safety and security of real people. As has been shown, other calamitous market realities of the early 2000s, such as the inflation and eventual collapse of the real estate market, are also found written into the burlesque of *Arrested Development*. In a very real way, however, the unscrupulous real estate economy which these episodes parody endangered real families, and destabilized the entire United States economy as mortgage backed derivatives were traded in "the biggest floating craps game of all time" (McLean and Nocera 5). To be sure, the complexities of the Great Recession of 2008 are still debated, and will likely prove to be just as complex as those of the Great Depression. However, such monstrosity most certainly played a part.

The Liminal: Should I Laugh or Should I Cry?

Given the real world monsters that lay behind the comedy of the Bluths, what insights do the fields of philosophy and cultural studies offer to help make sense of how we can laugh at those things which are quite horrific? The things that provoke dread and the things that provoke laughter both find their genesis in the strange realm of the liminal. Latin at its root, the word liminal comes from the word *limen*, which is an architectural term referring to the threshold of a door. It is the threshold between two clearly defined structural spaces, and as such it is neither part of one room nor the other, but unites them both. This seemingly unimportant architectural term has since developed into a complex theoretical concept, helping social scientists and cultural theorists understand all manner of social situations and important rituals. In many ways the Bluths themselves are liminal, being neither wealthy elites nor "commoners," and George Sr. is stuck betwixt and between as he is neither imprisoned nor free—indeed, hiding in the attic, George Sr. is in the house and yet not quite in the house.

Arnold van Gennep first developed the concept of the liminal in his book *Rites of Passage*. There he used this term of architectural transition to analyze the period of *social* transition occasioned by Rites of Passage such as puberty rites, weddings, and funerals. In moving from one clearly defined position to another, one must necessarily traverse a period where one temporarily stands outside of these social roles. A bridegroom on the eve of a wedding is neither a member of the unmarried nor the married, and a corpse waiting to be interred belongs neither to the living nor to the realm of the ancestors. They are something else entirely. They are in transition. They are liminal.

van Gennep looked to ancient Greece and the rites individuals had to undergo when traveling from one city-state to another as a helpful conceptual model for the liminal as a place of social transition. Unlike modern territorial boundaries, where the edge of one state is the beginning of another, ancient Greek city-states were separated by vast expansions of uninhabited or perhaps marginally inhabited land. These vast expansions of "no place" might be deserts, marshes, forests, battlefields, or other inhospitable and *uncivilized* terrains. Thus, passage between city-states was essentially a passage "between two worlds," and this same pattern, asserted van Gennep, is exhibited when an individual moves from one social identity to another. Accordingly, these landscapes of "no place," transitional, and on the way to somewhere safe and civilized, were also home to all manner of terrifying and dangerous entities—either real or mythical—an aspect of the liminal explored later by Victor Turner.

Turner developed van Gennep's conceptual framework further, and used it to analyze a wide variety of social and cultural times of transition and flux. He calls the liminal a time and space of "anti-structure," because it stands outside of social structures and categories, such as gender, family, or social status (Turner, *The Ritual Process*). The liminal is the place of paradox, indistinctness, and confusion. Between categories, and on the way from one category to another, it is a non-category; it is an anti-category. However, it is both threatening, and freeing. As the liminal is the place that occasions important transformations, the liminal is also a place of great power. In its terrifying ambiguity, it offers the necessary contrast to established order and conventional categories because it illustrates their limits and makes it clear why they are needed. However, in the dissolution of necessary categories and systems, which provokes such terror, the liminal also provides the pregnant, creative space wherein other ways of categorizing existence can be found. The liminal is at the same time the place of awful ambiguity and awe inspiring possibility.

The liminal stage in many rites is full of terrifying masks, threatening deities, and purposeful violations of otherwise sacred cultural taboos (Turner, *The Forest of Symbols*). For example, the liminal pubescence of Maeby and George Michael occasions their flirtation with the taboo of "kissing cousins." Turner also discusses moments of the liminal in the face of tumultuous social crises, or sometimes accompanying important calendrical changes or life cycles of the community, where rituals purposefully undo the social order and evoke what Turner refers to as generative powers of primordial, mythic time (Turner, "Images of Anti-Temporality"). Turner asserts, "it is in liminality and also in those phases of ritual that abut on liminality that one finds profuse symbolic reference to [strange entities] … structural life is snuffed out by animality and nature, even as it is being regenerated by these very same forces" (Turner, *Dramas* 253). The liminal threatens, but the liminal also transforms and creates.

Monsters

The liminal can be found at all those mythical places upon which it has been scrawled "Here there be monsters." Theories of liminality have made tremendous contributions to the study of monsters, which seem to embody that threatening "anti-structure" which Turner discusses. The study of monsters, as with any field of study, is quite broad. However, despite the many nuances and variations, for the purposes of this chapter it is enough to note that there are various points of general continuity; monsters and the monstrous are that which confront, conflate, and invalidate important categories of understanding. A zombie is both alive and dead—it is betwixt and between, it is undead.

Many scholars focus on what might best be described as monsters of the imagination, such as the mythical beasts of folklore and legend, or even the dreamed up terrors of contemporary cinema. Drawing upon a host of cross-cultural data from myths, legends and folklore from a variety of cultures, anthropologist David D. Gilmore offers some helpful insights into the commonalities found in the many different monsters that cultures contrive. As creations of the imagination, what is important for Gilmore, and others, is their hybrid or recombinant nature (Halberstam). The classic dragon of European lore is a popular example of this category-shuffling, and Buster Bluth realizes monstrosity when he acknowledges he is both part human and part machine. As embodiments of the liminal breakdown of categories by category shuffling, in the language of anthropologist Mary Douglas, monsters are "interstitial." Monsters *violate* important social categories precisely because they exist between them, and because of this they are objects of impurity (Douglas, *Purity and Danger*).

Violating our categories and bringing impurity, monsters always emerge from peripheral places such as caves, forests, swamps, or seas, and are consistently presented as wreaking havoc on the civilizations they neighbor. They are characterized by an insatiable appetite for destruction. Buster destroys his mother's home, wounds his uncle-father, and even the stair car's dashboard ("The Ocean Walker" 3:6) without intending to; he is now a monster, so he must be destructive. This need for destruction is not only insatiable but, more to the point, it is "the quality of inherent *evil*, that is, unmotivated wickedness toward humans" (Gilmore 6). Parodying the monstrous Godzilla, when Tobias dresses like a giant mole to fool potential Japanese investors, he destroys the fake model town, resulting in a parody of scenes from numerous Godzilla films ("Mr. F" 3:5). As a fake monster, he cannot help but destroy the tiny, fake village. However, building on the insights of psychoanalysis, as creations of the imagination monsters also have a great deal to teach as well, since they always reveal something about the cultures that construct them. These imaginary monsters derive from deep within the unconscious of humanity and are prolific, archetypal symbols of repressed fears and sublimated, threatening desires.

Whereas Gilmore and others may be more interested in imaginary or mythical monsters, many others have taken explorations of imaginary monsters as merely a starting point for exploring monsters and the monstrous as concepts within cultural thinking. Jeffrey Jerome Cohen has written extensively on monsters and the monstrous as a hermeneutical, or interpretive, tool for "reading culture." In Cohen's edited collection, *Monster Theory: Reading Culture*, he brings together an array of post-modern theorists and philosophers who explore ways in which monstrosity breaks down and conflates our cultural categories of time (monsters as primordial beasts come back to haunt, declaring that the past is always encroaching on the present), gender, identity, and even language itself. Other scholars have found monsters to be fertile ground for exploring questions about gender construction and sexuality in contemporary culture, much like the ambiguously gay Tobias Fünke whose own monstrosity is alluded to frequently, not least of which during his harrowing graft versus host experience. Moreover, in "Burning Love" (2:9) the classic werewolf motif, well-known for its specifically sexual overtones, is parodied. And when Tobias mistakenly shoots his wife, Lindsay, the entire episode is framed within the ongoing narrative of the Fünkes' decidedly asexual marriage, wherein the ambiguity of Tobias sexuality is its root. Although Maeby seems to welcome the always-impending divorce of Lindsay and Tobias, the monstrosity of Tobias' ambiguous sexuality is a constant threat to the security of his own family, or perhaps even the institution of marriage itself, as some more conservative voices might assert.

Imaginary monsters also serve important social functions, albeit frequently xenophobic functions, but what does monster theory say about monsters of a less fantastic nature? Neither the Bluth family nor their real-world, white-collar counterparts are monsters in any mythical sense. Instead, the Bluths and the cultural realities they represent are best described as metaphorical monsters, in that their monstrosity is expressed in terms of ethical and moral depravity. Historically, many xenophobic and ethnocentric interpretations of monsters, which developed throughout the Middle Ages, explained nature's monsters theologically as signaling a lack or a flaw on the part of the individual creature, such as moral depravity or resistance to God's divine will (Asma 26–44; 74–93). And although some saw monsters in more positive ways, such as expressions God's infinite and wondrous creativity, the more disparaging interpretations of moral lack would win out, informing even the metaphorical meanings of the word monster today. For example, Lucile Bluth is frequently regarded as monstrous due to her decided lack of motherly warmth and affection, and is literally made into a horror movie creature as the hideous "Gangie" ("Making a Stand" 3:8). Indeed, referring to the activities of humans as "monstrous" implies that there is something less-than-human, or perhaps even anti-human about them. It also seems quite fair to say that, at least in regard to corporate or financial monsters, that these terrifying qualities are in fact born of the darker aspects of an economic culture of greed and arrogance. Thus, even metaphorical monsters can still be understood as exploding our cultural categories—categories including motherhood and acceptable business practice—and thereby representing a kind of interstitial cultural impurity.

In this interstitial impurity, monsters—even metaphorical monsters—always bring with them important messages. A monster is always a text to be read (Cohen). Monsters warn and monsters teach. The Latin *monstrum* referred to a warning, a portent, or an omen, specifically to prodigious events in nature, either celestial or terrestrial. As Gilmore writes, "The ancient Romans tended to use *monstra* to mean all abnormal phenomena regarded as warnings or omens of the will of the gods, not just monsters, and, as such, the Latin term constituted a very important element of the Roman religion" (9). As Christianity emerged from within Roman cultural and intellectual traditions, the sacred preoccupation with divining God's messages to humanity from the prodigious and anomalous was continued within various branches of Christian theology, reaching its peak during the medieval and scholastic periods (Asma 74–93). Buster Bluth's prodigious birth is such a *monstrum*, as George Sr. recounts, "Maybe it was the eleven months he spent in the womb. The doctor said there were claw marks on the walls of her uterus, but he was our miracle baby." ("Bringing Up Buster" 1:3). Was Buster meant to bring a message to George Sr., or the rest of the Bluth family? Perhaps Buster's birth was a portent about George Sr.'s impending imprisonment, as Buster was trapped, held against his will, and clawing to escape in much the same was as George Sr. Or, perhaps it was an omen about the struggle of the Bluth family's own 'arrested development.' Regardless of the intended message, it went woefully unnoticed as George Sr. concedes, "I was just too burned out on raising you guys to care.... Maybe I just ignored the guy."

The Comedic

As with monsters—and arguably, more so—discussions of comedy are difficult, because there are many variations within this broad category. Humor, satire, wit, or even jokes of a more stereotyped nature, all seem to have their important differences for the scholars that investigate them. In general, the comedic, in its various forms, stems from some kind of incongruity, either with regard to expectations of common experience or the cultural assumptions of social situations.

The comedic signals the liminal rupture of categories by bringing together multiple sets of expectations and thus disrupting categorical assumptions. This can be as simple as a mundane category mistake where two things that share something in common are swapped, such as a young child, just learning the social importance of simple words and categories, might laugh excitedly at the notion of putting a sandwich on her head and calling it "hat." A hat is an object, and it goes on the head; a sandwich is an object, but it is a category mistake to put in on the head. This category mistake causes a comical juxtaposition. Similarly, when Lindsay Bluth excitedly shows Michael what is supposed to be a photocopy of the Volvo she wants to buy, but inadvertently hands him a revealing photocopy of herself sitting on the copy machine, the category mistake is signaled to the audience by Michael's characteristically deadpan response, "[T]his is not a Vol-*vo*" ("The Cabin Show" 3:1). Both are objects of importance to Lindsay, and they share certain phonal characteristics, but only one of them is appropriate as an object of public knowledge, let alone excited conversation with a sibling. By "bringing together ... images which have contrary additional ideas, as well as some resemblance in the principle idea," contrast is established "between ideas of grandeur, dignity, sanctity, perfection, and ideas of meanness, baseness, [and] profanity" (Francis Hutcheson qtd. in Carroll 153). While these examples are fairly benign, when taken further still, the incongruity of the comedic can also upset important elements of social life if the incongruity disrupts hierarchical relationships or the relational proprieties which buttress all manner of interactions.

Within the writings of Sigmund Freud, it is the work of the Super Ego to uphold these categories of social propriety and social organization. To do this, however, the Super Ego must continually repress the selfish and animalistic impulses of the Id. Thus, according to Freud it is only through the repression of Id forces that social life does not devolve into anarchic nihilism. Not surprisingly, many theories of monsters utilize a psychoanalytic perspective and consider monsters to be expressions of the Id. Within this perspective, the threat of the monster is precisely the threat of the Id on the stability maintained by the Super Ego (Jones). Quite tellingly, Noel Carroll, who has written extensively on monsters and horror, has pointed out that Freud's theory of the uncanny (1919), which is generally looked to as a starting point for monster theory, is strangely similar to his theory of humor and jokes. According to

Freud, humor and jokes evoke such pleasure because they temporarily allow the release of the psychological energy which tirelessly works to keep the Id under such strict control (Freud, *Wit*). Like the sweet relief of Atlas given a momentary reprieve from holding steady the structures of the world, laughing at the shamelessness of Gob Bluth's sexual exploits, for example, allows the Id to be given temporary vicarious expression. More importantly, Freud's theory of humor concerns itself with any instance of the comedic in which societal roles and expectations are threatened or breached, such as when Lucille Bluth states "I love all my children equally," speaking as a good mother ought, and yet in a moment of honest Id expression, "I don't care for Gob" ("Pilot" 1:1).

In addition to her work on the interstitial, which is critical for understanding the impurity of monsters, Mary Douglas has also explored the form and function of jokes in several of her works (*Implicit Meaning*; "The Social Control"). Douglas finds Freud's theory of humor and jokes crucial to expressing the fundamental relationship between the comedic and systems of power; the comedic subverts important mechanisms of control. Elsewhere, discussing the rituals which are the very manifestation of the Super Ego, Douglas writes, "The rite imposes order and harmony, while the joke disorganises [sic] ... [R]ituals create unity in experience. They assert hierarchy and order... But jokes have the opposite effect...They do not affirm the dominate values, but denigrate and devalue. Essentially a joke is an anti-rite" (*Implicit Meanings* 155). The comedic undermines the authority of prevailing systems, categories, and assumptions.

Many instances of the comedic involve the expectation of what is considered proper for a given scenario or social relationship, juxtaposed with behaviors or attitudes that are not only *im-proper* but appear to stand opposed to the social order itself. Much like the monster that threatens the stability of the village, the comedic often threatens civility with the expression of the Id. This can be seen in Gob's persistent attempts to sleep with women for the sole purpose of getting back at Michael for trying to date his Spanish-soap-opera girlfriend, Marta, not even taking the time to learn their names and without regard to romantic (or even physical) chemistry ("Shock and Aww" 1:14). In this way Gob embodies the Id, and there is something both freeing and despicable about his anti-social, utterly libidinal behavior. However, the audience only laughs precisely because his behavior is recognized as being improper (Eco), and thus, a category mistake. Laughter ensues, not because Gob's behavior is celebratory but *only because* it is understood that his behavior is reprehensible. This makes the comedic fundamentally bound up in relationships of power.

Umberto Eco, in his essay "The Frames of Comic 'Freedom,'" also explores the relationship of the comedic to systems of power and social control, and looks to the medieval celebration of Carnival as a starting point. Carnival is a Christian celebration that occurs right before the season of Lent—Lent being a period of personal sacrifice and abstinence. The medieval celebration of Carnival was instead a time of over-indulgence and gratuity before, and in contrast to, the strict self-denial of the Lenten season. But, as Eco illustrates, the celebration of Carnival was much more than just a time of over-eating and drunkenness, it was also a time where many of the strictures of medieval Catholic society were suspended and important customs and taboos were turned upside down. Despite the Church's historically prudish teachings, sexuality and licentiousness were celebrated, and "counterrituals [sic] such as the Mass of the Ass or the coronation of the Fool were enjoyable" (Eco 6). Carnival was only enjoyable precisely because the rituals and customs it mocked were understood to be of central importance throughout the rest of the calendar year; "an entire year of ritual observance is needed in order to make the transgression enjoyable" (ibid). Much like the freedom of the liminal, comic freedom is not always opposed to the social order it undoes but offers creative, re-imagined social orders instead, where those that are given ascendency are fools and inspire empowering laughter rather than demand disempowering subordination. In its allowance of the expression of the anti-social, the liminal freedom of the comedic carries with it the power to subvert (Eco 7–9). This is why many oppressive political regimes throughout history have gone to great lengths to suppress insubordinate jokes or humor, and the secret telling of jokes has been observed to be a strong, if closely guarded, source of psychological resistance (Speier; Oring).

Conclusion

The monstrous and the comedic give psychological primacy to those things which stand outside of, and sometimes opposed to, important social categories. In so doing, both the monstrous and the comedic challenge assumptions about whom or what is acceptable to our social sensibilities and redress this imbalance either by mockery or by might. Threatening or laughable in their liminality, the construction of the monster and the construction of the comedic are inherently social enterprises. And in instances of the comedic, who does the laughing and who is the fool is an entirely political one.

Juxtaposed against real-world horrors, the unholy union of monstrosity and comedy functions within *Arrested Development* as a mechanism of creative subversion. Expressing the potentiality within the liminal to provide a time and space in which can be fathomed new ways of ordering the world, in the telling of the Bluths' story, that which threatens is transformed into that which is subordinated and left open to critique. As out-of-touch elites, the Bluth family is forced to rejoin the "real world" when their company collapses under charges of fraud and comes under government scrutiny. Used to the complacency and frivolous consumption of high society, Michael Bluth constantly reproaches the rest of the family to "get a job." Ironically, this is the same refrain often heard in American culture, touted by socio-economic elites about the lower-class, glossed as freeloaders. In the comedic inversion of the Bluth family, however, it is so-called elites that are forced to find jobs and, with the exception of Michael and George Michael, display inherent laziness and the lack of marketable skills after a lifetime of expecting their money to work for them. *Arrested Development* utilizes the liminal union of monstrous-cum-comedic, betrayed in Buster's contemptuous wails, to critique the threat of economic instability due to corporate malfeasance by way of the fumbling buffoonery of a fallen, "once prominent" family.

One cowers from monsters because in their presence one feels vulnerable and weak. However, in the mockery of the fool, it is those that do the laughing that are empowered. Thus, in *Arrested Development* the comedic inversion of liminal play confronts the audience with an empowering and subversive re-imagining of corporate and socio-economic realities. The early 2000s, leading up to the Great Recession of 2008, seem to illustrate that there is something truly horrific when those responsible of corporate misconduct evade justice—when dangerous monsters roam free. However, within the comedic frame of *Arrested Development*, the Bluth family is not a threatening embodiment of corporate excess but the laughable buffoons of social satire. Outside the televised frame corporate giants and vampiric free-market capitalism exist as real threats, but within the subjunctive space of comedic play their power is subsumed and subverted, left open to the carnivalesque gaze of the public.

Works Cited

Asma, Stephen T. *On Monsters: An Unnatural History of Our Worst Fears.* New York: Oxford University Press, 2009. Print.

Carroll, Noel. "Horror and Humor." *The Journal of Aesthetics and Art Criticism* 57.2 (1999): 145–160. Print.

Cohen, Jeffrey Jerome. *Monster Theory: Reading Culture.* Minneapolis: University of Minnesota Press, 1996. Print.

Colbert, Stephen. *American Again: Re-Becoming the Greatness We Never Weren't.* New York: Grand Central Publishing, 2012. Print.

Cruver, Brian. *Anatomy of Greed: The Unshredded Truth from an Enron Insider*. New York: Carroll and Graf Publishers, 2002. Print.

Douglas, Mary. *Implicit Meanings: Selected Essays in Anthropology, 2nd Edition*. New York: Routledge, 1999. Print.

_____. *Purity and Danger: An Analysis of Concepts of Pollution and Taboo*. New York: Routledge, 1966. Print.

_____. "The Social Control of Cognition: Some Factors in Joke Perception." *Man*, New Series 3.3 (1968): 361–376. Print.

Eco, Umberto. "The Frames of Comic 'Freedom.'" *Carnival!* Ed. Thomas A. Sebeok. New York: Mouton Publishers, 1984. 1–9. Print.

Feder, Barnaby J., and Michael Brick. "Enron's Many Strands: The Documents." *The New York Times*. 30 Jan. 2002. Web. 24 Jan. 2014. http://www.nytimes.com/2002/01/30/business/enron-s-many-strands-documents-enron-says-shredding-records-was-not-stopped.html

Freud, Sigmund. *The Uncanny*. Penguin, 1919 [2003] New York: Print

_____. *Wit and its Relation to the Unconscious*. Dover, 1916 [1993]. New York: Print.

Garson, Barbara. *Down the Up Escalator: How the 99 Percent Live in the Great Recession*. New York: Doubleday, 2013. Print.

Gilmore, David D. *Monsters: Evil Beings, Mythical Beasts, and All Manner of Imaginary Terrors*. Philadelphia: University of Pennsylvania Press, 2003. Print.

Halberstam, Judith. *Skin Shows: Gothic Horror and the Technology of Monsters*. Durham: Duke University Press, 1995. Print.

Jones, E. Michael. *Monsters from the Id: The Rise of Horror in Fiction and Film*. Dallas: Spence, 2000. Print.

Krugman, Paul. *The Return of Depression Economics and the Crisis of 2008*. New York: W. W. Norton, 2009. Print .

Kuttner, Robert. *The End of Laissez-Faire: National Purpose and the Global Economy after the Cold War*. New York: Alfred A. Knopf, 1991. Print.

McLean, Bethany. "Is Enron Overpriced?" *Fortune*. 5 March 2001. Web. 24 January 2014. http://money.cnn.com/2006/01/13/news/companies/enronoriginal_fortune/index.htm

McLean, Bethany, and Peter Elkind. *The Smartest Guys in the Room: The Amazing Rise and Scandalous Fall of Enron*. New York: Penguin Group, 2003. Print.

McLean, Bethany, and Joe Nocera. *All the Devils Are Here: The Hidden History of the Financial Crisis*. New York: Penguin, 2010. Print.

McNally, David. *Monsters of the Market: Zombies, Vampires and Global Capitalism*. Boston: Brill, 2011. Print.

Oring, Elliott. "Risky Business: Political Jokes under Repressive Regimes." *Western Folklore* 63.3 (2004): 209–236. Print.

Pace, Gina. "Time to Move Enron Case." CBSNews.com. 5 Jan. 2006. Web. 24 Jan. 2014. http://www.cbsnews.com/news/time-to-move-enron-case/

Speier, Hans. "Wit and Politics: An Essay on Power and Laughter." *American Journal of Sociology* 103.5 (1998): 1352–1401. Print.

Stein, Nicholas. "The World's Most Admired Companies." *Fortune*. 2 Oct. 2000. Web. 24 Jan. 2014. http://money.cnn.com/magazines/fortune/fortune_archive/2000/10/02/288448/

Turner, Victor. *Dramas, Fields and Metaphors: Symbolic Action in Human Society*. Ithaca: Cornell University Press, 1974. Print.

_____. *The Forest of Symbols: Aspects of Ndembu Ritual*. Ithaca: Cornell University Press, 1967. Print.

_____. "Images of Anti-Temporality: An Essay in the Anthropology of Experience." *The Harvard Theological Review* 75.2 (1982): 243–265. Print.

_____. *The Ritual Process: Structure and Anti-Structure*. Ithaca: Cornell University Press, 1969. Print.

van Gennep, Arnold. *Rites of Passage*. Chicago: University of Chicago Press, 1960. Print.

Narrative and the Narrator in the Politics of Memory

Dustin Freeley

In between the appropriately titled episodes "Out on a Limb" (2:11) and "Hand to God," (2:12) the third-person, omniscient narrator (voiced by Ron Howard) informs us that Buster Bluth loses his hand in a loose-seal accident. This moment is, at once, both a lesson for Buster, who defies his mother, and a testament to *Arrested Development*'s apparent stance against character development, as losing the hand does nothing to alter Buster's childlike demeanor as the series progresses. In the past, characters on television had been regarded as vehicles to move the story along, possessing no psychological qualities and existing solely to convey the message inherent to the episode (e.g. that children should obey their parents, or parents should trust their children, or honesty is the best policy). In contrast, television series like *Breaking Bad* (2008–2013), *Dexter* (2006–2013), *The Walking Dead* (2010–present), and even comedies like *The Big Bang Theory* (2007–present) and *Parks and Recreation* (2009–2015) spend entire episodes devoted to a character's actions and how these actions impact or create plot lines in subsequent episodes. The establishment of the serial sitcom has shifted the focus from the message conveyed in each episode to a cohesive narrative wherein the breaks between episodes become breaks in the characters' lives and the moments on screen perpetuate the arc of the narrative. However, *Arrested Development* blends these molds of past and contemporary television shows, in that it portends to be a cohesive narrative about the trials and tribulations of the Bluth family, regardless of the fact that, the characters—as the title of the series suggests—fail to develop.

Repeat viewings of the series reveal that it should come as little surprise that Buster loses his hand, as his loss is foreshadowed throughout the first two seasons: the recurrence of J. Walter Weatherman, who routinely loses his prosthetic arm during staged events in which George Sr. is attempting to teach his children a lesson ("Pier Pressure," 1:10); in "¡Amigos!" (2:3) when Buster, believing he is in Mexico, laments "I never thought I'd miss a hand so much" upon seeing a large, red hand-chair; Buster's adeptness at using the arcade claw machine to retrieve various stuffed animals—including a seal wearing a t-shirt embroidered with "Good luck" ("Afternoon Delight" 2:6); in "Out on a Limb" (2:11) Buster sits on a bus bench, obscuring most of an advertisement, save a portion that spells "Arm Off." In these examples, the repeated foreshadowing is subliminally located in various disguises of other characters, furniture, arcade games, and advertising, respectively. Within these disguises, the fate of Buster's hand becomes less surprising, insomuch as the representation of a hand is, more often than not, disconnected in Buster's presence. One rationale for this absence in presence can be taken from Gilles Deleuze, who asserts that "Repetition is truly that which disguises itself in constituting itself, that which constitutes itself on by disguising itself" (*Difference and Repetition* 17). Buster's failure to recognize the various omens leads to his ultimate mangling, which is one occurrence in a long series of repetitions of similar events. Buster's mangled hand signifies an arrested *physical* development, as if his inability to evolve and recognize the inevitable compels a devolution, wherein he becomes *un*developed.

Interestingly enough, he is not the final Bluth to lose an appendage. Three episodes later, in "Sword of Destiny," (2:15), Buster's brother Gob loses the middle and index fingers on his left hand, while Buster's other brother Michael is admitted to the hospital to have his appendix removed. The cycle of repetition that begins with Buster and encircles his brothers also creates a circuit of time in which, as Deleuze suggests, "there is no longer a future, present and past in succession, in accordance with the explicit passage of presents which we make out" (*Cinema 2* 100). For Deleuze, the present and future are only perceived, as they are just manifestations of past events repeating themselves in different forms. Throughout *Arrested Development*, these circuits are fashioned through both a witty narrative and the omniscient narrator. In combination, these devices limn *Arrested Development*'s mordant commentary on society's collective memory born from postmodern schizophrenia, and the ways in which, collectively, we fail to recognize or learn from past mistakes.

In his look at the intersection of television and postmodern theory, Paul Booth claims that "For theorists of the postmodern, the contemporary era creates a certain temporal misalignment. There is no sense of the 'past' or 'future' but rather an instantaneous and vacuous sense of the 'present'" ("Memories"

374). Within this framework, Buster's lost hand is an amalgam of what has always been present, but what Buster fails to recognize. Because of Buster's repeated failure to recognize the signals around him, he becomes an embodiment of postmodern schizophrenia, a phenomenon characterized by "an age of uber-simultaneity where we experience many different temporalities all at once" (Booth, "Memories" 374). When Buster sees the hand-chair, he recalls the past, laments its absence in the present, and misunderstands its future significance. When he plays with the claw game, he reverts to the state of a child, but he is unaware that he is, ironically, honing his dexterity with what will be his future hand—and trying to retrieve a stuffed symbol of what ultimately amputates his hand, a seal. In *Arrested Development's* fourth season, Buster is provided with a new hand, but with rather destructive results ("Off the Hook" 4:14). By attaching a new hand, doctors provide Buster the opportunity to relive the past, thus recreating his present, but the way in which Buster is unable to control his new, giant hand suggests that the past is unlivable and altering it only reinforces a foreboding warning on the prospect of change, thus trapping Buster in a circuit of *un*development.

Furthermore, Buster's very existence is an embodiment of different temporalities insomuch as he is a thirty something-year old man stuck in the progress of perpetual college student whose studies have included archaeology and cartography. While intriguing, both of these disciplines revolve around the past. In the case of archaeology, Buster is unearthing remnants from the past, and cartography is veritably obsolete, something not lost on Michael who asks, "Hasn't everything already sort of been discovered, though... by, like, Magellan and Cortés?" ("Pilot" 1:1). Furthermore, we find that he is not adept in either discipline. In "Charity Drive" (1:6), Buster smashes a skull with his rock hammer, which he blames "90 percent" on "gravity," and when given a nautical map to aid the Bluths in their escape from the Securities and Exchange Commission, he notes, "obviously this blue part here is the land" ("Pilot" 1:1). With the smashed skull, Buster's education actually allows him to destroy an element from the past so that less can be learned, while his inability to distinguish water from land slows the Bluths' potential escape, thus leaving them trapped in the present conundrum.

Time, Temporality and the Narrator

While multiple temporalities exist in the framework of specific characters like Buster, a further exploration of time and repetition are present in the presence of the narrator. The presence of a narrator, in combination with the single-camera style of filming, immediately creates the impression of *Arrested Development* as documentary. In its satirical and farcical nature, it also fits into the mockumentary genre. As such, *Arrested Development* ostensibly focuses on the figurative and literal trials of the Bluth family after the CEO of the Bluth Company, George Sr., is arrested by the Security and Exchange Commission for "using the company as his personal piggy bank" ("Pilot" 1:1) and perhaps some "light treason." But by the sixth episode ("Charity Drive" 1:6), there are clear allusions to the 2003 invasion of Iraq, a war that similarly mirrored an invasion that took place just over a decade prior. A few of the players were the same: Dick Cheney, Colin Powell, and a President Bush. While this chapter is not guided by a political agenda, it's important to note a few of the differences—and at least one glaring similarity—between the two conflicts in the Middle East. In 1990, George H.W. Bush "assembled an international coalition with consummate skill and unleashed a daunting, dazzling military offensive that established America as the sole superpower, the most powerful nation in history" (McDaniel). After entering southern Iraq and pushing back Saddam's troops, Bush slowed the progression, fearing "that the allies would not support the occupation of Baghdad. Concerns were raised that if Saddam's regime were toppled, the entire nation could disintegrate into a civil war" ("Operation Desert Storm"), a fear not exclusively held by the senior Bush. Critics warned that the "partial partitioning of Iraq could destabilize the region," while others warned of a "quagmire: escalation that leads to U.S. ground forces being pinned down amidst a hostile population ... if the Administration returned to its indecisive ways, groping at half solutions" ("Re-Engaging Saddam" 18–19). In the end, Bush decided against an all-out invasion of Iraq, for the most part because there was no exit strategy from a region in which there was an "absence of democratic forms of government; the disparity in the distribution of wealth and natural resources; the impressive buildup of conventional and nonconventional arms in the region" and "a major overriding issue, namely, the Arab-Israeli conflict" (Pamir 284).

Jumping forward to 2003, a number of the same concerns reemerge in a newly invaded Iraq, this time by George W. Bush. However, the decision to invade in 2003 was not backed by an international coalition, did not garner the support of the United Nations, and a popular topic of conversation became the "exit strategy," or lack thereof, which brings us back to *Arrested Development*'s parody of the war narrative. In "Charity Drive" (1:6), Lucille Bluth hires a new maid that cleans the floor from the outer-edge in, leaving her stuck by the fireplace, compelling Lucile to implore "Tell me you've got an exit strategy!" Here, *Arrested Development*'s narrative arc blurs the lines between past and present. It is at once contemporary in its ridiculing of 2003 politics, but also refers to the political discourse of 1990, linking the moments through two characters, one who recognizes the importance of anticipating an exit strategy (Bush Sr.) and one who does not (George W.). At the same time, the war narrative demonstrates a further disconnect between the two wars, one produced through the medium of television itself. Jason Mittell puts forth the idea that "While the Gulf War demonstrated the ability of television to offer war coverage with unprecedented moment-to-moment detail, it also revealed the nature of such reporting as overly reliant on official sources, focuses on compelling and potentially misleading action footage, and offering reassuring narratives at the cost of complexity and accuracy" (*Television and American Culture* 136). The coverage of the invasion of Iraq on George W.'s watch was such that it was inescapable, whereas the coverage in 1991 was relegated—for the most part—to nightly news broadcasts and to CNN, the only outlet able to communicate from inside Iraq. That said, the years between the wars produced a wealth of 24-hour news channels as well as expanded access to countries in conflict, which, in turn expanded our knowledge (perceived or otherwise) of the conflicts as well.

As the narrator relays events in the series in the past tense, the show itself actively blurs the lines between past, present, and future. This mode of telling a story is quite antithetical to most contemporary television shows, wherein "The experience of film imagery is generally taken to be in the present tense, the spectator apparently experiences action as it happens" (Shaw 82). The difference with *Arrested Development* is that each of the characters acts in what appears to be the present, but the narrator's voiceover remains in the past tense, once again reverting any contemporary allusions to the war in Iraq, issues in education, the housing market, or social media to the past, as if the show itself is offering signals and warnings about the propensity for the past to repeat itself. Thus, our typical experience watching television and understanding the narrative is challenged, as is our understanding of our contextual time and place.

When *Arrested Development* purposefully merges the past and present, the show's narrative arc and its narrator are playing with our role as the viewer. In a present sense, we are aware of the contemporary politics, but we are also immersed in a constructed memory of the characters' pasts in a time that is familiar to the present setting but allocated to a past existence. Such constructed memory is common when considering the politics of news and television, in which memory and historical self-consciousness are "particularly demonstrable in the age of media capitalism in the way that news selects stories worthy of representation and discards others" (Currie 101). As a result, we have one character, Lucille, whose choice of words derives, consciously or subconsciously, from contemporary events, particularly a popular rhetorical synecdoche used to sum up a primary point of discourse about the war. With Lucille's reference to an "exit strategy" in "Charity Drive" (1:6), her language mirrors the ways in which a common war rhetoric permeated social awareness and language, wherein "people's lives imitate stories rather than the other way around" (Currie 102). In turn we, as viewers, draw the same connection, but are coerced to do so in the context of both the past and the present, inasmuch as the narrator keeps us in the past.

Perpetuating the circuitous war narrative, *Arrested Development* provides an additional example in "The One Where They Build a House" (2:2), an episode that lampoons Bush's swift "Mission Accomplished" declaration in Iraq. Mirroring an apparent overzealousness to emerge victorious, the Bluths throw together the frame of a house with nothing really supporting it, only to have it fall apart almost immediately after the banner is revealed. Similarly, in "Good Grief" (2:4), when George Sr. is found living in an underground bunker, he bears a striking resemblance to the image of a bearded, disheveled Saddam Hussein. These examples are demonstrations of how global politics become edited and disseminated through constructed media narratives that emerge in everyday imitations.

Archived Imitations

In the same way that the Bluths' actions often imitate the conflicts in Iraq, the Bluth family itself becomes an imitated product that structures the Bluths' family history, its publically perceived present, as well as its foreseeable future. After George Sr. is arrested in the pilot episode, a news broadcaster suggests that it was for "using the company as his personal piggy bank." Soon after, we find out this isn't necessarily true and that George Sr. "was setup," and is in more trouble for some "light treason" ("Spring Breakout" 2:17). In "Sad Sack" (2:5), supposed evidence of weapons of mass destruction—another buzzphrase—is found in a Bluth email, which compels the same broadcaster to announce "We've obtained photographs that officials call definite proof of WMDs in Iraq." Of course, these turn out to be "balls," but the confidence with which the broadcaster offers definitive proof, replete with the headline "We Knew It!" fosters a false reality and veers far away from unbiased journalism. In tandem, when the photos are revealed as "balls," the headline, "We Blew It," is one ripe with sexual innuendo and a glib apology that is not offered to the Bluths, but the viewers. Effectively, the Bluths still remain a public enemy associated with the conflict in Iraq, while the broadcast can conjure a laugh with its punny headline. In a similar way, the events of George Sr.'s discovery are dramatized and distorted when Tobias plays George Sr. in *Scandalmakers'* "Blurred Truth: The Bluth Family Scandal" ("Spring Breakout" 2:17). In this particular exposé, the *Scandalmakers* narrator suggests George Sr. was found "under one of the homes that he himself built," something that is untrue. Rather, as *Arrested Development*'s narrator clarifies, "he was actually found in a hole near the house." Playing the role of George Sr., Tobias fictionalizes history, altering George Sr.'s speech and the events that lead him into the Bluth family's attic by inserting the line "Perhaps an attic shall I seek." Here, Tobias rewrites history, perpetuates George Sr.'s (and the Bluths') negative stigma, and misunderstands how the negative connotations also reflect on him. With the possibility of a big acting break, Tobias is blinded by potential success, but his depiction is wicked in that it aids the archiving of false history. As Derrida and Prenowitz note in a lecture on past and present abilities to archive history, "The archivization produces as much as it records the event. This is also our political experience of the so-called news media" (17). Simply put, the recording of an event is just as important as the medium through which it is recorded. And Tobias' butchering of events becomes the most widely disseminated starting point, thus decreasing the odds of re-archiving or altering the information.

Therefore, Tobias' depiction of George Sr. plays with the concept and understanding of past and present. Tobias acts as George Sr. who acts as Saddam Hussein, but the actions of all three occur within a small window of time. Saddam is captured at the end of 2003 and Tobias and George Sr. offer their imitations in a season that runs during the last few months of 2004 and the first few months of 2005. George Sr.'s imitation of Saddam brings a past reference to the present, but Tobias' imitation pushes George Sr.'s actions further into the past, offering a new variation of history, despite the short timeframe between the discovery of George Sr. and Tobias' depiction of it. Referring to the "media exhaustion of news" and its influence on our understanding of history, Frederic Jameson explains, "that the very function of the news media is to relegate such recent historical experiences as rapidly as possible into the past" (179). This jettisoning of present and near past into the further past exists in Tobias' depiction, and it, more importantly, skews our understanding of history and its purpose as a guide in our future. It transitively alters memory by showing people "not what they were, but what they must remember having been" (Hanke 62). If Gary R. Edgerton is correct when he writes, "Television must be understood ... as the primary way that children and adults form their understanding of the past" (1), then *Arrested Development*'s agenda in these depictions is meant to challenge our own understanding of history and how it has been altered before it has been archived.

Lessons in Pastiche

Often, we watch television in such a way that we follow the narrative from the understanding of "earlier and later," where events happen chronologically from A to B to C. In the case of *Arrested Development*, we are forced to evaluate and make connections between events that occur in different parts of various episodes, while performing the same task based on the past, present, and future within the individual episode. We encounter this in "Charity Drive" (1:6) in Lucille's request for an exit strategy that plays on the past and present simultaneously. *Arrested Development* also forces us to evaluate the past, present, and future within each episode in the context of the entire series. Through flashbacks, George Sr. notoriously teaches his children lessons, most often with the help of the prosthetic-armed J. Walter Weatherman, who would lose his arm as fake blood spurted from a stump in a rather terrifying moment that created a loose connection to the Bluth children's actions. To teach the children to "always leave a note," George Sr. piles the children into the car under the guise of going to the store ("Pier Pressure" 1:10). Along the way, George Sr.'s car strikes Weatherman, whose arm flies onto the windshield and frightens the children. This idea of "teaching a lesson" pervades *Arrested Development* as a recurring phrase and an action. In the pilot, Maeby suggests that she and George Michael kiss to teach their parents a lesson; in "In God We Trust" (1:8), Michael and Lindsay want to teach Lucille a lesson, so they spring George Sr. from prison for a day so that he sees her attending the Living Classics Pageant with Wayne Jarvis; in "The One Where They Build a House" (2:2), Buster joins the army to teach Lucille a lesson; in "Pier Pressure" (1:10), Michael wants to teach George Michael a lesson to prevent him from smoking pot and later in the same episode, George Sr. teaches Michael not to teach his son lessons. The common denominator in these episodes is that the characters' actions have little or nothing to do with the lesson intended to be taught. Maeby is frustrated by her parents' obliviousness, which is unrelated to George Michael; George Sr. has never encountered Wayne Jarvis and is stuck on stage playing God, so the connection that Jarvis and Lucille are on a date would be improbable; Buster reluctantly goes to sign up for the army, but has no intention of joining, so when the army accepts him because he "had miscalculated the army's current need for personnel" ("The One Where They Build a House" 2:2), Buster is the one who is punished; in "Pier Pressure" (1:10), one of the Hot Cops sent to frighten George Michael is his algebra teacher, so the ruse is immediately blown; and, in the same episode, Weatherman's arm flies off, which frightens Michael, but has no connection to Michael's desire to teach his son a lesson. Rather, the arm functions as a symbol of frightening moments from childhood when a lesson was *supposed* to be taught. If the shock of the amputated arm overshadows the lesson being taught, then the inappropriate actions (not leaving a note, yelling, etc.) are destined to repeat themselves—and they obviously do when Michael discovers that Lindsay, Gob, and Tobias have been driving George Sr.'s car while he's in prison and have left it in shambles ("Pier Pressure" 1:10). Throughout their lives, Michael, Lindsay, Buster, and Gob associate the amputated arm with a lesson, but it takes Weatherman's gruff voice to articulate just what the lesson is supposed to be. All told, this creates a circuit of "lessons" in which nothing is learned. There is no clearer personification of this circuit than Buster and his missing hand.

In a morbidly ironic sense, Buster would be taught a lesson about his mother's controlling nature, if only he "could remember why he went into the ocean" ("Beef Consommé" 1:13). Similarly, Gob might be taught a lesson by this missing arm—perhaps one about avoiding feeding kittens to seals so that they don't get the taste for blood. Perhaps even Lucille might learn a lesson about how to treat Buster. The converging narratives centered on a missing limb can be interpreted as a stream of consciousness "drawing upon disparate time elements to bind itself together into one stream of experience. Equally, it is a succession of acts, coalescing as phases that comprise a unified, self-manifestation" (Shaw 82).

While the repetition of lessons fails to teach any of the Bluths, the repetition of such moments throughout the series leads us to what Jameson refers to as "pastiche," wherein "the stylistic innovation is no longer possible, all that is left is to imitate dead styles, to speak through the masks and with the voices of the styles in the imaginary museum" (180). Working through this lens, George Sr.'s lessons can be seen as lacking style or nuance, thus failing because of their redundancy. In Weatherman's arm, the past and present are linked together, and the lesson is caught up in the imagery of the arm, rather than the primary intention, which ultimately leads to what Jameson refers to as "the failure of the new, the imprisonment in the past" (180). Michael becomes a victim of this imprisonment when George Sr., from prison, hires Weatherman to teach Michael a lesson in "Pier Pressure" (1:10). As George Sr.'s hired police surround the pier on which Michael believes George Michael is purchasing pot, shots are fired and a prosthetic arm lands at Michael's feet. Instantly, he realizes that he's being taught a *lesson*, but he is jettisoned back in time to when he was a young boy being taught lessons in the same "dead style."

As a result, Michael learns little more than how to teach lessons poorly. This is apparent in the way that he tries to teach George Michael a lesson, but also in the way that he tries to teach his family a lesson by routinely fleeing the family only to return without them really knowing that he's gone, as in both "Pilot" (1:1) and "The One Where Michael Leaves" (2:1). In a sense, George Sr.'s lessons, as well as Michael's actions, parallel *Arrested Development*'s indictment of the present's failure to learn from the past. Much in the same way that television-as-history creates the war narrative, George Sr.'s lessons impact his children in such a way that "produces forgetfulness, not memory, flow, not history" (Heath 279).

In its exploration of forgetfulness, *Arrested Development* is often comprised of moments that "randomly cannibaliz[e] styles and images from the past" (Anderson 19). That has, in one sense, been discussed in the linking of past and present surrounding the conflicts in Iraq. At the same time, many of these images derive from pop culture. A prime example of this is "Good Grief" (2:4), the episode titled after Charlie Brown's common catch phrase. George Michael, George Sr., Tobias, and Gob ultimately walk sullenly with their heads down to the tune of Charlie Brown's dejected-walk music; a black and white beagle rests on top of a red dog house as George Michael trudges home; two people can be seen carrying a meager tree in homage to *A Charlie Brown Christmas* (1965). However, the most interesting part of "Good Grief" is the repetition of the phrase "Good grief!" in certain episodes that precede it. "Pilot" (1:1), "Charity Drive" (1:6), "Public Relations" (1:11), and "Marta Complex" (1:12) each feature an exasperated exclamation of "Good grief!" à la Charlie Brown. However, once we reach the episode "Good Grief," the exclamation ceases to exist within the episode or through the rest of the series thus far. It's almost as if the repeated presence of the exclamation culminates in an imitation of the character that it parodies, thus suggesting an underlying, ingrained connection to disseminated pop culture that forces the past into the present through language and action. Through a Lacanian lens, we can see the shared expression as a part of language that is "simultaneously non-being and insisting to be" (Lacan 326). "Good grief!" is both symbol of exasperation and a phrase that recalls a group of pop culture characters. By default, the Bluths are similarly likened to cartoon characters, adding themselves to the various imitations present throughout *Arrested Development*, as well as characters living their present through representations recalled from the past.

While "Good grief!" remains unspoken after its namesake episode, *Peanuts* references remain present in the narrative. Buster's genitals are often referred to as his "Charlie Browns" ("The One Where They Build a House"; "¡Amigos!"; "Hand to God") or his "Linus" ("Spring Breakout"; "Hand to God"). Similarly, in season four, we are privy to Michael, Tobias, and Buster all revisiting Charlie Brown's dejected walk when they are respectively rejected ("Flight of the Phoenix," 4:1; "A New Start," 4:5; "Off the Hook," 4:14). In addition to persistent references to *Peanuts*, the titles of *Arrested Development* episodes in season three parody classic James Bond films, categorizing this serial as part of the spy genre ("For British Eyes Only," 3:2; "Notapusy," 3:4; "Mr. F," 3:5). Beginning in "The Immaculate Election" (2:14), Tobias becomes Mrs. Featherbottom, an older British nanny incepted from the exact plot of *Mrs. Doubtfire* (1993), but with a musical accompaniment like *Mary Poppins* (1964). In the introduction to his exploration of genre studies, Jason Mittell asserts that "genres can be seen as key ways that our media experiences are classified and organized into categories that have specific links to particular concepts like cultural value, assumed audience, and social function" (*Genre and Television* xii). This mash-up of genres problematizes how we understand the serialized adventures of the Bluth family. We are unable to categorize the Bluths because they are often unable to categorize themselves. They exist as imitations in a world of imitations. As the narrator notes in "The Immaculate Election" (2:14), Tobias's ruse is the "exact plot of *Mrs. Doubtfire*," and, as such, indicts Tobias as both creatively bankrupt and the product of a culture that thrives on imitations. All told, *Arrested Development*'s use of transparent allusions to other films, styles, and use of varying genres further traps the characters and the audience in a veritable circuit of repetition.

On the Next Arrested Development

Within the circuits of time and repetition present in each episode of *Arrested Development*, so too is a narrative complexity present that intentionally misleads and frustrates the audience. As Booth notes, "A show is narratively complex if it rejects the need for closure after every episode, allows for the development of an overarching story to develop across episodes, and creates an elaborate, interconnected network of characters, actions, locations, props, and plots" ("Memories" 371). While *Arrested Development* creates an overarching story that might exist across episodes, the rejection of closure occurs most often *between* episodes, where, beginning with the pilot, the narrator deceives us by offering what happens "on the next *Arrested Development*." However, the subsequent episode doesn't elaborate on the moments offered at the preceding episode's closing sequence. Rather, the moments offered from "the next" episode are left tangential and fragmented. Here, *Arrested Development* disrupts and problematizes how we often view television serials, wherein "the main action of any given episode tends to be resolved. Most typically, certain questions go unanswered for episode after episode, but they are not the kind of questions that obstruct narrative clarity" (Newman 20). Within these moments, we are again subjected to a manipulated form of archiving in which we see glimpses of what happens and are forced to accept the truth as it comes without the buffering contexts of *before* and *after*. Take for example Buster's amputation, a seemingly rather important moment insomuch as it involves the mangling of a main character, but one that also becomes the inception point for jokes that run the duration of the series. Regardless, this moment is quickly exposed by the narrator ("a seal bites off his hand") but not offered within what might be considered the episode proper ("Out on a Limb" 2:11). And it is within moments like this that *Arrested Development* insists on playing with our concept and understanding of time through the presence of the narrator. First and foremost, the ending of each episode is the only part of the overall narrative that is relayed in the future tense, with the narrator looking forward to the next episode, while every other moment throughout the series is relayed to the viewer in the past tense. Within each episode, we are simultaneously robbed of the present, as we follow a story that happened in the past, and promised moments in the future that go unfulfilled and instead are relegated to the past once the next episode begins. This continuous jettisoning of the future to the past is "a type of time compression," in which "the quickening cycle of narration and renarration reflects the time compression of commercial life in general where the pressure to renew the style of commodity is part of the process of renewing markets" (Currie 105). For each moment of renarration, the viewer is asked to understand their own place and consciousness within the narrative. If Shaw is correct when he writes that "Consciousness is characterized by time, it is a temporal experience" (81), then *Arrested Development* challenges our consciousness by asking us to separate compacted moments found within each episode among flashbacks and imitations while simultaneously requiring us to unpack moments presented as future events that we will never fully witness (81).

This constant separating and unpacking can be understood as the further reflection of a schizophrenic culture driven by media sound bites, and can also be viewed as a challenge to the viewers' historical self-consciousness, or "the sense that one is a narrative, or that one is part of the narrative history so that the present is experienced as if it were always already narrated in retrospect" (Currie 101). As noted above in the discussion of "Charity Drive" (1:6), each episode forces us to re-contextualize our understanding of contemporary events and displace them in the past. In doing this, the viewer is also forced to anticipate the ultimate results of past events presented in the series as well as anticipate the future results of contemporary events imitated in a past narration.

Further problematizing this merger of past, present, and future is the actual narrator, a presence that cultivates trust, in that he is presumably omniscient, and also familiarity insomuch as he is Ron Howard. Regarding the narrator's omniscience, trust is formed because he is the source of both flashbacks that further establish the present events in the narrative but also because both the flashbacks and his interjections provide corrections to the characters' personal narratives that often function as a way to manipulate the truth. In the pilot, Lucille Bluth claims, "I love all of my children equally," before the narrator reminds us that Lucille confessed "I don't care for Gob," earlier that day; Michael's claim that he "used to love" working in the banana stand during the summer is immediately contradicted by an image of him unhappily covered in chocolate from 1989 ("Top Banana" 1:2); to save face, Gob repeatedly insists that he has "closed that deal" with his wife, but the narrator reminds us that "he really didn't" ("Altar Egos" 1:17). The flashbacks and narrator-corrections define the characters as unreliable narrators of their own lives, but they also expose the characters as attempting to rewrite their past through a self-psychoanalysis that understands "The past was a lie, and the present is the cure in the form of truthful, reliable self-narration" (Currie 119). Here, the inability for the characters to recognize their own blatant deceit holds them in a circuit of untruth and forces them to perpetuate this same circuit. There is thus an increased sense of cultural schizophrenia in an inherent split that exists between the I of the *past* and the I of the *present*.

Strangely enough, by the fourth season, the narrator becomes victim to this self-psychoanalysis and schizophrenia himself when Ron Howard-the-narrator becomes Ron Howard-the-character. As a character, he is recontextualized and the familiarity forged for the first three seasons is tarnished, primarily when we meet his fictionalized daughter, Rebel Alley. While Rebel's presence is often amusing, her introduction further complicates the "viewer's reconciliation that what he or she sees as a narrative is actually another person's memory of that (fictional) narrative. Indeed, not just issues of narrative complexity but also issues of fictionality are at stake here" (Booth, "Memories" 377). As such, we are forced to question the accuracy of the narrative corrections present in the first three seasons. Admittedly, some of these lies are exposed through flashbacks, but others are corrected through a narrative voice over that offers a re-interpretation. If it's true that "It must be the person (re)-interpreting the events in the text that creates the narrative structure," then the narrator and his coinciding corrections forces the viewer to question whether the characters within *Arrested Development* are the only ones caught in circuits of repeated time and imitation, or if their circuits are partially construed by the narrator as well (Booth, "Intermediality" 400).

The Blue Dot, the Blurred Truths and the Bluths

In total, *Arrested Development* disjoints relationships, disrupts temporalities, and displaces memories. The intertwining depictions of the past, present, and future depict an overall blurring of the truth that challenges our understanding of archived history and the ways in which pop culture and media permeate our society. As it is the title of the *Scandalmakers'* exposé of the Bluths' supposed misdeeds, the "Blurred Truth" becomes an inchoate facet to the *Arrested Development* narrative. It feels there is little coincidence that the act of blurring is similarly recurrent. Memories are blurry as are the half-truths that are told, as are the familial ties between George Michael and Maeby, Michael and Lindsay. Even the namesake Bluth feels more akin to a truncated buzzword birthed from the marriage of "blurred" and "truth." Meanwhile, the homophonous "blue" appears in one form or another recurrently throughout the series. Tobias attempts to join the Blue Man Group, and while he awaits their phone call, he uses the blue paint to hide himself in blue areas throughout the city while following Lindsay around in "The One Where They Build a House" (2:2). In the same episode, a blue dot is used to conceal the obscene. In previous episodes, nudity was hidden with the traditional blur, but here a blue dot is used, as it is again in "Good Grief" (2:4) and "Queen for a Day" (2:8). Similarly, the cutoff jeans that enable Tobias's "never nude" affliction are also blue ("In God We Trust" 1:8). In combination, the Bluths represent the disjointed, the disrupted, and the displaced. They are stream of consciousness blend of the past, present, and future with a constantly revolving archive of memory and temporality.

Works Cited

Anderson, Steve. "History TV and Popular Memory." *Television Histories: Shaping Collective Memory in the Media Age*. Eds. Gary R. Edgerton and Peter C. Rollins. Lexington: University Press of Kentucky, 2001. 19–36. Print.

Booth, Paul. "Intermediality in Film and Internet: *Donnie Darko* and Issues of Narrative Substantiality." *Journal of Narrative Theory* 38.3 (2008): 398–415. Print.

_____. "Memories, Temporalities, Fictions: Temporal Displacement in Contemporary Television." *Television New Media* 12.4 (2011): 370 -388. Print.

Currie, Mark. *Postmodern Narrative Theory*. 2nd ed. New York: Palgrave Macmillan, 2011. Print.

Deleuze, Gilles. *Difference and Repetition*. London: Athlone Press, 1994. Print.

_____. *Cinema 2: The Time Image*. Minneapolis: University of Minnesota Press, 1989. Print.

Derrida, Jacques, and Eric Prenowitz. "Archive Fever: A Freudian Impression." *Diacritics* 25.2 (1995): 9–63. Print.

Edgerton, Gary R. "Introduction: Television as Historian: A Different Kind of History Altogether." *Television Histories: Shaping Collective Memory in the Media Age*. Eds. Gary R. Edgerton and Peter C. Rollins. Lexington: University Press of Kentucky, 2001. 1–18. Print.

Hanke, Robert. "*Quantum Leap*: The Postmodern Challenge of Television as History." *Television Histories: Shaping Collective Memory in the Media Age*. Eds. Gary R. Edgerton and Peter C. Rollins. Lexington: University Press of Kentucky, 2001. 59–78. Print.

Heath, Stephen. "Representing Television." *Logics of Television: Essays in Cultural Criticism*. Ed. Patricia Mellencamp. Bloomington: Indiana University Press, 1990. 267–302. Print.

Jameson, Fredric. "Postmodernism and Consumer Society." *Modernism/Postmodernism*. Ed. Peter Brooker. London: Longman, 1992. 163–179. Print.

Lacan, Jacques. *The Seminar of Jacques Lacan: Book II: The Ego in Freud's Theory and in the Technique of Psychoanalysis 1954–1955*. Ed. Jacques-Alain Miller. Trans. Sylvana Tomaselli. New York: Norton, 1991. Print.

McDaniel, Ann L. "What Went Wrong—Campaign '92." *Newsweek*. 23 Aug. 1992. Web. 25 Oct. 2013. http://www.newsweek.com/what-went-wrong-campaign-92–198168.

Mittell, Jason. *Television and American Culture*. Oxford: Oxford UP, 2009. Print.

_____. *Genre and Television: From Cop Shows to Cartoons in American Culture*. New York: Routledge, 2004. Print.

Newman, Michael Z. "From Beats to Arcs: Toward a Poetics of Television Narrative." *The Velvet Light Trap* 58 (2006): 16–28. Print.

"Operation Desert Storm." *USHistory.org*. Independence Hall Association. n.d. Web. 27 Jan. 2014. http://www.ushistory.org/us/60a.asp.

Pamir, Peri. "Peace-Building Scenarios After the Gulf War," *Third World Quarterly* 13.2 (1992): 283–300. Print.

"Re-Engaging Saddam" *National Review* 44.18 (1992): 18–19. Print.

Shaw, Spencer. *Film Consciousness: From Phenomenology to Deleuze*. Jefferson: McFarland, 2008. Print.

Families with Low Self-Esteem

The Fünke Dynamic

Bethany Yates Poston
and Crisman Richards

The Fünkes are self-absorbed, inattentive parents—neither capable of functioning independently, nor as a cohesive unit. The Fünke dynamic, therefore, revolves around the dysfunctional role reversal amongst formerly-noted psychiatrist, Dr. Tobias Fünke, his wife Lindsay Bluth-Fünke, and their daughter, Maeby. Tobias is highly dependent on the acceptance of others: he is riddled with denim cut-offs and negative expectations, and he pathologically avoids intimacy to subvert anticipated rejection. This pathology causes a great deal of confusion for Tobias, leading him to form a skewed understanding of his role in Maeby's life. Delusions of grandeur envelope Tobias' psyche in the form of obsession with an imagined life as an actor, and indeed he is motivated to succeed, but his strategy for breaking in to show business is ill-conceived and poorly executed. This misguided energy only exacerbates his inadequacy as a husband and father. Lindsay's mothering is equally ineffective and characterized by preoccupied feelings of unworthiness and an extreme dependence upon outside approval. Lindsay is a veritable cornucopia of insecurity, courtesy of her egotistical parents, George Sr. and Lucille. Her father praises her physical appearance while her mother ridicules Lindsay unrelentingly about her weight: Believing her worth to be only skin-deep, Lindsay battles with feelings of inadequacy. She fills the void left from a lifetime of maternal rejection by ignoring her daughter and instead focusing her short attention on a plethora of "good causes." As a result of these numerous and damaging psychological issues, it is Tobias and Lindsay's obstinate un-parenting that allows Maeby to feel that she is above the law. Indeed, within the Fünke family, Maeby *is* the law. As such, *Arrested Development* offers three generations worth of psychosocial dysfunction stemming from the overbearing Bluth dynamic. In spite of genetically deep psychological shortcomings plaguing the surrounding adults, daughter Maeby develops into the only truly self-sufficient member of the Bluth clan.

Deception is a cherished Bluth family tradition, established during the pilot episode when lies are the first lines we hear from each of the Fünkes. Tobias lies about his job search then immediately confesses he has yet to look for a job. Lindsay fibs about the family's flight just arriving before quickly admitting they've been in town for a month. Maeby's lies throughout the series are more ambitious and take fraudulence to impressive lengths. The audience's introduction to Maeby occurs after she cuts a fox foot off her grandmother's fur coat and then uses the foot in an attempt to scam her cousin George Michael out of a frozen banana. George Michael sees through the ruse and immediately recognizes his relative. The teenagers blame the adults for keeping the family apart. "We should teach them a lesson," suggests Maeby ("Pilot" 1:1), who faces adolescence with the burden of parenting two delusional adults who cannot be bothered to notice their daughter blossoming into a competent grown up. Frustration is evident when Maeby suggests she and her cousin George Michael "make-out" in front of her mother, only to have the lesson go parentally-unnoticed in the kerfuffle of George Sr.'s arrest ("Pilot" 1:1). Maeby is consistently left behind in the whirlwind of Bluth drama and her parents' self-involvement. Armed with conniving instincts and a confidence otherwise foreign to her relatives, Maeby finds security on her own.

As pathologically inattentive parents, Tobias and Lindsay become so consumed by their own problems that Maeby is left to develop independence out of emotional necessity while incidentally taking control of her finances through the rebellious act of gainful employment. Lindsay's self-centered apathy causes her to essentially ignore and occasionally forget Maeby's existence. But while Lindsay remains unaware of her striking behavioral similarities to Lucille, Maeby's personal work ethic ensures she will never be like her own lazy mother. Lucille's harsh criticism of every minute detail of her daughter's life innately compels Lindsay to oppositionally develop a subconscious habit of forgetting that Maeby exists. Struggling to compensate with a lower socio-economic status than they are accustomed, Tobias and Lindsay become consumed by their own vortex of complacency. Lee and Shrum offer helpful insight into reactionary behavior associated with social exclusion, warning that:

> Being ignored reduces one's power to gain attention from others. Unlike explicit rejection, in which a rejected person can attempt to argue with a rejection decision (and thus assert control), being ignored is unilateral and provides no control mechanism unless the attention is gained. Being ignored (ostracized) has also been likened to being invisible and having no existence [532].

To compensate for persistent neglect, Maeby forms a professional attachment to the fickle embrace of Hollywood, and since lying comes naturally to Maeby, she quickly earns prominence as a media executive. Maeby gets the attention she has been denied, at last, from a film studio and develops a control mechanism to empower the inner security and behavioral competence that elude her parents. Maeby no longer considers herself to be invisible, as she can see her name on the silver screen as her work blossoms into hit movies. She finds validation beyond the given family structure, even when her parents don't notice. Tobias and Lindsay are too self-involved to see their young daughter obtain the success and recognition they crave for themselves. Maeby oppositionally develops a more self-focused response to living as a mere afterthought in her parents' day-to-day existence. Her entrance into the workforce stems from an adolescent need to distance herself from her unemployed parents, and she goes out to get her first job after overhearing Michael warn Lindsay that unless she set a better example, her daughter is going to grow up to be just like everyone else in the family—self-absorbed and lazy ("Shoot me when that happens" protests Maeby ["Top Banana" 1:2]). Once Maeby equates her own behavior to Lindsay's slothful ways, she shakes off genetic lethargy and goes to work under George Michael at the banana stand. Inevitably, though, Maeby's hereditary kleptomania sets in; she grows bored of work during her first shift and intuitively begins stealing from the family business. Her lack of scruples against lying or stealing serves her well, and Maeby uses those skills to become more productive, confident, and financially successful than either of her parents. Though inadvertently achieved, Tobias and Lindsay should be credited for denying their daughter feelings of a meaningful existence. The void left by her parents leads Maeby to gain control over her finances, laying the groundwork to subversively become the most powerful member of the Bluth family.

In addition to being responsible for her own financial independence, Tobias and Lindsay's irresponsible lack of structure leads Maeby to assume the patriarchal role of family disciplinarian. The Bluth tendency to "teach lessons" skips over Lindsay, instead transferring from George Sr. to Maeby. As the narrator explains, "George Sr. had used his considerable means to stage intricate scenarios to teach his children what he considered valuable life lessons" ("Pier Pressure" 1:10). Lindsay's residual trauma from George Sr.'s elaborate lessons could possibly explain her lax parenting method. But the Fünkes' decided lack of discipline is primarily a result of Tobias and Lindsay's selfish apathy: they are often seen napping undisturbed by the family drama bustling around them. To their credit, the other family members haven't failed to notice Tobias and Lindsay's lethargy and are quick to comment on it: Lucille informs Lindsay that Michael has referred to her as a "stay-in-bed mom" ("In God We Trust" 1:8) and Tobias is chastised by Michael for laying around the house all day watching entertainment news and setting a bad example for Maeby ("Not Without My Daughter" 1:21). It appears that for Tobias and Lindsay, teaching lessons is simply too much work. Mayseless, Bartholomew, Henderson, and Trinkle offer interesting parallels to the Fünkes' role reversal in their article, "I Was More Her Mom than She Was Mine." The authors suggest that role reversal develops when families are "unable to maintain hierarchical generational boundaries" (78). For example, Tobias and Lindsay's consistent refusal to work leads Maeby to develop a diligent work ethic; this reactionary rebellion is consistent with what Mayseless et al. found in women who engage in maternal role reversal relationships, such as the mother-daughter dynamic Maeby and Lindsay share. This oppositional motivation plays out when Lindsay offers self-righteous protest to the bulldozing of surrounding trees as part of the Bluth Company's Sudden Valley development only to change her mind when she realizes she will make money off such expansion. Lindsay chooses potential material gain over environmental conviction. In response, Maeby launches a rebellious campaign to save a tree under threat of her mother's vacillating protest ("Key Decisions" 1:4). Maeby becomes the antithesis of Lindsay's capricious protests, waging opposition as dictated by her mother's carousel of charitable cause. While George Sr.'s traumatizing practice is likely what initially compels Lindsay to adopt a contradictory parenting method in which no effort is made whatsoever to teach lessons to children, it is important to remember that the Bluths are also extraordinarily lazy creatures. Lindsay's apathy provides a consistent lack of follow-through necessary for such obtuse parenting. Tobias' debunked psychiatric skills, on the other hand, grant him enough displaced confidence to self-affirm his choices as a distant husband and father. As a result, Maeby adopts the role of disciplinarian in her adolescent effort to keep the family together or, at the very least, teach them a lesson.

The decidedly elusive parenting approach Lindsay and Tobias employ is in stark contrast to Michael's overbearing method. When Lindsay accuses her brother of suffocating his teenage son, Michael responds, "Maybe I should be a little bit more like you when it comes to parenting. No borders. No limits. 'Go ahead, touch the Cornballer. You know best.'" ("Bringing Up Buster" 1:3). Conversely, Fünke parenting philosophy allows Maeby to live an unsupervised life while Tobias gets "the pleasure of guessing what that might entail" ("Bringing Up Buster" 1:3). Michael's relationship to the Fünkes could be characterized as a perpetual state of intervention. When a pajamaed Maeby is found celebrating Take Your Daughter to Work Day in front of the television with her father, Uncle Michael interjects with what he believes is a better example of fathering than Tobias in his bathrobe presents. McHale and Huston note that fathers, more than mothers, spend less time with children, and that any time spent together is more often in play rather than caregiving (1350). In the past, when Maeby was young and Tobias was employed, Take Your Daughter to Work Day was perhaps the only father-daughter tradition to involve the mutual enjoyment of quality time. This practice began at the height of Dr. Fünke's psychiatric success "on the forefront of the self-esteem movement" ("Not Without My Daughter" 1:21). The fact that Tobias still honors this ritual, despite unemployment, shows both his occupational delusion and his earnest desire to occasionally spend time with his daughter. Still, Michael orders Maeby to get dressed, baffling Tobias when she responds promptly to a stern directive. Michael believes that "kids love boundaries" ("Not Without My Daughter" 1:21) and warns Tobias that without boundaries, Maeby could wind up in a *Girls with Low Self-Esteem* video. Maeby remains open to occasional parenting in the odd moments when she finds her parents behaving in a respectable manner. McHale and Huston suggest that "individual differences in attitudes are more likely to make a difference in behavior when an individual is free to decide about whether to engage in activities" (1360). On Take Your Daughter to Work Day, Maeby has a myriad of options at hand: she can go to school, to her own job, or spend her time with one morally-questionable adult or another. McHale and Huston offer that "correlations between parents' characteristics and their activities also are important in that they provide additional evidence for the coherence of the particular dimensions of mother and father roles" and that, "the result, in terms of behavior, is to move them more into line with the activity patterns traditionally displayed by the opposite-sex parent. Thus, nontraditional mothers decrease the frequency of their child care" (1360). Since childcare is low on Lindsay's priority list as is, Maeby and Tobias are able to compensate by initiating time together without even noticing Lindsay has taken a job. Lindsay is uncomfortable with adopting a non-traditional role in the workplace, and thoroughly ashamed of employment as a shopgirl.

Rather than face the humiliation of pleasing Michael, Lindsay lies about obtaining a legitimate job, claiming to have shoplifted the new wardrobe she obtains as a result of working. For once, Maeby is impressed with her mother. Here, the Bluth values system causes an inversion of familial expectation: most families would likely prefer employment over thievery, but not the Bluths. They are far more ashamed of a hard day's work than of any amount of money stolen by a member of the family, and Maeby's values align accordingly. When she learns that Lindsay has successfully shoplifted her wardrobe, Maeby takes the rare initiative to spend time with her mother. Michael intervenes and adopts Maeby as his daughter for the day so she can have a positive role model "who is honest, who doesn't steal, doesn't lie, and, I don't know, watch entertainment news" ("Not Without My Daughter" 1:21).

While members of the Bluth-Fünkes experience individual motivations to operate as a functional family, internal neurosis perpetually battle to drive them apart. Tobias is paralyzed by intimacy issues and cannot provide Lindsay with the spousal support she desperately requires. As Tobias and Lindsay's marriage falls to ruin, Maeby is marginalized. Tobias' role is characterized by his ironically misguided understanding of the psychological machinations at play within his own mind and family, most notably dramatized when Michael interjects unsolicited marital counseling by forcing Tobias and Lindsay to leave the comforts of the nursery (where they sleep comfortably in parallel twin beds designed for two little girls) and into the master bedroom to live like "a normal couple" and share a Queen-size bed ("The One Where Michael Leaves" 2:1). Maeby, meanwhile, shares a bunk bed with her cousin down the hall where she can come and go undetected as her filming schedule dictates. Terrified at the prospect of a night alone with Lindsay, Tobias proposes an admittedly delusional attempt to save the marriage without the hassle of physical intimacy. Borrowing from his failed psychiatric experiences, Tobias initiates an open marriage in which he and Lindsay may remain emotionally-committed whilst free to explore extramarital encounters ("The One Where Michael Leaves" 2:1). Tobias believes a permissive approach is the best way for the family to bond, and his motivation to then immediately call a family meeting and inappropriately involve Maeby can be understood through McHale and Huston's research on the roles of sexual orientation in parenting. By examining mothers' and fathers' sex role orientations and employment situations in connection with their involvement in child-oriented activities, McHale and Huston theorize that while a father's non-traditional views of gender roles in society have little correlation to their perceived skill in childcare, "it is possible, for example, that men who think of themselves as "liberal" in sex role attitudes tend to overestimate the extent of their day-to-day involvement with their children" (1351). In this way, Tobias sees his "great experiment" with an open marriage as a way to bring the family closer together. McHale and Huston would argue that since Tobias considers himself sexually-liberal enough to declare an open marriage, it stands to reason that he also considers the fleeting moments he spends with Maeby to be incidental quality time. In the Fünkes' case, Tobias' feelings of incompetency correlate with his absence in Maeby's life.

Despite being involuntarily distanced from her emotionally unstable parents, Maeby gains independence under the Fünke regime of inconsistency. Amidst their individual journeys for independence, the Fünkes do develop a gentle codependence that continually brings them back together. For example, Tobias' delusion that an open marriage will bring the family closer together spurs Maeby's manipulation; she quickly recognizes the more time her parents spend apart, the more time they individually devote to negatively impacting her life. Maeby preys on her parents' flagrant insecurities as means to more alone time. "The important thing is that you guys don't lose focus on yourselves," Maeby tells her parents with the gusto of a fatherly pep talk ("¡Amigos!" 2:3). Ultimately, however, Lindsay and Tobias each lack the emotional fortitude necessary to carry out the logistics of an open marriage. Years of marital strife have left Lindsay and Tobias crippled by fear, resulting in a destructive pattern in which Tobias rejects Lindsay sexually and Lindsay abuses Tobias verbally. Despite the ever present terror of becoming her mother, Lindsay adopts Lucille's caustic nature by employing verbal barbs meant to inflict maximum pain through minimal, vodka-flavored effort while Tobias takes to frequent crying in the shower. Neither possesses the confidence necessary to succeed in the dating world nor the determination to form legitimate independence. Lindsay mistakes attention for affection while inherently believing she is undesirable. Tobias appears to be trapped in the closet. Maeby uses the chasm created by her parents' marital woes to her advantage, taking the extra time she has to herself to jumpstart her career.

The result of their warped independence is Lindsay and Tobias' collective breakdown, which in turn causes Maeby to affect a dispassionate approach to her parents' emotional shortcomings. Lindsay's primary motivation is to garner external validation through affectionate attention from the opposite sex, while Tobias' modus operandi remains performing the art of everyday theatrics without facing the potential rejection of pursuing a career on stage. Maeby retains a visible level of skepticism over her father's idea for an open marriage and responds only by rolling her eyes and disappearing until the end of the episode

("The One Where Michael Leaves" 2:1). When his plan runs instantly afoul, Tobias seeks the comfort of what he believes to be a support group for depressed men and is dazzled instead to discover performance artists The Blue Man Group. Tobias is swept away in a swirl of delusion and blue paint. Instead of going through the audition process, Tobias subverts anticipated rejection by focusing his energy on painting himself blue and going about his daily routine. As the great experiment digresses, Maeby remains ostracized by her parents' displaced intentions and the Fünkes must face inevitable separation. Lindsay loses patience with her state of perpetual sexual frustration and evicts Tobias from the model home, declaring, "I don't know why, but that's it" ("The Immaculate Election" 2:14). On his own, Tobias playfully grapples with gender-identification on top of his already skewed understanding of his role as Maeby's parent, further alienating his daughter with a confusing masquerade. Left to the lonely graveyard shift at the studio (a job secured by Maeby herself), Tobias explores his feminine side by creating the character Mrs. Featherbottom and hatching a classic plot as an excuse to spend time with his daughter. McHale and Huston note that in these types of situations, "fathers who feel skilled or who have nontraditional ideas about parenting roles are more involved in child-oriented activities, and the nature of their involvement includes proportionately more caregiving relative to play and leisure activities with their children (i.e., a nontypical pattern of father involvement)" (1357). Borrowing heavily from *Mrs. Doubtfire* (1993) and *Mary Poppins* (1964), Tobias dresses as a dowdy British maid and gets a job keeping house for the Bluths. While in this ridiculous disguise, Mrs. Featherbottom works diligently as a housekeeper and, for once, the Bluths are impressed (and mildly amused) by Tobias. Though the family is pleased to have an impeccable house, Maeby is frustrated by her father's ludicrous dishonesty. For Maeby, transparency within the nuclear structure of the family is more important than the domestic functionality of the home. Disgusted by his poorly-executed dishonesty, Maeby tries to signal that she can see right through Tobias' ruse, referring to him as "Mister Fingerbottom." He corrects, "I'm sure wherever your father is right now, she loves you very, very much," to which Maeby sincerely responds, "Not enough to be honest with me" ("The Immaculate Election" 2:14). Maeby appears to have grown bored with her parents' poor attempts at deception, and in so doing reaches a new level of maturation in which she communicates frankly with her recalcitrant father. Lindsay and Tobias struggle to maintain emotional health while Maeby learns to effectively manage narcissistic behavior, a skill she is then able to successful apply to her professional life in the entertainment industry.

Interestingly, Maeby learns both compassion and manipulation from observing the juxtaposition of Lindsay's absenteeism and Lucille's piercing criticism, thereby developing an appreciation for Lindsay as her mother. Maeby forms relationships based on the manipulative self-interest governing the Bluth family, adopting her grandparents' divide-and-conquer attitude. Maeby learns that family unity can be weaponized to make sibling rivalry more closely resemble troubled alliances between warring nations. If there is one thing Bluths don't trust, it is other Bluths getting along. Maeby is cognizant of this tenuous reality and uses it to her advantage, playing her symbiotic relationship with Lucille against Lindsay at every opportunity and effectively capitalizing on her parents' insecurities. While her parents struggle to cope with external forces shaking their internal neurosis, Maeby adapts to and learns from the rampant sociopathy. Lindsay fails to notice that by constantly berating Tobias she has already taken on Lucille's most hurtful trait. Tobias, consequently, develops an impressive ability to psychologically block the verbal assaults. When Tobias suggest Lucille is evincing denial, she tells him he is a worse psychiatrist than he is a son-in-law and will never work as an actor because he has no talent. In response, Tobias blinks disappointedly and states that if Lucille is "not going to say anything," he "certainly can't help her" ("Out on a Limb" 2:11). Tobias represses the overt criticism to form an iron-clad force field of denial. Maeby watches her father's humiliation play out and is struck with the notion that the best way to inflict pain is to involve Lucille; Lindsay applies this same tactic when she struggles to exert control over her daughter. Lindsay, however, lacks the psychological intellect required to execute calculated maneuvers on par with Lucille and Maeby, one a seasoned tormenter, the other a bright adolescent teeming with vitriol. Lindsay's only defense is to deflect Lucille's critical eye to Maeby. Lindsay questions their progressively aloof parenting method and attempts to discipline Maeby for receiving poor grades ("Pier Pressure" 1:10). Forced to correct her daughter's behavior under the scrutiny of Lucille's critical eye, Lindsay punishes Maeby by making her spend the afternoon with her Gangie. Inevitably, Gangie's acerbic tongue lashes at Maeby's freckles and "chubby little wrist" ("Pier Pressure" 1:10). A few hours of Gangie's verbal abuse, however, grants Maeby a new level of compassion for Lindsay. Maeby tries to alleviate some of Lindsay's own unresolved parental issues by giving her an elephant brooch—a family heirloom passed from unfaithful father to spiteful mother, then on to rebellious granddaughter and at last to entitled daughter. Maeby's newfound empathy for Lindsay is successfully communicated in a language Lindsay understands: jewelry. Lindsay's unhealthy response is juxtaposed against Maeby's healthy approach to create the desired result in which Lindsay finds validation as a mother and finally teaches her daughter a valuable lesson.

Tobias and Lindsay leave the nest when it should be their daughter's turn to fly, leaving Maeby to deal with an apogee of neglect while her parents individually pursue independence and assume their only daughter is in the other's care. This desertion is reckless as Tobias and Lindsay simultaneously give up their responsibilities and expose Maeby to a new level of psychological rejection at a pivotal point in her young adult life. Lee and Shrum conclude that such ostracization seems to threaten four particular needs simultaneously: belongingness, self-esteem, control, and meaningful existence (540). Upon learning that she was adopted by George Sr. and Lucille, Lindsay is in the throes of psychological crisis when she tells Tobias that her "life is a fallacy" ("Indian Takers" 4:3). Tobias responds by spontaneously breaking into song and dance. Somehow watching her husband dance while she is in existential crisis allows Lindsay to see her marriage as a total sham. Lindsay tells Tobias it is time for them to give up on the dreams that aren't working, suggesting they set out to discover what they are meant to be individually. "We're chasing things that aren't real," Lindsay tells her husband ("A New Start" 4:5). Tobias is perplexed to discover that everyone thinks he is gay and further broken-hearted to discover he is the butt of a running family joke. In the scope of one conversation, Tobias has lost control of his marriage and his sense of familial belonging while remaining pathologically deaf to his perpetually homoerotic double entendre. Eventually Tobias and Lindsay part ways in search of self-actualization, neither noticing Maeby playing dead on the other side of the room ("Señoritis" 4:12). Maeby responds by clipping her own wings and intentionally failing the twelfth grade. Psychologically, Maeby is unprepared to gain full independence until her parents acknowledge her accomplishments.

Maeby compensates for deepening abandonment issues by eschewing self-pity and instead focusing on her burgeoning career as a Hollywood hit-maker after Tobias and Lindsay separate for good (it appears the distance the Fünkes' keep from each other is correlative to Maeby success). As a clear signifier that they are complete in their abandonment of Maeby, just before they leave, both Tobias and Lindsay fail to find room in their suitcases for pictures of their daughter. Lee and Shrum contend that while "being ignored does not immediately convey rejection" (532), the shift to rejection now threatens Maeby's self-esteem, something Lee and Shrum predict as a possibility "when the intensity or duration of being ignored makes the social exclusion explicit" (532). The Fünkes embark individually on what they each believe to be a family-free vacation. Lindsay sets out on a spiritual quest while Maeby is at the helm of a big budget horror film and Tobias attempts to get as far away from his wife as possible. Tobias processes Lindsay's explicit rejection while struggling to understand why he is misunderstood, christening his journey with a vanity license plate to remind him of his fresh beginning: ANUSTART ("A New Start" 4:5). Exiled from his family, Tobias loses his sense of belonging and responds accordingly by attempting "to straighten out his image." In his attempt to distance himself from his wife, Tobias also loses touch with Maeby. Maeby contends with more parental distance than she is psychologically prepared to handle by focusing on her increasingly successful career.

The shift in Maeby's defense strategy and subsequent success are mandated by her advantage of being the only Fünke aware of her surroundings, a trait she presumably developed while Lindsay and Tobias focused intently on their own individual desires. A lifetime of orchestrating increasingly elaborate lessons grants Maeby the theatrical skill set tantamount to the detail-oriented experience of a seasoned movie producer. When Maeby arrives in India, she spots her mother in the lobby of their shared hotel. Maeby is unable to resist the opportunity to teach Lindsay a cinematic lesson and avails herself to her professional film makeup crew in order to appear before her mother as a bearded shaman. Lindsay does not recognize her daughter's intricate disguise and believes momentarily the shaman is hitting on her. Maeby is stung when Lindsay says that she does not have any children. Though Lindsay is unaware she is speaking to her only daughter, her behavior directly rejects Maeby. Maeby's transformation into a wise old shaman is symbolic of a more forthcoming approach in her language toward Lindsay. In costume, she advises Lindsay to live truthfully, to pull her head out of the sand, and that she is "full of shit" ("Indian Takers" 4:3). This is the second instance in which Maeby is confronting a parent's lie, although both cases involves subterfuge and disguises on her or her parents' parts. Lindsay is initially disheartened by the shaman's harsh ridicule, but then decides to process the criticism as compliment. Still, she follows the shaman's advice and returns home to reunite with Tobias, but only after Lucille offers to pay the Fünkes to feign family togetherness in a court of law. Following their collective return from India, the Fünkes reunite briefly as Lindsay would rather pretend to be a functional family than get an actual job. Despite initially good spiritual intentions, world travel has not afforded Tobias and Lindsay enough perspective to notice their daughter. They remain debilitated by self-involvement and delusions of grandeur. The Fünkes concoct an ill-conceived plan to redouble their efforts to "achieve the unachievable dream" ("A New Start" 4:5) and mortgage a house they can neither afford nor furnish. Lindsay and Tobias cling to delusion, habitually denying Maeby's existence, often when she is right in the same room. When Lindsay and Tobias both momentarily forget they have a daughter while mortgaging a massive mansion, Maeby chimes in from the corner of the office: "I could've spoken up but I just wanted to see if you guys got there" ("Indian Takers" 4:3). The Fünkes become so fixated upon the prospect of a luxurious house, they neglect to acknowledge Maeby, which in turns causes her to exercise her well-honed disciplinary instincts and consequently fulfill her own emotional needs independent of parental encouragement. Despite her parents' heightened myopia, Maeby's new disciplinary approach has the transformative ability of subversively manipulating Tobias and Lindsay while also keeping herself in a surreptitious position of power.

Delusionally, Lindsay and Tobias assume that by keeping the family physically together, they are somehow fulfilling their parental obligations, when in all actuality their abandonment affords Maeby illimitable opportunity. Maeby arrests herself developmentally as a senior in high school for a superfluous five years (a feat similarly accomplished by her cousin/ex-boyfriend, Steve Holt). Maeby's desire to teach her parents a lesson arguably backfires when she forgoes obtaining age-appropriate independence in a stunted, years-long effort to get Lindsay and Tobias' attention. Maeby learns persistence in dealing with her parents and appears to have developed a distant optimism that someday, somehow Lindsay and Tobias will take enough time to notice she has not graduated high school. While Maeby enjoys the self-esteem boost from several bonus years of being a high school senior, the Fünkes remain solely interested in fulfilling their own selfish whims. Tobias and Lindsay fail to recognize Maeby's passive-aggressive pleas for parental recognition, and as a result, Maeby intentionally fails to graduate until her parents care enough to take an interest in her scathing lack of accomplishment.

Lindsay and Tobias make one last attempt at saving their relationship by attending a methadone clinic that Tobias has mistaken for an acting class and each meet other people with whom they share an emotional connection. Swept away in opiates and the romance of it all, once again neither bothers to say goodbye to Maeby before running away. She hears the news, instead, from the answering machine, along with their eviction notice. Technically, they are all homeless, but Maeby has been upwardly mobile for several years and adapts by returning to the vacant model home and enrolling in another year of high school. After their inevitable split, Tobias and Lindsay blunder unsuccessfully on their own before each crawling to Maeby for shelter. Maeby exerts more control over Lindsay and Tobias when they each find they cannot function on their own. In keeping with her self-involved method of parenting, Lindsay's protective maternal instincts only kick in when she thinks Lucille is financially interfering in Maeby's life. When Lindsay arrives at the luxury detention center's tennis courts to confront her mother, Lucille does not immediately recognize her daughter, though she maintains the Bluth tradition of referring to Lindsay as a prostitute by complaining about there being "another high end hooker" in their private lady prison ("Red Hairing" 4:8). Taking on a self-righteous tone, Lindsay asserts that she is nothing like Lucille by claiming to love Maeby just the way she is. Lucille calmly forces Lindsay to admit that she has not seen Maeby in a year as she has presumably been living with Tobias. Lucille cuts through her daughter's insincerity and warns "the apple does not far from the tree fall," to which Lindsay protests, "I am like you nothing" ("Red Hairing" 4:8). Now confronting her own inadequacies as a mother, Lindsay is poised to complete her transformation and verbally reject Maeby to her face. Later in the same episode, Maeby unexpectedly bumps into her estranged mother and briefly enjoys a fleeting moment nearing respect when Lindsay confesses her impending act of glittery nonviolent protest. Unfortunately, cynical Lindsay does not believe a word her daughter says, and immediately rejects Maeby's truth. "I tried," she says, "Tell your therapist I tried" ("Red Hairing" 4:8). Maeby is left dealing with a fresh sting of rejection as her mother walks away and responds by orchestrating a profitable lesson. Instead of retreating into a self-pitying pout, Maeby confronts Lindsay. This forthright approach is consistent with Lee and Shrum's theory that "motivation to reconnect with others is likely to be more dominant than a motivation to assert power or control" (532). "You're a whore," Maeby declares ("Red Hairing" 4:8) before taking on her most dominant role as her own mother's pimp. What is important here is not so much that Maeby is profiting from her mother's affair, but that she continues to speak authentically, if abrasively, and remains committed to teaching Lindsay a lesson. Maeby is empowered enough by her parents' rejection to verbally challenge her mother and then clever enough to capitalize on Lindsay's desperate need for intimacy. Regardless of the Fünkes' deep psychological misgivings, Maeby displays a resilient nature capable of healthy emotional response while also maintaining the morally-bankrupt Bluth value system of exploitation.

The Fünke dynamic maintains an overall positive result in Maeby's confidence, even when she faces setbacks in the professional arena. The Fünkes remain egotistical, distracted parents despite years of Maeby's escalating attempts to teach them otherwise. Delusions of grandeur keep Tobias and Lindsay incapable of functioning as independent adults, even when the pretense of family togetherness is dropped. Maeby remains resilient thanks to her parents' self-centered neglect. Tobias' motivation is characterized by a misplaced drive to succeed, regardless of perpetual rejection. Lindsay abandons maternal notions altogether for a life in public self-service, choosing to work out her feelings of unworthiness by depending exclusively upon outside approval. Role reversal within the Fünke dynamic has proven to increase the overall functionality of individual members of the family while simultaneously encouraging them to develop confidence independent of flagrant parental flaws. Perhaps, in time, the Fünkes will mature enough to appreciate the positive effect their imperfections have had on one another.

Works Cited

Lee, Jaehoon, and L. J. Shrum. "Conspicuous Consumption Versus Charitable Behavior in Response to Social Exclusion: A Differential Needs Explanation." *Journal of Consumer Research* 39.3 (2012). 530–544. Print.

Mayseless, Ofra, Kim Bartholomew, Antonia Henderson, and Shanna Trinke. ""I Was More Her Mom Than She Was Mine": Role Reversal in a Community Sample." *Family Relations* 53.1 (2004). 78–86. Print.

McHale, Susan M., and Ted L. Huston. "Men and Women as Parents: Sex Role Orientations, Employment, and Parental Roles with Infants." *Child Development* 55 4 (1984). 1349–1361. Print.

"Obviously this blue part here is the land"

The Bluths, Decadence and Logic Adrift

Joseph S. Walker

"The forms of art as of life seem exhausted, the stages of development have been run through."—scholar Jacques Barzun defines decadence

"Well, obviously this blue part here is the land."—cartography student Buster Bluth reads a map ["Pilot" 1:1].

"Stealing the *Queen Mary* comes under maritime law, which, I just found out, is an actual thing."—lawyer Barry Zuckerkorn delivers bad news ["Borderline Personalities" 4:2].

How do we read a television series which actively works to make the act of reading itself appear, at best, misguided, or, at worst, the target of unbridled mockery? Similarly to other texts which engage in the hyperbolic representation of a heightened and stylized version of reality (for example, *Alice in Wonderland* or the films of the Coen brothers), *Arrested Development* simultaneously invites close, even obsessive, attention and challenges rigorous analysis, making any attempt to engage in serious interpretation stand only as evidence that the text has been fundamentally misunderstood. Like perpetual student Buster Bluth smashing a skull at an archeology dig ("Charity Drive" 1:6), we risk destroying the very thing we set out to study. After all, given a show in which nearly every line of dialogue is a joke and in which multiple viewings are required to register every sight gag (even new viewers probably notice Tobais's blue handprints all over the model home immediately, but how many viewings are required to register Lupe's mistimed holiday sweaters?), how can we take anything seriously enough to warrant, let alone authorize, analysis? If it is commonly understood that a joke that must be explained is a bad joke, it would seem to follow that the audience member who can't resist explaining a good joke is a bad viewer. This must be particularly true of a show, such as *Arrested Development*, in which the misreading of signs and the absurdity of asserting privilege are among the most frequent sources of humor. Confronting such a text, how can critics claim any critical privilege to articulate a reading of signs with any degree of confidence?

It may be necessary to accept that simply by articulating a reading of such a text, we make ourselves ridiculous. Contemplating a scholarly approach to Mitchell Hurwitz's densely packed, excessive carnival of a sitcom brings us back, again and again, to the figure of Buster, the most ineffectual and powerless of the Bluths. While all the members of the Bluth family frequently (indeed, persistently) misunderstand what is happening around them, this is usually because of their extreme levels of self-absorption and self-delusion. Buster alone actually sees what is happening and, for the most part, perceives reality accurately; witness the fact that he is the only Bluth who actually reads all of Michael's letter about the unfrozen Bluth Company stock, and thus does not sell his shares ("Queen for a Day" 2:8). Buster's understanding, however, is almost always meaningless, because it cannot be translated into significant action. Faced with a crisis in the pilot episode, the Bluths call upon Buster to act, but his cartography studies have not equipped him to read a map, and his knowledge of 18th century agrarianism has not prepared him to run the Bluths' business; he can only collapse into inarticulate panic attacks. Incapable of truly engaging the world, Buster is simply shunted into increasingly esoteric and useless fields of study. These are merely diversions; ultimately he seeks only a nurturing maternal presence to shield and protect him from the world that is a series of terrifying threats. On at least one of its seemingly endless metatextual levels, *Arrested Development* suggests that studying it casts us into the role of Buster, mastering esoteric knowledge that has no application to reality.

Acknowledging the numerous ways in which *Arrested Development* resists interpretation, however, does not negate the fact that a series which has achieved such widespread acclaim and fan devotion must have something of significance to say about the culture in which it is embedded. The very vigor with which the series resists easy or reductive "meaning"—the zeal with which it proclaims itself to be only about itself, an endlessly self-referential snake swallowing its own tail—ultimately testifies to its very real thematic concern with addressing late-stage American consumer culture at a period when it has become similarly self-absorbed. *Arrested Development* is, above all else, a show about decadence in the sense outlined by Jacques Barzun as "a very active time, full of deep concerns, but peculiarly restless, for it sees no clear line of advance. The loss it faces is that of Possibility. The forms of art as of life seem exhausted, the stages of development have been run through" (xx). It is difficult to conceive of a more fitting description of the Bluth family than "peculiarly restless" but with "no clear line of advance"—and it need hardly be pointed out that development which has been completely run through must also be arrested.

Specifically, *Arrested Development* is about the decadence of America at the start of the twenty-first century, a period when the nation's global dominance seemed to become irrelevant at the very moment that it also seemed to become assured. Like a model house stocked with HomeFill simulated products disguising troubling and persistent structural weaknesses, the American experiment has lost sight of lofty, substantial goals—the establishment of global democracy, humanitarian efforts, space exploration, the universal well-being of its citizens—and become mired in mindless consumerism, falsified narratives of success, and the celebration of empty beauty, unearned fame, and unexamined privilege.

This concern is perhaps most obviously visible in the show's devastating lampoon of the American campaign in Iraq, where the long-sought weapons of mass destruction turn out to be HomeFill fakes planted by the CIA in a Bluth model home filled with Saddam Hussein impersonators (and, evidently, the "real" Hussein, although this "reality" is rendered purely arbitrary by the presence of his mob of imitators). Initially, the show's appropriation of the language and images of the war might seem to be just another of its many playful references to contemporary culture. When George Michael examines a bearded George Sr.'s teeth after finding him hiding in a hole ("Good Grief" 2:4), the visual echo of similar images of Saddam Hussein being examined after being found in just such a hole is clearly deliberate and would immediately be recognized as such by the audience of the time. The episode first aired in December of 2004, almost exactly a year after Hussein's capture, and the images from the incident were still fresh in the public's mind. The passage of time, however, blunts any impact such simple echoing might have; like the multiple discussions of the Atkins Diet in the episode "Let 'Em Eat Cake" (1:22), this is a reference that will probably require some form of annotation for many future viewers. It is more difficult to overlook the explicit satire of the "Mission Accomplished" banner that Gob unfurls on the false front of a hastily-erected home immediately before it collapses ("The One Where They Build a House" 2:2). By the time the Bluth brothers are on the verge of being executed for uncovering a CIA plan to falsify a cause for the war, however ("Exit Strategy" 3:12), we have left behind entirely the realm of superficial and easily dated references being used simply for the pleasure of recognizing them; there is real, pointed political content here.

By the time *Arrested Development* returned for its belated fourth season on Netflix in 2013, the war in Iraq was over, at least in terms of public perception (this perception is, of course, frequently unreliable, as Lindsay demonstrates in "Whistler's Mother" [1:20] when she is surprised to learn there is an actual war going on). It has been displaced by an ongoing, and still less publicly visible, "war on terror." This provides the show with the occasion for perhaps its most pointed and overt satiric attack on American policy, as Buster, newly returned to the army, becomes a drone pilot, under the mistaken impression that he is playing video games ("Off the Hook" 4:14). Although he is part of a newly gay-friendly military and reporting for duty in an innocuous mini-mall, Buster is fully engaged in an American campaign which has been marked by controversy and deep misgivings, its worst moments recalled in his gleeful "Take that, Taliban wedding!" When he realizes that he has in fact been piloting an actual drone and firing real weapons at living people, Buster once again collapses in panic. This is easily the darkest moment ever generated by the program: its most innocent, passive character has been prolifically killing people, brought to this point precisely because of his guileless acceptance of any assertion of authority and discipline. We are very far removed from simple, referential farce here; this is satire so dark that it virtually edges into horror. Indeed, the show itself seems incapable of fully containing or acknowledging what we have seen in this moment, retreating into the absurdity of Buster's adventures with his new, oversized prosthetic hand. Nonetheless, the moment stands as the decisive rebuttal of the idea that *Arrested Development* is simply a series of absurdities with nothing of significance to say.

Still, the show's most frequently evoked thematic concerns are not political, but cultural (of course, the line between the political and the cultural is always blurred). As Ethan Thompson has pointed out, *Arrested Development* participates in the trend of "comedy verité" in a way which allows it to sharply parody the worst aspects of a popular culture which has turned fully toward "reality" television and celebrity worship. Tobias's insistence on seeing everything that happens to him through the prism of his "acting" career (thus a therapy session becomes an acting exercise, and a real estate agent is tasked with finding him roles) and Gob's unceasing efforts to launch and maintain his identity as a successful magician are only the most obvious examples of the degree to which the language and tropes of entertainment permeate the show.

At one time or another nearly all the Bluths actively pursue success and fame in the entertainment industry; Oscar writes songs, George Sr. sells his *Caged Wisdom* tapes, George Michael tries to create a musical app, and so on. By the fourth season even Michael, initially the only Bluth actually interested in making a legitimate success of the family's traditional business, has become more invested in the process of making his family's story into a movie. Perhaps the only significant exception to this rule is Lucille, who is always more comfortable exercising power from behind the throne, but even she ends up with a starring role in the reality series *Real Asian Prison Housewives of the Orange County White Collar Prison System*, where she is happy to give technical advice to the camera crew and offers to do retakes ("Queen B." 4:10). The actual operations of the Bluth Company are increasingly marginalized and irrelevant to the show and, indeed, much of what it actually *does* remains unspoken and mysterious (it's worth noting that both the Bluth Company set and the banana stand are absent from the show's fourth season). Though it often appears to be a highly diversified, multinational corporation, the only thing we ever actually see the company doing is building houses, which turn out to be shoddy simulations. The critique of the contemporary American economic system here is direct and unmistakable. It is the same critique expressed by an angry union leader contemplating the collapse of his industry in the far more overtly engaged series *The Wire* (2002–2008): "We used to make shit in this country" ("Bad Dreams" 2:11). Now, it would appear, the only concrete, physical product the Bluths can imagine actually producing is a frozen banana—but even that idea was stolen from Korea, and at any rate they are far more interested in negotiating the animation rights to the Mr. Bananagrabber character.

The show's self-reflexive obsession with show business, however, is only one manifestation of a deeper, defining concern with the decadence of America in the wake of the exhausted collapse of its age of expansion and self-confidence. America is decadent because there is no longer a clear way forward, no longer a path to meaningful new creation; confronted with that absence, American culture can only engage in the endless, self-perpetuating process of reexamining and recycling what has gone before. Structurally, this theme is represented by the endless self-referentiality of the program (thematically, it is represented in the frequent jokes about incest that run throughout the show). Many of the jokes in *Arrested Development* are funny not in and of themselves, but rather because of the ways in which they echo, reference, foreshadow, or invert other moments in the show, creating an increasingly rich and complex shared language between show and audience—or, perhaps more accurately, a mythology. When Gob mishears Lindsay's statement that she is going to start a bead business, leading to a confused "Bees?"/"No, beads" exchange, we laugh because their shared confusion is grounded in their mutual narcissism and in the easily misheard words ("Let 'Em Eat Cake" 1:22). When essentially the same exchange occurs between Gob and George Sr. years later, just before Gob's bees are freed from his limo to wreak havoc, we laugh less for these reasons than because we recognize the callback to the earlier exchange; the show is essentially rewarding us for our attention and memory ("Colony Collapse" 4:7). The fourth season of the show invests heavily in this aspect of its relationship with the fans; virtually every significant element of the season, down to passing lines of dialogue, is either a reference to some moment in the first three seasons or a deliberate effort to create new moments for such references and revision. Recognizing all these connections requires almost obsessively rewatching the show to uncover new connections and callbacks, and fans have dutifully created dozens of websites that catalogue every moment of the show in exacting detail. It's possible, for example, to trace the frequent appearances or mentions of ostriches in the fourth season, and specifically Lindsay's unintended involvement with an ostrich farm, to her tossed-off comment "Well, I don't care about *ostriches*" when Michael challenges her environmentalist claims by noting that she is wearing ostrich-skin boots—an exchange that occurs in just the fourth episode of the series ("Key Decisions" 1:4).

Of course, self-referentialism in television is nothing new; by the early 1990s it was already possible for David Foster Wallace to observe that in some shows "Every character and conflict and joke and dramatic surge depends on involution, self-reference, metatelevision. It is in-joke within in-joke" (32). In the intervening decades more and more shows have engaged in such practices, largely in response to shifts in viewing patterns. Viewers are no longer restricted to watching their favorite shows once a week, or only once per episode; thanks to syndication, DVD sets, and now Internet streaming, they can engage in marathons, consuming entire seasons in a weekend and returning to earlier episodes as often as they like. Such viewing patterns enable shows to become more ambitious and complex in a multitude of ways, depending upon the viewers' intimate familiarity with the series as a whole, not just with a basic situation that remains fundamentally unchanged from one week to the next. *Arrested Development* clearly anticipates this kind of attention from its viewers, and the fourth season particularly, freed from network restrictions and commercial breaks and released in its entirety simultaneously, is designed with binge watching in mind.

Discussing the final episode of *Seinfeld* (1989–1998), Joanne Morreale writes that increasing numbers of sitcoms "are no longer simply self-referential, but they also incorporate intertextuality, parody, and play with the sitcom form, indicating an even greater emphasis on the discursive relationship set up between text and viewer" (110). This relationship is in flux, as "Identification and commitment ... occurred with the discourse of the text, perhaps more than the characters within it" (114). *Arrested Development* takes this relationship with the audience to its most extreme level, creating a viewing experience almost entirely disassociated from the experience of the characters themselves. In *Seinfeld*, the catalog of self-referential allusions (the contest, hand, Superman) were grounded in the experiences of the characters and told us something about them—their interests, their experiences, their characteristics. Jerry and his friends knew what "the contest" was, and understood the role it played in their life. The same cannot be said for the characters of *Arrested Development*; for the most part, the characters here are simply oblivious to the network of allusions, references, coincidences, foreshadowing, and echoes which structures their existence. It's highly unlikely that Lindsay, finding herself on an ostrich farm ("Indian Takers" 4:3), remembers her comment about ostrich boots, or would see any connection between the two incidents if she did. Buster, upon losing his hand to a loose seal, probably did not reflect upon the irony of his earlier statement "I never thought I'd miss a hand so much" when he comes across his old hand chair in his housekeeper's home ("¡Amigos!" 2:3). When George Michael sees an attractive redhead at the Opies and leers "Gentlemen, start your engines" ("It Gets Better" 4:13), he has no way of knowing that his father makes the exact same comment upon seeing the exact same redhead at the Balboa Towers ("Flight of the Phoenix" 4:1), let alone that the woman is his aunt in a wig. Often the referential connections do not even occur within the characters' plane of existence. When Argyle says that "They used to call me Mr. Fantastic," he does not hear the "Mr. F" musical sting that follows his statement, and would not understand its significance if he did ("Smashed" 4:9).

Lacking the perspective granted to both the narrator and the audience, the characters of *Arrested Development* are trapped in an elaborate structure that they have no way to recognize. Their lives are given meaning not through traditional character arcs, but through structures of repetition, reference and similarity entirely outside the boundaries of their perception. The result, again and again, is frustration, confusion, and anxiety as the characters' plans and aspirations are repeatedly foiled or rendered absurd by forces beyond their comprehension. This confrontation with the limits of meaning and creation is frequently embodied through encounters with the Pacific Ocean—the border that marked the limits of the expansion which defined the first two centuries of the American project, and which in this show marks the limits of logic, security, knowledge, and power.

We begin to get some sense of the symbolic significance of the sea in *Arrested Development* from a very early, and seemingly minor, moment in the series. In just the second episode ("Top Banana" 1:2), Gob has been tasked by Michael with the job of mailing a letter—the only thing Michael finds simple enough to entrust to his older brother. Lucille tells Michael that Gob has mailed the letter, but her assertion is immediately undercut by the narrator: "Gob had not mailed the letter, but in an act of defiance dramatically hurled the letter into the sea. This proved a more difficult dramatic gesture than he'd anticipated." As the narrator tells us this we see Gob attempting, several times, to throw the envelope into the sea, only to have it blown back by the wind; increasingly frustrated, he eventually has to run fully into the water (and is summarily knocked over by a wave) before he is satisfied that the letter is gone. On the face of it, this is little more than one of the show's funnier moments of physical comedy, but seen in the context of the show as a whole, the scene offers a microcosm of the larger functions of the sea in the series. Michael's authority, Lucille's knowledge, and Gob's intentions are all frustrated here; only the narrator, operating from a higher narrative plane, can fully understand and describe what is happening and why. Minor as it is, the letter is an artifact of the world of reason, logic, responsibility, and law; it is a symbol of Michael's attempt to align his company and his family with the rules of normality and to exercise some measure of control over his fate. And of course, the letter is not so minor after all; it's an insurance payment for the banana stand, and his belief that it has been mailed is what enables Michael to attempt to bond with his son by burning the stand down (here again Michael's knowledge fails him, as he does not realize that his father has hidden money in its walls).

Similar moments involving the sea, as well as the adjoining border regions of the beach and boardwalk, occur at various other points throughout the series. When Gob sinks the family yacht as part of an illusion, he is again abusing something Michael has given him, again with consequences he does not intend. When he releases a seal into the ocean, he has no way of knowing it will eventually claim Buster's hand. When Lucille kisses Oscar at the beach, she has no way of knowing that she will be seen as giving CPR to a homeless man and that a picture of the encounter will drive her husband to return from Mexico in a jealous rage. The banana stand, located at the boardwalk, is frequently the site of particularly visible disruptions of order and intention; although it is meant to be the cornerstone of the Bluth empire, they cannot prevent it from being seen as the "big yellow joint" that provides a center for the local drug culture ("Pier Pressure" 1:10) or from annually being vandalized and dumped into the bay as part of a Newport Beach Christmas tradition ("Afternoon Delight" 2:6).

In moments such as these the ocean is the visible representation of the limits and frustrations *Arrested Development's* emphasis on self-referential structure imposes upon its characters. That is to say, it is a realm outside the authority and control of human agents. When *Arrested Development* is resurrected for its fourth season, we learn that the characters, in fact, often depend upon the sea functioning in just this way. In a flashback during the episode "Borderline Personalities" (4:2), young lawyer Barry Zuckerkorn (played, in one of the show's typically self-referential gestures, by Max Winkler, the son of Henry Winkler, who plays the "present day" Barry) tells George Sr. and Lucille Bluth that crimes they commit or plan in international waters cannot be prosecuted: "Take to the sea! Three miles out, and it's a free-for-all. No rules, pirate radio laws." As is typical for Barry, this is, of course, entirely wrong, and yet it is the advice the Bluths apparently model the deeply fraudulent management of their company on for years afterwards. Barry's vision of international waters figures the sea as a place utterly beyond the knowledge or reach of American authority and surveillance. Although this proves incorrect, it can be taken as retroactively explaining elements of the program dating all the way back to the first episode—for example, Gob and Buster's surprise at the realization that the SEC has boats (why would they, if the sea is essentially a place without law?). Even before the SEC arrives to undercut the "take to the sea" strategy, however, the yacht has already been the site of breakdowns in communication, understanding, identity, and convention. It's on the yacht, within the first twenty minutes of the *Arrested Development* saga, where Michael learns that he has radically misunderstood his role in the company and the family; on the yacht where George Michael and Maeby begin their endless circling of incestuous taboos; on the yacht where Lindsay fails to recognize her own husband, wearing her own clothes, across a few yards of water; on the yacht where Buster and Gob, called upon to act in their self-proclaimed roles of cartographer and magician, fail miserably while somehow not recognizing their own failures; near the yacht where Tobias decides to reject his previous identity as a medical professional and embrace a new career as an actor. The major plot threads of the first three seasons of the show are all set in motion during these key moments, and they all depend upon characters confronting breakdowns in their identities and the places they understand themselves to occupy in the world.

From the very beginning of the series, then, the sea (and the shoreline which represents the still more unstable border region) is where the Bluths encounter the limits of their worldviews and identities, sometimes with terror, sometimes with enthusiasm. It's not insignificant that this first series of such encounters is set on a yacht—one of the ultimate symbols of power, excess, prestige, and privilege in the American pantheon of signifiers. If the Bluths are themselves representative of the American state of decadence, it is only fitting that we first see them in this context of luxury—particularly when we are armed with the knowledge that this luxury is entirely unearned, except through criminal means. One of the most alarming characteristics of America in its decadent stage is the division—greater than at any point in our history— between the privileged few and the increasingly beleaguered many. Paraphrasing John Steinbeck, Ronald Wright famously suggested that "Socialism never took root in America because the poor see themselves not as an exploited proletariat but as temporarily embarrassed millionaires" (124). *Arrested Development* is in many ways the story of this collective delusion, and the yacht is the first and most powerful symbol of it. On the surface it extends our power and prestige into the sea, beyond their natural bounds; in reality, it exposes the degree to which we are merely continuing to delude ourselves.

In addition to positing the sea as a realm free from the rule of law, the fourth season also establishes, in its opening moments, a new focus for the Bluths' symbolic encounters with the sea: "the annual celebration known as Cinco de Cuatro" ("Flight of the Phoenix" 4:1). Started in 1982 by Lucille Bluth in an effort to keep her household staff from taking a day off on May 5, this holiday attempts to deplete the local supply of Hispanic foods and party supplies by dumping them into the bay. Of course, like any scheme hatched by a Bluth, this has gone wrong, and the local community has come to embrace the new "holiday" for the opportunities it offers for profit, turning the fourth of May into a carnival celebrating the elements of destruction and disruption, and an opportunity to dispose of anything unwanted in the waters. Thus we see, for example, Dr. Norman using the holiday as an opportunity to dump his massive supply of illicit drugs and incriminating patient records into the sea—accomplishing efficiently what Gob struggled to achieve with the letter. The name of the celebration, of course, translates into the essentially meaningless "five of four," not the "fourth of May" Lucille presumably intended; this continues the pattern that runs throughout the series of the Bluths knowing no Spanish, despite living in a community with a large Hispanic population that they frequently interact with. The Cinco celebration, as it is familiarly called, is (along with the night of the Opie Awards and the strategy session in the penthouse) one of the focal events of the fourth season, drawing together the characters who, for most of the fifteen episodes, are isolated from each other. It marks the culmination of the plots which have run through most of the season, and the initiation of the event which will mark the starting point of any further continuation of the narrative: the disappearance of Lucille Austero. With its carnival atmosphere and its central theme of destruction, Cinco represents the ultimate expression of the sea's symbolic position in *Arrested Development* as a marker of chaos and disorder.

Of course, as the Bluths also discover in the fourth season, the sea is not, in fact, a realm completely separate from human control and authority; as Barry discovers to his shock, maritime law "is an actual thing" ("Borderline Personalities" 4:2). The invocation of maritime law initially seems to be just another of the show's seemingly endless callbacks, in this case to the legal specialty Michael claimed for himself when he posed as the lawyer Chareth Cutestory during his affair with Maggie Lizer in season one ("Altar Egos" 1:17). In this case, however, the concept is expanded upon to become a completely new point of reference for the show. Lucille is tried under this set of laws for her hijacking of the *Queen Mary* at the end of season three, and her trial is another of the focal points the season continuously returns to although, for various reasons, all the other members of the family miss it. Their presence, at any rate, could hardly render the "trial" any sillier than it is, as the exercise of "maritime law" quickly becomes one of the most cartoonish elements in a series that specializes in the absurd. The trial is conducted in a seafood restaurant on the pier, presided over by a judge played by Bernie Kopell, the actor best known for his role as "Doc" on the series *The Love Boat* (1977–1986). While awaiting the trial, the Bluths are required to accept special "maritime" surveillance cameras in their apartment, installed by men equipped with hoses. Barry calls his witness not to the stand, but to "the oyster bar thing where they sit" ("Indian Takers" 4:3); when Lucille awaits her verdict she does so in a literal cooler, the restaurant's walk-in refrigerator; her verdict is put on a chalkboard at the front of the restaurant next to the day's specials. When "Judge" Judge Reinhold presided over *Mock Trial* in the third season of *Arrested Development*, it was merely a reality show; here, nobody seems to question that there is real legal force behind the farcical proceedings. Lucille is indeed convicted, largely on the basis of her antagonistic interrogation of Lucille Austero, and sentenced to prison, though it is a "white collar prison" run like a luxury spa. The entire trial, in other words, resembles something from *Mad* magazine, exposing the arbitrary nature of the exercise of any authority. "Maritime law," as expressed through this trial, is less a system of knowledge and power than an acceptance of their limits and irrelevance in a decadent world.

In fact, however, the same can be said of virtually any system operating in the world of *Arrested Development*. The irrationality of Lucille's trial is self-evident, but it is really little different from the only marginally more realistic legal perils faced by George Sr. in the first three seasons of the program. A trial held in a seafood restaurant differs in degree, not kind, from a prosecution conducted by a woman who has spent years pretending to be blind in order to pass the bar and curry sympathy from juries, and which presents a close-up photograph of a scrotum as its key piece of evidence. This is, in fact, the central truth of *Arrested Development*: there is no aspect of the reality it represents which is not deeply marked by the absurd. It is not the Bluths who are mad, but the world—the decadent world—which they occupy.

For example, the show has occasionally been criticized for its representation of homosexuality, and it is true that it's easy to be disturbed by the fact that essentially every gay man on the show conforms to the broadest possible stereotype of the mincing fairy, barely a step above the heavily feminized dancers Mel Brooks gave the world in 1974's *Blazing Saddles*. Even members of the military, once it begins openly accepting gays, can be identified by their mastery of Stephen Sondheim trivia ("Off the Hook" 4:14). Is the show's version of homosexuality, however, really any more cartoonish than its representation of heterosexuality? Is it any more cartoonish than the "Mexican" scenes, complete with burro and cactus, which are transparently shot on a backlot "village square" set? If there are no dignified gays or Hispanics in *Arrested Development*, this is less because the show is practicing outdated gender and racial politics and more because the show lacks any figures that possess any degree of dignity whatsoever. In the world occupied by the Bluths, everyone—regardless of their degree of power or privilege—is ridiculous. This applies as well to the various forms of authority operating in the world. We have already seen the various ways in which the law and the military are rendered outlandish. Essentially the same case can be made for every system of authority and order the Bluths might conceivably have to answer to. Their own knowledge of religion is, of course, laughable (in "Justice Is Blind" [1:18] we see that none of the Bluths can accurately quote a single one of the Ten Commandments), but religion itself is rendered hollow by the pious hypocrisy of the Veals and the bland ditherings of *And As It Is Such, So Also As Such Is It Unto You*. The news media are routinely shown in the series to be unreliable, sensationalistic, and easily manipulated. The operation of capitalism is undermined not only by the continued existence of the Bluth Company despite its overwhelming incompetence and illegality, but by the dishonesty and short-sightedness of essentially every other economic entity (consider, for example, the NINJA loan—No Income, No Job and No Assets—that Lindsay and Tobias easily obtain to buy a mansion before the housing crash).

In short, the world represented by *Arrested Development* is one in which individuals, trapped within an elaborate system of references, have no control over their own fate and no ability to engineer progress toward their goals; it is, moreover, a world in which every conceivable form of power and discipline has been rendered equally inept and impotent. What we are left with, then, is a single authority that appears to order existence, from top to bottom: narration. The narrator's is the first voice we hear at the start of the series, and his orientation and knowledge continue to guide us through every scene of every episode of the show. He is privy to the inner thoughts of each character, and able to call our attention to connections and additional information that the characters themselves are never aware of. Aided and abetted by the editing which moves us from scene to scene, the narrator gives order, direction, and shape to a series of events which, seen from within, must seem to represent nothing more than chaos, instability, and the arbitrary whims of fate. *Arrested Development* is ultimately a testament to the power of telling stories, and it is ultimately the force of narrative necessity that compels the characters to act as they do and achieve the outcomes they reach. In this context, the fourth season can be seen as an exercise in complicating a narrative to the greatest extreme possible while maintaining absolute authority over the events contained within that narrative (to quote the song George Michael records to showcase his woodblock skills, keeping "those balls in the air"). Consider the narration accompanying the opening credits in each episode of the first three seasons: "Now the story of a wealthy family who lost everything, and the one son who had *no choice* but to keep them together" (emphasis added). Michael is robbed, here, of the fundamental aspect of agency; his actions are regarded as inevitable, compelled by the nature of the story he lives within. Given the number of times he leaves for Phoenix in the show, only to be drawn back into the insane orbit of his family, it would seem difficult to argue the point.

Except, of course, that Michael does argue the point; in his speech at the party on the *Queen Mary* at the end of season three, he tells his family and the assembled crowd that "three years ago, *I made a choice* to keep this family together" ("Development Arrested" 3:13; emphasis added). It's possible to see this as just another instance of Michael deluding himself, but the fact is that the narrator is not infallible; the narration of the show is not a seamless demonstration of perfect authority. There are, for example, moments when the narrator confesses that he does *not* know what a character is thinking, as when Michael, in the vote to see who will leave his son's dorm room, opens the meaningless fourth vote ("Flight of the Phoenix" 4:1). There are also instances when the narrator reveals that his perspective on events is far from objective or unbiased, as when Jessie, the public relations expert Michael hires, disparagingly refers to George Michael as "Opie": "Jessie had gone too far, and she had best watch her mouth," the narrator comments ("Public Relations" 1:11). What is primarily occurring here is one of the show's innumerable metatextual references, reminding the audience that Ron Howard—performing the voice of the narrator—began his career with his childhood part as Opie on *The Andy Griffith Show* (1960–1968). *Arrested Development* frequently includes sly references to the real lives and other roles of its cast, but what sets moments such as this apart is the recognition that the narrator is not simply describing events, but acknowledging his place in their creation—a recognition that depends upon the viewer knowing that Ron Howard is not just another cast member, but actually one of the show's producers as well. The joke, in other words, demands a momentary recognition of the very circumstances of the show's production, and in so doing sacrifices the illusion of reality any story depends upon. What could more fundamentally undermine the authority of narration than such reminders that it is itself an artifice?

If the show's narration is thus limited, biased, and artificial, these limitations are most regularly exposed in the "On the next *Arrested Development*" sequences which appear at the end of almost every episode. On their simplest level these snippets parody the common convention of showing such scenes at the end of many television shows, but the scenes they contain, with very rare exceptions, never actually appear in the following episode. Often, in fact, they are scenes which directly contradict events that we know occur in the main storyline of the series, or which provide additional narrative branches that are never followed up on or definitively shown to have happened. Consider, for example, the end of "The One Where Michael Leaves" (2:1), an episode where Tobias, wearing his dark blue makeup at walking and night, is struck by a car driven by Barry. In the final scene from the "on the next" sequence at the end of the episode, Michael visits Barry in jail and learns that he's having the time of his life and is happy that Tobias is pressing charges. The scene is, in part, one of the show's trademark callbacks, directly echoing the first time Michael visits his father in prison. More importantly for our purposes, it's a scene that we cannot be sure actually happens; we never again see Barry in prison, and never again hear any reference to Tobias pressing charges against him. The scene is presented with the full authority and confidence of the narrator, but it seems completely disconnected from anything else he ever tells us. As such scenes appear in almost every episode, the cumulative effect builds, undermining the absolute authority the narrator seems to have; if we cannot trust the "on the next" sequences to actually be what they appear to be, then why should we trust any other sequence we are shown to be reliable? Presented as a masterful exercise in the ability of narrative to shape the world and our experience of it, *Arrested Development* ultimately reveals in these moments that the power of narration is as flawed, partial, and arbitrary as any other power it represents, and equally unable to generate new meaning in a decadent world.

Works Cited

Barzun, Jacques. *From Dawn to Decadence: 500 Years of Western Cultural Life: 1500 to the Present.* New York: HarperCollins, 2000. Print.

Morreale, Joanne. "Sitcoms Say Goodbye: The Cultural Spectacle of *Seinfeld*'s Last Episode." *Journal of Popular Film and Television* 28.3 (2000): 108–115. Print.

Thompson, Ethan. "Comedy Verité? The Observational Documentary Meets the Televisual Sitcom." *The Velvet Light Trap* 60 (2007): 63–72. Print.

Wallace, David Foster. "E Unibus Pluram: Television and U.S. Fiction." *A Supposedly Fun Thing I'll Never Do Again: Essays and Arguments.* Boston: Little, Brown 1997. 21–82. Print.

Wright, Ronald. *A Short History of Progress.* Toronto: House of Anansi, 2004. Print.

COMPARATIVE DEVELOPMENTS

Hamlet's Ghost Meme
Accidental Shakespeare, Repetition Compulsion and Roofie Circles

KRISTIN N. DENSLOW

> Thus, every new revival of *Hamlet* is doubly haunted, on the one hand, by the memories of the famous *Hamlets* of the past (some within the living memory of audience members, others known only through historical reputation) and, on the other hand, by memories of the new interpreter, who comes with his own particular style and technique, in most cases also familiar to the audiences. The successful new Hamlet will add his unique voice to the tradition and join the ghosts with whom Hamlets of the future must deal.
> —Marvin Carlson, *The Haunted Stage*

> And you tell me you've got some P.E. teacher directing? That just makes me want to puke all over your head, sir. Give me a chance to tell the Bard's tale, and I give you my word on humble knee, whence you shall not say it wasn't e'er to be.
> —Tobias Fünke ("Bringing Up Buster" 1:3)

That *Hamlet* keeps coming back in various stage and film productions and references in comic strips, novels, music, and art is by now a cultural truism. As Marvin Carlson indicates in the epigraph, *Hamlet* is an archive of cultural memory, and the play's haunting of contemporary culture is visible even in phrases and images that creep into ordinary conversation and visual rhetoric. On the one hand, mentioning the play can conjure a resentment of highbrow culture or memories of high school boredom, yet, on the other, *Hamlet's* key

moments—"To be or not to be...," Yorick's skull, the appearance of the Ghost—
are cited regularly as part of the cultural ether. This tension between dismissal
and reverence exemplifies the popular cultural stance on Shakespeare in the
20th and 21st centuries in which allusions to and citations of Shakespeare typically present an unswerving ambivalence towards the plays. Beyond the many,
many cultural invocations of *Hamlet*—from now-canonical films by Olivier,
Zeffirelli, and Branagh to more derivative forays through diverse genres including television, graphic novels (including Ryan North's choose-your-own adven-
ture comic *To Be or Not to Be*), fiction, and abundant references in news articles,
political cartoons, advertisements, and iPad apps—*Hamlet* also encroaches
silently into culture in moments that one might describe as accidentally Shakespearean. Indeed, Douglas Lanier's argument that the boundaries of what constitutes as Shakespearean are always in flux is particularly valuable in these
moments. How might the constant renegotiation of Shakespearean boundaries
play out when the "Shakespearean" appears as accidental, both inessential and
coincidental? What happens when the designation "Shakespearean" is applied
to an artifact not appealing to Shakespeare's cultural power and value, and
that label is assigned not by the author but by the critic? Might it be that
"Shakespearean" is a label appropriated primarily by scholars who operate
within a broader knowledge and heightened awareness of the Shakespearean
text(s)?

Subtle, unacknowledged references to *Hamlet* in the television series
Arrested Development embody this idea of "accidental" Shakespeare and begin
to address some of the questions outlined above. In addition to its densely
tangled web of intertextual cultural references, the series contains a version of
a Shakespearean "meme" which replicates the narrative of Hamlet's haunting
by his deceased father. In this Ghost meme, the undead, frequently-absent
father, George Sr., haunts multiple sons, and the Bluth sons collectively form
a composite sketch of Hamlet's character. Though this *Hamlet*-like narrative
is picked up periodically throughout the series, it registers as an apparently
accidental citation of Shakespeare. In contrast to the show's other Shakespearean invocation of *Much Ado About Nothing* ("Bringing Up Buster" 1:3),
Hamlet is never directly referenced by the series, giving its appearance a meme-
like quality. In other words, like a meme, *Hamlet* circulates continuously and
unconsciously, and it can be picked up unintentionally by cultural artifacts.
The meme is a unit of doubling and repetition; it proliferates wildly, spawns
both replications and mutations, and never moves in a linear fashion. These
issues of originlessness and unceasing replication appear throughout *Arrested
Development* in moments separable from the Ghost meme, making the series

not only an example of a particular meme but also symptomatic of the broader ramifications of meme theory. Reading the "accidental" Shakespearean moments in *Arrested Development* through the lens of memes suggests that Shakespeare's "stickiness" in contemporary popular culture is a matter of cultural circulation, selective thematic and narrative uptake, and memetic survival, traits which indeed are characteristic of all forms of Shakespearean adaptation.

The term meme originates from Richard Dawkins' 1976 book *The Selfish Gene* in which he defines the meme as a unit of cultural transmission, roughly analogous to the gene. His now-famous examples of potential memes include "tunes, ideas, catch-phrases, clothes fashions, ways of making pots or of building arches" (192). Like genes, memes are replicators; they function solely to replicate cultural units. According to Dawkins, a successful meme possesses three properties: copying-fidelity, fecundity, and longevity. In other words, the meme that survives faithfully copies its predecessor (though there may be important mutations that also enable memetic success), copies frequently, and continues copying itself for a long period of time. Mutations of a meme encourage the preservation and long-term survival of the source though in slightly different, more resilient forms. Linda Hutcheon applies this theory of biology and mutation to narratives, suggesting that stories work through adaptation and "travel to different cultures and different media" (31). In addition, "like genes, they [stories] adapt to those new environments by virtue of mutation— in their 'offspring' or their adaptations. And the fittest do more than survive; they flourish" (32). For Hutcheon, these biological, genetic principles of adaptation apply directly to how stories spread and evolve culturally, though she does stop short of describing this activity as memetic (see Bortolotti and Hutcheon). The meme has also been taken up in a range of academic disciplines including oral literature, performance studies, psychology, computer and information sciences, and marketing, even as it's scientific validity remains a source of dispute.

In spite of these sometimes polemical critiques and defenses of the meme in more scientific circles, its contemporary Internet usage provides an important intersection given its current relevance and popularity. The Internet meme, typically defined as the viral spread and eventual repackaging of an image, a phrase, a video, or any transmittable content on the Internet, is typically viewed as completely distinct from what Dawkins, et al., conceived, thus redeeming the concept from its debatable origins. Internet memes emphasize the digital transmission of and connectivity between individual memes, as well as the social and public expression of the meme. Internet memes are a highly participatory genre in which each meme contributes to a larger collection of texts, causes, events, and ideas. As Limor Shifman points out, though memes begin as virals rapidly transmitted from user to user, the viral becomes a meme when multiple users simultaneously imitate, interpret, and repackage the "original" text as well as its copies. A popular example of this would be Beyoncé's 2008 hit video, "Single Ladies," which first spread rapidly as a viral Internet sensation but then was modified, repackaged, and refilmed by both professional and amateur interpretations and parodies of the pop sensation. Metaphorically, Shakespeare's plays work like Internet memes in that they always spread as groups of texts, performances, revisions, and memories that are continuously repackaged by "users," (i.e., directors, editors, scholars, and fans). For example, the famously unstable text of *Hamlet* is fraught with inconsistencies between quartos and folios. Therefore, all editions, readings, and adaptations must do the interpretive work of recombination, revision, and repackaging based on the available texts. Thus, when Kenneth Branagh claims to have filmed the "full text" of *Hamlet* for his 1996 film, even he follows a conflationist model of combining sources, patching together pieces from the Second Quarto, First Folio, and other sources which amplify the First Folio text.

The meme, as defined here, connotes constant, compulsive circulation combined with both purposeful and accidental repackaging. In a Shakespeare and adaptation context, the meme draws from Dawkins' trinity of memetic transmission. A successful Shakespeare meme copies some unit of the Shakespearean text faithfully and that meme then spreads prolifically and for a long time. The Internet definition focuses more on the repackaging element of a Shakespeare meme; as Shakespearean texts are taken up, they are reworked and revised across a variety of media and for a variety of purposes. Though recent scholars of Internet memes (most notably Shifman) argue that memetic activity and transmission is always purposive, the analysis of pre-digital memes, such as a Shakespearean meme, demonstrates that memes can and do exist without direct reference to the source. As products of cultural circulation, memes are bound to be taken up without intent. The study of Shakespearean memes demonstrates that any unacknowledged adaptation, whether the result of political suppression, psychological repression, or sheer coincidence, can still participate in memetic activity because memetic activity is about endless circulation and repetition, not about intent.

Though there are numerous Shakespeare memes worthy of study, the Ghost meme's frequent appearance in 21st century television deems it a particularly suitable example. In contrast to some other memes within the *Hamlet* memeplex (memeplex being shorthand for meme complex), the Ghost meme is primarily narrative-based. Its reduction and oversimplification of both the plot and criticism of *Hamlet* results in a thematic, rather than linguistic, presentation. In other words, very broad, limited readings of *Hamlet*'s themes of haunting, revenge, and inaction surface more frequently than other themes. The Ghost meme works differently than cultural uptake of a given speech, such as Hamlet's "To be or not to be" speech, which is reduced to a Shakespearean sound bite removed from its context. The Ghost meme's content consists primarily of the (perceived) appearance of the Ghost of the father visiting the son. Of course, ghostly visitations exist as narrative devices apart from *Hamlet*, so other related thematic registers must be considered. Thematically, the Ghost meme may involve such issues as vengeance, guilt, and psychological trauma. The Ghost meme possesses some sort of narrative storytelling element (again, in contrast to a Shakespeare meme that signifies more linguistically or symbolically, like the hoisting of Yorick's skull). The Ghost meme's flexible narrative content makes it an ideal study in accidental Shakespeare because its narrative and thematic content do not automatically register as Shakespearean.

Fittingly, the Ghost meme raises issues of repetition, compulsion, the uncanny, and psychoanalysis that relate not only to *Hamlet* but also to the concept of the meme more broadly. That is to say, the reading of this particular meme reinforces an understanding of memes in general, as well as a definition of accidental Shakespeare. The examples referenced here from *Arrested Development* are notable because even though *Arrested Development* explicitly references Shakespeare, particularly in the context of the theatrical, it also embeds *Hamlet*-like Ghost narratives with no acknowledgment of a Shakespearean source. To refer to this Ghost narrative as reference, spin-off, or citation would be inaccurate because the narrative arcs are never grounded in *Hamlet*.

The (potentially accidental) presentation of the Ghost meme in *Arrested Development* relies on psychoanalytic undertones fitting with the common cultural shorthand that substitutes *Hamlet* for "daddy issues." The series presents Hamlet in terms of fractured masculinity in that the presence of a haunting father results directly in the son's failure. Like *Arrested Development*, other popular 21st century television series present this meme without acknowledging its source, including the series *Six Feet Under* (2001–2005), *Lost* (2004–2010), and *Gossip Girl* (2007–2012). Notably, each television repetition of the Ghost meme tells the story in terms of young, wealthy, white, straight men struggling with overbearing or distant fathers whose death and return (typically through some form of "haunting" relationship) provokes the son's inaction, indecision, and ennui. The lack of racial, ethnic, gender, and socioeconomic diversity is quite striking, as if Hamlet's haunted relationship with his father is only applicable to individuals within this very narrow demographic. Though television women are also occasionally subject to ghostly visits, they typically are haunted by lovers (*Grey's Anatomy* [2005–present]) and friends (*Veronica Mars* [2004–2007], *Buffy the Vampire Slayer* [1997–2003]) rather than parents. An informal survey of 21st century U.S. television reveals that the Ghost meme's intergenerational father/son haunting dynamic is not replicated in father/daughter, mother/son, or mother/daughter pairings.

The shows *Lost* and *Six Feet Under* each deploy the Hamlet meme in fairly faithful (and totally unacknowledged) forms. In each of these examples, the hero must die (or disappear) to end the story, making this death the only logical end for a son haunted by his father. In these two shows, the Hamlet analogue is found in the main character. In *Lost*, Jack Shephard sees visions of his father while trapped on a purgatory-like island after a plane crash. In fact, he was on the flight in the first place because he was transporting his father's body from Australia to the U.S. His father's ghost haunts him both on and off the island; his depressive streaks are punctuated with these ghostly visits. On *Six Feet Under*, Nate Fisher, whose father, Nathaniel, dies in an accident in the show's pilot, has recurring conversations with the deceased. His father's sudden death leads Nate to move home and help with the family funeral business. Through his post-death conversations with his father, Nate realizes he wishes he had known Nathaniel better. Nate, like *Lost*'s Jack, struggles with many family dynamics and "daddy" issues, and none seem resolved by the show's completion. Nate's own death in the final season seems to be the logical end for the series' melancholy lead.

A more complicated example of the Ghost meme occurs in *Gossip Girl*, which engages with the Ghost meme more extensively, ultimately rewriting the narrative and offering the son a way out through the second death of his father. Unlike Hamlet, who contends with a supernatural spirit, *Gossip Girl*'s Chuck Bass deals first with a spectral father, projected from Chuck's unconscious, then with a father returned to life who haunts Chuck's ability to manage his own destiny. The first haunting, which follows Bart Bass' untimely death, consists of Chuck imagining the Ghost of his father chastising him. Later, after Bart is shown to have faked his own death, the living Ghost sends Chuck into despair and depression. When Chuck and his father ultimately have a rooftop confrontation, a fitting scenario for any engagement with Hamlet and his father, Chuck's Hamlet can finally move on from the scripted dramatic trajectory of Shakespeare's text. Whereas in *Lost* and *Six Feet Under* the Hamlet characters inevitably fail in reckoning with the Ghost of the father, *Gossip Girl* subverts the narrative, allowing the Hamlet character to ultimately conquer both the uncle and the Ghost of the father. Furthermore, this narrative arrives silently; in contrast to the show's heavy-handed inter- and meta-textual references, including an extensive engagement with Punchdrunk's *Macbeth*-based performance experience, *Sleep No More* ("The Big Sleep No More" 5:7), Chuck's extended narrative arc is never announced as *Hamlet*.

That *Arrested Development* picks up on the Ghost meme may be unsurprising given the show's notorious density in terms of its narrative and web of references. As Jason Mittell points out, *Arrested Development*'s complexity, in fitting with a contemporary American television tendency towards "prime-time episodic seriality" (33), ties spectacle to narrative. The audience is engaged in the narrative experience that is mediated by the show's push towards self-reflexivity and breaking the fourth wall. Mittell writes that in these moments, "we watch the process of narration as a machine rather than engaging in its diegesis" (35). Thus, the audience of *Arrested Development* becomes more interested in making connections, applying pet theories, and following the show down its intertextual rabbit hole than in losing itself to the show's characters and plot. The show's engagement with *Hamlet* reflects its other intertextual, citational moments, including sometimes obscure, sly references to *My Mother the Car* (1965–1966) ("My Mother, the Car" 1:8), *Mystery Science Theater 3000* (1988–1999) ("A New Start" 4:5), and various projects of Imagine Entertainment.

Briefly, the Fox/Netflix comedy follows the story of the Bluth family, or to quote the introduction: "This is the story of a wealthy family who lost everything, and the one son who had no choice but to keep them all together." The very first episode sets up this family struggle with the arrest of their patriarch, George Sr., at a Bluth Company party. Michael Bluth, who expected to be named his father's successor, is thrown into the role of keeping his very dysfunctional family together and keeping the family business afloat. The series' title applies equally to each of the family members, Michael included; the family's arrested development makes them self-absorbed, manipulative, and incredibly naive. Intergenerational family dynamics and incestual undertones abound in this family. There are no heroes here.

The overtly Shakespearean material in *Arrested Development* consists primarily of one episode, "Bringing Up Buster" (1:3), in which cousins George Michael and Maeby (along with Steve Holt) perform in the school's rendition of *Much Ado About Nothing*, directed by Maeby's father Tobias. The romantic mishaps of the play, coupled with the direct mention of Renaissance theater norms in which female roles were played by boys (Cue Tobias: "Did you know that in Shakespeare's day, that the women's roles were played by men? Fancy that!"), fits with the show's themes of acting across gender norms. Tobias, a character known not only for his Never Nude problem but also for constant homosexual double entendres, confuses parts. He originally casts Maeby as Beatrice and Steve Holt as Benedick, but then, through a series of mix-ups, reverses the roles, making George Michael into Benedick and Steve Holt into Beatrice. He thinks he is playing Cupid, matching up his nephew George Michael with Steve Holt. In reality, though, George Michael volunteered for the play only because of his forbidden, taboo love interest: his cousin Maeby. Tobias eventually resolves the mix-up by matching Maeby with the more suitable partner, Steve Holt, later revealed to be yet another cousin. While the show's overtly Shakespearean material is contained to that classic high school scenario of staging the school play, the humor it draws from taboo topics marks another thematic similarity with Shakespeare's oeuvre. One need look only at *Much Ado* to recognize the double entendre and sexual innuendo that Shakespeare deploys. *Arrested Development* takes part in this longstanding tradition of using comedy to push the envelope.

Other moments in the series also allude gently to *Hamlet*, though not explicitly engaging in the Ghost meme narrative arc. One such moment is the one-off quotation in which Michael and Maggie Lizer quote what they take to be the 7th commandment: "Be true to thineself and to thine own self be true" ("Justice Is Blind" 1:18), a Shakespeare-speak paraphrase of Polonius' line "This above all: to thine own self be true." The show also alludes to the Jacobean revenge genre through the revelation that George Sr. was the 1970s serial killer "The Muffin Man" who killed his children's teachers with baskets of poisoned muffins ("S.O.B.s" 3:9), though this detail more properly resembles Thomas Middleton's *The Revenger's Tragedy*. Finally, the recurring reference to "Uncle-Father Oscar" echoes Hamlet's reference to his "uncle-father and aunt-mother."

In contrast to these passing references, the show's largely unacknowledged Ghost meme material carries across the entire series, influencing both plot and character development. George Sr. functions as the Ghost who haunts his son(s). Even though he remains alive throughout the series (in spite of a fake Mexican funeral and burial), his presence (and frequent absence) serves to prevent his sons from ever actually taking control of the company. His sons keep getting called up to run the company, but George Sr. eventually returns to put them in their places. George Sr.'s haunting qualities transcend to his physical location in the attic of the Bluth family model home, reinforcing the verticality often associated with *Hamlet* (see Olivier and Zeffirelli film adaptations for examples). As family members go about their days, their father's spirit dresses in outdated maternity clothes and hosts tea parties for dolls he finds in attic boxes while simultaneously making demands of his children.

If George Sr. is the Ghost equivalent (albeit deeply flawed and very much alive), then one must ask whom he haunts. In many ways, the series sets up Michael as the show's main character, and thus, logically, the Hamlet analogue. And, indeed, Michael portrays some of these traits: he is the son who holds the family together after his father's first disappearance (an arrest) and later his (faked) death. Michael attempts to be the voice of reason throughout the series, and clearly he sees himself as the sanest family member. Yet, as the show repeatedly reveals, his delusional behavior and self-absorption rivals that of his siblings. In spite of his insistence to his son, George Michael, that family is the most important thing, he frequently criticizes his family and threatens to leave them.

Though Michael may seem to be the protagonist (and Michael certainly sees himself in this role), the other brothers(-in-law) can equally be described as Hamlet-like. Youngest son Buster, for example, represents the Oedipal angles of the storyline; he is the coddled son who, through seasons-worth of Freudian slips and erotic references to his mother, clearly demonstrates both the Oedipal desire as well as the need to remove the father (and uncle) from the picture. In season four, when Lucille is incarcerated, Buster hunts for alternative mother-figures, beginning with a stuffed doll of Lucille, then trying out Lucille Austero (his mother's best frenemy), Army, and the aptly-named Ophelia Love ("Off the Hook" 4:14). Buster experiences a crisis of father-identification as he learns that his father's twin brother, Oscar, is his biological father and thus his Uncle-Father Oscar. His mother's ongoing affairs with both men, as well as his own paternal confusion, mean that Buster must try to supplant multiple father figures in the battle for his mother's affections. Beyond these Oedipal overtones, Buster spends years of his life in school, studying such esoteric subjects as medieval agrarian economies and cartography. Like Hamlet, who was studying at Wittenberg at the time of King Hamlet's death, Buster discontinues his studies when the family is thrown into crisis.

Gob (George Oscar Bluth) puts on the more melancholy aspects of Hamlet's personality. He takes on the names of both the father and uncle, and his personality reflects both the vanity of George Sr. and the self-loathing of Oscar. He is the outcast son, referred to as Lucille's least favorite offspring. He tries to make up for his family status by womanizing and through his magic career, but he inevitably fails in these ventures. Gob is the Hamlet of "To be or not to be" though his reflections are staged not in terms of an actor-ly monologue but with Gob staring into the distance while Simon & Garfunkel lyrics play in the background. Whereas Gob takes on Hamlet's ennui, son-in-law Tobias exhibits the dramatic side of Hamlet's persona. Tobias' manic character resulted in him abandoning his career as a therapist to become an actor, in spite of his complete lack of acting skill. Tobias is pulled in multiple directions, torn between his family and his desire to act. In order to obtain a part playing George Sr. in an episode of the reality series *Scandalmakers*, Tobias sells the rights to his family. While preparing for the role though, the real George Sr. comes back into the picture, giving him notes on the correct way to play the part and insisting that Tobias play him "like a man" ("Motherboy XXX" 2:13).

By each taking on one facet of Hamlet's character, these four brothers form a composite sketch. And in each of these personas, the brothers are beholden to and haunted by the "ghost" of George Sr. Each exists in a state of arrested development produced by a combination of withheld affection, lack of trust, and general family trauma at the hands of their distant, then absent father. When they think their father has died, they have difficulty expressing their grief, which is inconvenient since George Sr. eavesdrops on his funeral from the attic. As each gradually becomes aware of George Sr.'s presence, each must find a way to appease him but none can ever succeed. *Arrested Development* repackages the narrative of *Hamlet*, reducing the sons to a state of indecision and inaction due to the death, disappearance, and subsequent reappearance of the father figure. The Bluth sons remain trapped in a circular narrative that resembles one of Gob's roofie circles; every time one might break free from the family drama, he is drawn back into pattern of repetition and failure.

This *Hamlet*-like Ghost meme plays out in a show that in its narrative structure and thematic resonances embodies the theories of the memetic. That is to say, even as *Arrested Development* contains an example of a Shakespearean meme, the themes and structure of the series help to define how memes work, demonstrating a symbiotic relationship between the theory and the analysis. *Arrested Development* often seems to be caught up in a roofie circle full of looping narratives, confusion based on doubling of roles, characters, personalities, or words, and an investment in the processes of theater and therapy, models of a theory of surrogation that is also emblematic of memes in general. The series is invested in multiple forms of repetition simultaneously, and the storylines, though often tied together, frequently devolve into a dizzying array of references, performances, and interconnections. These qualities, groundbreaking in *Arrested Development* but increasingly common in twenty-first century television characterized by "episodic seriality" (Mittell), reflect the movement of memes in culture. So, even as the series offers the alert reader a version of the *Hamlet* story that may be referred to as a meme, it simultaneously reinforces the mechanisms that make memetic principles a worthy object of study.

Arrested Development, as a series, demonstrates an obsession with and anxiety about twins, doubling, and repetition, which is fitting for a show exemplifying the work of memes. The show repeatedly emphasizes a doubling of, and thus confusion of, family roles, perhaps to be expected in a family with arrested development. This doubling of family roles includes an Uncle-Father Oscar, kissing cousins, and fathers, sons, and brothers sleeping with the same women. In particular, when it comes to sex, the brothers (and fathers) are often interchangeable. Furthermore, there is a proliferation of twins (George Sr. and Oscar), mistaken twins (Michael and Lindsay), missing twins, Andy Richter twins, and campus twin clubs. Several non-twin characters also insist on their sameness: Michael suggests repeatedly that he and George Michael are just like twins, rather than father and son, and Gob plays a game of professional one-upping with fellow magician Tony Wonder that devolves into the repeated insistence of "same!" Words and phrases are also part of this ongoing play with sameness, including such memorable moments as the bees/beads incident and the Gothic Castle/Gothic Asshole debacle, and double meanings, such as George Sr.'s mantra: "There is always money in the banana stand" ("Top Banana" 1:2). The Netflix season (season four) is particularly obsessed with twinning and doubling, even as it insists on being the "same" as the original series which aired seven years earlier on a different network. This repeated insistence on the sameness of two slightly (or very) different people, words, or images embodies the spirit of the meme, which circulates through a combination of repetition and (often subtle) repackaging.

Furthermore, the show's interest in doubling extends to two processes of doubling and repetition that are brought up repeatedly by the series: therapy and theatricality. According to Abigail De Kosnik, television has historically been bound up with theater and therapy. While the theatricality inherent to both theater and therapy should lead to individual self-knowledge, in *Arrested Development* that path towards self-knowledge is always thwarted. Both theater and therapy partake in a repetition compulsion that ends in a loop of failure and shame. Here, Joseph Roach's explanation of "surrogation" might be particularly helpful. Roach writes that:

> In the life of a community, the process of surrogation does not begin or end but continues as actual or perceived vacancies occur in the network of relations that constitutes the social fabric. Into the cavities created by loss through death or

other forms of departure, I hypothesize, survivors attempt to fit satisfactory alternates. Because collective memory works selectively, imaginatively, and often perversely, surrogation rarely if ever succeeds...The intended substitute either cannot fulfill expectations, creating a deficit, or actually exceeds them, creating a surplus [2].

For Roach, the ongoing process of surrogation attempts to cover over communal wounds stemming from death, departure, or trauma, and performance represents one such type of replacement act; it "stands in for an elusive entity that it is not but that it must vainly aspire both to embody and to replace" (3–4), making it another form of circulation not grounded in an original. So, while performance, such as the performance of theater or of therapy, attempts to substitute for some type of loss or trauma, it cannot replace. Theater and therapy can only ever supplement. In a way, the idea of surrogation also gets at the concept of the meme, always supplementing and adding to without erasing the "original." Indeed, the original itself becomes irrelevant as surrogation constantly supplements for an original that does not exist.

In *Arrested Development*, the failed attempts at both acting and therapy exemplify this theory of surrogation and become interchangeable enterprises within the series. The two processes are exemplified in the character of Tobias, who is both a failed therapist and a failed actor. Tobias quits his career as "analrapist" (analyst+therapist) in order to pursue an acting career, though most of his actor-ly moments are variations on pseudo–Shakespeare-speak or poorly executed improv exercises, in which he adds "Yes, and..." in response to other characters. When Tobias returns to his career and works at Austerity, a drug rehabilitation facility run by Argyle Austero, he ultimately cancels group therapy in order to produce a (very bad) musical version of *The Fantastic Four*. Tobias is simultaneously a poor therapist and a misguided actor, going so far as to mistake a methadone clinic for a method acting class. Tobias constantly cycles back and forth between the authority of each career, alternately citing his expertise as a therapist or as an actor. Yet, in spite of De Kosnik's argument that theater and therapy, as Foucauldian "technologies of the self," should produce self-knowledge, neither performative mode offers Tobias any opportunities for growth. He is eternally stuck in a wildly spiraling performative mode that offers no cathartic relief or resolution, just endless repetition and failure.

Thematically, each of these instances of repetition, doubling, and interchangeability as they relate to twins, mistaken identities, theater, and therapy converge in season four. In this season, the narrative becomes increasingly circular, taking part in its own "roofie circle," a phrase that describes how Gob, known for making bad decisions, repeatedly ingests "Forget-Me-Now" pills in order to live with his shame. As the narrator explains:

And soon Gob found himself experiencing what on the street is referred to as a "roofie circle" whereby a roofie is taken the day after a degrading event, too late to erase the memory of the degrading event itself, but not too late to erase the prior day's attempt to erase the event. Thus, with no memory of taking the roofie but the memory of the event very much alive, the victim of the roofie circle finds himself constantly trying to re-erase the memory but only succeeds in erasing the memory of the attempt to erase the memory. Days turn into weeks, weeks turn into months, as relationships grow testy. And what begins in shame almost always ends in a Mexican hospital with stage 4 syphilis ["Colony Collapse" 4:7].

Gob's roofie circles are attempts at moving on by forgetting, but as with all of the show's neuroses and pathologies, resolution is denied. The roofie circle is symptomatic of season four's narrative style, in which the same story is told from different angles across fifteen episodes. One Coast Guard station scene comes back eight different times, and the audience gradually learns the relevance of each *mise-en-scène* detail from the first iteration, from Tobias' freewheeling vocal performance to the background sound of coughing. In *Arrested Development*, there is no background; all details are potentially relevant. In fact, the process of catching background details and vague references and then making connections has become an Internet pastime, a guilty pleasure for viewers caught up in their own fan culture loop.

This doubling and repetition compulsion that we see in *Arrested Development* in general and particularly in season four's narrative roofie circles loops right back to meme theory and the compulsion to revisit, rewrite, revise, and rework. As Shifman writes, all memes are works of creative repackaging that still retain the memory of the old meme. Revision doesn't erase the history; it only succeeds in producing a new spin on the old story. So, when shows like *Arrested Development* take part in the Ghost meme (either consciously or unconsciously), they take part in this process of repetition and doubling. *Arrested Development* repackages the Ghost meme and, through this replication, extends the longevity and fecundity of the Ghost meme, though with varying degrees of copying-fidelity. The extended longevity and fecundity leads to the meme being taken up by other artifacts and other genres, ensuring that the Shakespearean narrative will continue to appear "accidentally" in the future.

The presence of the Ghost meme in *Arrested Development* complicates an understanding of what is or is not Shakespeare, an issue that must constantly be addressed in a post-textual era. The show's narrative and its meta-narrative can be described as both Shakespearean and not–Shakespearean. The meme terminology allows for a more flexible form of fidelity to the Shakespearean source because it allows for an unacknowledged *and* fragmented form of narrative uptake. The Ghost meme, like other ideas, narratives, and literary themes, circulates constantly in culture. Because it contains a certain "stickiness," that ongoing circulation results in the frequent uptake of the Ghost meme in popular culture. This uptake then ensures the meme's long-term survival. This circular process continues indefinitely until the meme dies out. In the case of Shakespeare, it appears that this will not be the case for a very long time.

Works Cited

Aunger, Robert. *The Electric Meme: A New Theory of How We Think*. New York: Simon and Schuster, 2002. Print.

Blackmore, Susan. *The Meme Machine*. Oxford: Oxford University Press, 1999. Print.

Bortolotti, Gary R. and Linda Hutcheon. "On the Origin of Adaptations: Rethinking Fidelity Discourse and "Success"—Biologically." *New Literary History* 38.3 (2007): 443–458. Print.

Carlson, Marvin. *The Haunted Stage: The Theatre as Memory Machine*. Ann Arbor: The University of Michigan Press, 2001. Print.

Dawkins, Richard. *The Selfish Gene*. 2nd ed. Oxford: Oxford University Press, 1989. Print.

De Kosnik, Abigail. "Drama is the Cure for Gossip: Television's Turn to Theatricality in a Time of Media Transition." *Modern Drama* 53.3 (2010): 370–389. Print.

Dennett, Daniel C. *Darwin's Dangerous Idea: Evolution and the Meaning of Life*. London: Simon and Schuster, 1995. Print.

Distin, Kate. *The Selfish Meme: A Critical Reassessment*. Cambridge: Cambridge University Press, 2005. Print.

Hutcheon, Linda. *A Theory of Adaptation*. New York: Routledge, 2006. Print.

Lanier, Douglas M. "Post-Textual Shakespeare." *Shakespeare Survey* 64 (2011): 145–162. Print.

Mittell, Jason. "Narrative Complexity in Contemporary American Television." *The Velvet Light Trap* 58 (2006): 29–40. Print.

Roach, Joseph. *Cities of the Dead: Circum-Atlantic Performance*. New York: Columbia University Press, 1996. Print.

Shifman, Limor. *Memes in Digital Culture*. Cambridge: The MIT Press, 2014. Kindle.

The Family Business

Bluths, Corleones and the American Dream

KRISTIN M. BARTON

When it was announced that the fourth season of *Arrested Development* was headed to Netflix in an anthologized format, reactions from both fans and critics were mixed. For some, having the Bluths back in any format was a win, while for others the change of format signaled a departure from the blueprint that made the first three seasons so beloved. In addressing fans' concerns, series creator and writer/director Mitchell Hurwitz offered this comparison:

> It's difficult to make this comparison because it sounds self-aggrandizing and I don't mean it that way, but I remember when *The Godfather II* came out. People were like, "What? What is this? I want to see *The Godfather* where they shoot people, not this thing where they talk about Cuba" [Greene].

What fans of *The Godfather* films (1972, 1974, 1990) have come to appreciate, in retrospect, is that the elements that were initially considered un*Godfather*-like in the second film were necessary in order to convey the complete story of a man that built an empire and the ramifications those actions had on his family. The trilogy's director, Francis Ford Coppola, even stated that he wrote *The Godfather Part II* as the second part of the "family saga" of the Corleones, and that rather than viewing the second film as a sequel he sees the two films as a single story. Similarly, in order to continue the interwoven and multilayered story of the Bluths, Hurwitz abandoned the more traditional sitcom format for season four and elected instead to tell the story in a new format, one that would allow the audience to catch up on what each member of the Bluth family had been doing for the previous seven years while also servicing nine

163

characters the audience had grown to love. This was certainly born, to a degree, out of necessity, given the actors' busy work schedules, but it once again emphasizes how *Arrested Development* continues to break many of the sitcom tropes that have made the genre stagnant for so many years.

But storytelling techniques and narrative structures aside, comparing the Bluth and Corleone families provides insight into family dynamics, particularly as they apply in family-centric businesses. It is surprising that despite their contrasting genres (comedy versus drama), different media (television versus film) and methods of delivery (68 episodes versus three feature films), the depictions of these characters and the familial roles they play are remarkably consistent. In looking at these two highly-regarded examples of televisual and cinematic art, viewers gain insight into the confluence of felonious business practices, the attainment of the American Dream, and the impact these have on family.

Comparing Bananas and Oranges

On the surface it may seem absurd to compare the petty and selfish Bluths from *Arrested Development* to the violent and homicidal Corleone family from *The Godfather* films. However, closer inspection reveals more similarities exist between the two than one might expect. While the following are certainly more coincidence than intentional, it is still worth noting some of the numerous ways in which the members of the Bluth and Corleone families parallel one another in order to lay the groundwork for later analysis of their family dynamics. Indeed, the fact that these familial roles so closely align without any premeditation on the part of Hurwitz or his writers suggests a level of authenticity with regard to how these types of characters might exist in similar real-world circumstances.

The Patriarchs (George Bluth, Sr./Vito Corleone)

Two powerful and strong-willed men, George Sr. and Vito are the heads of their family businesses until they are forced (by incarceration or being critically shot) to relinquish control. Both have legitimate business ventures that serve as covers for their illegal activities, and while they each claims to put family above everything else, they continue to operate businesses that place their families in constant legal (if not mortal) jeopardy.

The Matriarchs (Lucille Bluth/Carmela Corleone)

Lucille and Carmela are both mothers of four children (both of whom loosely adopt a fifth; Lucille through her spiteful adoption of Annyong and Carmela through her care of a young and neglected Tom Hagen). While neither matriarch is part of their family business in any official capacity, both wield significant influence over their families and manipulate relationships within each. In discussing Carmela's role in *The Godfather* (but being applicable to Lucille as well), Tom Santopietro argues that this depiction of motherhood is dictated by "an Old World patriarchy in which women remain at home and carve out their sphere of influence on the smaller stage of family life" (205).

The Eldest Sons (Gob Bluth/Sonny Corleone)

Both Gob and Sonny, as the eldest sons, see it as their birthrights to take over the family businesses from their fathers, which both do for a brief time with clear ineptitude. Their inability to serve as leaders within the families largely stems from their impulsive tempers and their tendencies to make rash decisions.

The Responsible Sons (Michael Bluth/Michael Corleone)

While it may be coincidence that both sons are named Michael, they share an initial unwillingness to involve themselves in the family businesses, or at least the more corrupt aspects of them. Both attempt to divorce themselves from their unscrupulous families by striking out on their own (to Sitwell Enterprises and by joining the Marines, respectively), but as their families begin to disintegrate and problems arise that the other family members can't properly deal with, they each become, to use a familiar phrase, "the one son who had no choice but to keep them all together." Despite the moral high ground they initially claim to stand upon, each deceives, manipulates, and intentionally causes harm (either emotionally or mortally) to members of their immediate family.

The Younger Sons (Buster Bluth/Fredo Corleone)

Although Fredo is not the youngest of the Corleone brothers, he is the most childlike and naive in many ways. Both he and Buster ultimately have little interest in (and even less competency for) the family business, which, to some degree, leads them both to betray their families. Fredo turns on Michael and his family by working with Hyman Roth, while Buster is willing to turn over evidence to the authorities in exchange for a grilled cheese sandwich ("Justice Is Blind" 1:18). In the end, however, both brothers are basically powerless against their families. Also, both have ill-fated experiences on boats (Buster falls off of one, Fredo is killed on one).

The Daughters (Lindsay Bluth-Fünke/Connie Corleone)

While not actually involved with their families' businesses, both Lindsay and Connie enjoy reaping the rewards that their families' illegal activities afford them. Both feel entitled to the wealth they have not earned and play the part of loving sister when it is necessary in order to get what they want. Each is a neglectful mother to her child(ren) and marry men their families disapprove of.

The Sons-in-Law (Tobias Fünke/Carlo Rizzi)

The Godfather opens on Connie and Carlo's wedding day, the two meeting as a result of Carlo's emigration from Nevada to escape legal troubles. Similarly, while technically already part of the family, Tobias is more fully thrust into the world of the Bluths after losing his medical license due to his negligence in administering CPR to a person he erroneously thought to be having a heart attack. So as outsiders, both men are brought more fully into the family folds as a result of legal issues. Both men also have numerous marital issues, such Tobias' latent homosexuality and Carlo's physical abuse of Connie. Ultimately, both are largely disliked by their wives' families.

The Grandsons (George Michael Bluth/Anthony Corleone)

Without much argument, the grandsons in the Bluth and Corleone clans are perceived as the most moral and upstanding members of their families. Neither have any aspirations to be involved in the family businesses (despite George Michael's short tenure as Mr. Manager), and seek to strike out on their own using their passions for music—through the creation of a woodblock app and as an opera singer—to satisfy their creative impulses.

The Granddaughters (Maeby Fünke/Mary Corleonoe)

Maeby and Mary are given the least amount of screen time in their respective series, which results in their limited roles and interactions within their families. However, both initiate forbidden romantic relationships with their cousins (even if Maeby only does it to teach her parents a lesson) which result in strong reciprocal feelings from their male counterparts.

While on the surface these similarities are striking, it is a deeper examination that provides a more interesting look at the intersection of family and business. Whether committing murder or "light treason," audiences continue to root for these corrupt characters despite their continued immoral and illegal behaviors. This can, in part, be better explained by exploring the concept of the antihero; characters that are inherently flawed and, by almost every acceptable social standard, should be viewed as antagonists, not protagonists. The convention of the antihero is hardly a new development, and many notable and popular characters have risen from stories that feature lead characters circumventing (or often completely disregarding) the law to achieve their goals. These characters are peppered throughout the history of literature, and more recently have appeared in films such as *Death Wish* (1974) and *Falling Down* (1993) and are embodied in comic book characters such as The Punisher and Wolverine. On television, antiheroes have proven to be particularly popular as they have been featured on many critically-acclaimed series such as *The Sopranos* (1999–2007), *Dexter* (2006–2013), *Breaking Bad* (2008–2013), and *Sons of Anarchy* (2008–2014) among others. Audience attachment to and love for these characters embodies the type of cognitive dissonance media consumers face when cheering on characters that routinely steal, sell drugs, and commit murder. As Brett Martin notes, "These [are] characters whom, conventional wisdom had once insisted, Americans would never allow into their living rooms: unhappy, morally compromised, complicated, deeply human" (4). Dean Tavoularis, the production designer for *The Godfather* trilogy, in making a case for why audiences root for Vito Corleone and his unlawful offspring, makes a similar argument: "[Coppola] wanted the audience to see that these guys were in many ways like us—that's the paradox of it. Like Hitler holding a party...You can't relate to a guy blowing someone's brains out, but you can relate to a guy making spaghetti" (Lebo 92). By the same notion, George Sr., along with the rest of the Bluths, enjoy the paradoxical position of being depicted as generally reprehensible human beings while at the same time engendering the good will of the audience, which is to say that we largely root for them to succeed even when they engage in activities we find immoral or unethical. Because they experience some of the same trials and tribulations we all do—addiction, marital problems, financial difficulties—the Bluths are people that we can (unfortunately) relate to.

With all this said, the characters from *Arrested Development* and *The*

Godfather are worthy of further exploration for two reasons. First, both of these fictional families feature multi-generational criminal lineages, where behaviors are passed down from parent to child (George Sr., his daughter Lindsay, and granddaughter Maeby are each scam artists and extortionists). Second, the impetus for the continued illegal activities of both families initially or primarily stems from the family businesses, which were once symbols of power and prestige but both of which eventually collapse into near ruin. By exploring the complex relationships that emerge between family, business, and ethics, we can see that these two narratives feature families whose bonds are continually strained given the extreme adversity they routinely endure, but that at the same time represent a new way of looking at the traditional nuclear family.

The Family Unit

Both *The Godfather* series and *Arrested Development* revolve around the conflict that arises between trying to keep a family together and the achievement of personal success through the acquisition of money and power. This conflict is best exemplified by the eldest sons and how they balance the responsibilities of family with their inherited leadership of an organization in turmoil. During his time as acting don in *The Godfather*, Sonny wreaks havoc by lashing out at members of the other families in retribution for his father's shooting without stopping to consider the impact these actions will have on the safety of both his biological and criminal families. Although less violent, Gob spends much of his time as president of the Bluth Company acting selfishly (redecorating his office to include a pool table) while shrugging off any actual work that might help the company succeed, thereby earning money for his family and providing financial stability. Both choose to act out of selfish desires rather than act in the best interests of either the family or the business.

While Sonny and Gob exhibit impulsive and agitable tendencies, these are not qualities learned from their measured and level-headed fathers. Both George Sr. and Vito generally counsel and practice composure in the face of adversity, most noticeably in the calm both men exhibit after being incarcerated (George Sr.) and being shot (Vito). For Don Vito, his measured disposition is likely the result of an embattled and turbulent childhood, plagued with the trauma of seeing his family killed and setting out to America on his own at age nine: There is little left in the world that can break a man who's already experienced so much (the exception to this being his breakdown after learning of Sonny's death). Although George Sr.'s childhood is never shown over the course of *Arrested Development*'s four seasons, viewers *are* given a look into his and Vito's early forays into their illegal and immoral business practices, which again affords us with some understanding as to why these men behave the way they do. During season four of *Arrested Development*, a young George Sr. (played by Seth Rogen) creates Babytock as a way to sell the loud, metronomic timers from his banned Cornballers, providing insight into how his manipulative business practices emerged. In a strangely similar way, *The Godfather Part II* flashes back to a young Vito Corleone (played by Robert De Niro) and reveals the catalyst for his first forays into theft, hijacking, and murder. Yet for all the power and notoriety their status brings them, George Sr. and Vito possess relatively calm demeanors. They are men who walk softly but carry big sticks. Or, more appropriately, the men who work for them have big sticks. Careful not to get their own hands dirty, the family patriarchs have the means to take care of problems, such as George Sr. hiring T-Bone ("the flamer") to burn down the family storage unit in order to destroy evidence ("Top Banana" 1:2). Coincidentally, both men also have agents who use dismemberment as a method of "teaching lessons": J. Walter Weatherman's missing arm and the decapitated horse's head found in Jack Woltz's bed each manage to convey messages to those who refused to listen to reasonable requests.

But despite their ruthlessness when it comes to their business endeavors, George Sr. and Vito have a passion for life that their children do not share. They enjoy the simple pleasures of good food (such as fresh fruit and ice cream sandwiches), and exhibit a passion for family—particularly their wives—that is unmatched by their children. As Vito tells Johnny Fontane in *The Godfather*, "A man who doesn't spend time with his family can never be a real man." In fact, it is only after their sons take over for them that family unity begins to unravel, highlighting the discrepancy in the importance of family within a single generation. This isn't to say that the patriarchs themselves don't have family issues (George Sr. and Oscar have never been particularly close), nor is it to say that the subsequent generation shoulders all the blame (Michael Bluth can hardly be blamed for the Bluth Company's financial ruin that creates so much havoc within the family), but while both Michaels focus their energies on solidifying their families' business ventures, their lack of guidance with regard to family relationships causes more serious problems for each of them in the long term.

This is, perhaps, one of the reasons that Michael Corleone moves his family from New York to the estate at Lake Tahoe. With family issues surfacing, as well as the need for increased security after murdering the dons of the Five Families at the end of the first film, Michael's motivation in relocating is, at least in part, as a means of regaining control. This seems to conform with Coppola's intention, who stated that, "The whole idea of a family living in a compound—that was all based on Hyannisport [*sic*]" (Santopietro 179), a reference to the Kennedys' compound in Massachusetts. Isolated and secluded, the Kennedys, like the Corleones, preferred to quarter off their family from the outside world in order to control not only who got in, but also what got out. Santopietro makes the case that "the Corleones chose to live in a compound so that family could form a buffer against the outside world" (180). Weary of rival families and various members of the law enforcement community, the Corleones have essentially elected to disengage from society in order to protect themselves. By contrast, the Bluths have also been insulated from society, but, unlike the Corleones who purposefully shun society, for the Bluths it is society that has shunned them. Resigned to their singular model home in the vast expanse that will someday become Sudden Valley, the Bluths have no neighbors and remain sequestered away from the world despite multiple attempts to raise the capital to build on the barren land. When, in season four, Sudden Valley is completed, it remains in isolation as a modern-day leper colony for sex offenders that, like the Bluths, decent society has excommunicated. If, as Coppola has stated, *The Godfather* is a film about "a king with three sons" (Santopietro 179), then the Lake Tahoe compound is a fitting kingdom for a monarch with legitimate power. It is also fitting, then, that the Bluths, whose patriarch's power is negligible and whose sons are hardly princes, find their "kingdom" to be a shoddily constructed model home outfitted with HomeFill products. While the Corleones have influence and power, the Bluths' kingdom is (as Gob might say) an illusion.

But the Bluths' collective delusion about their current social status (they continue to hold to the belief that they are still upper-crust elites) does little to diminish the family bonds that tie them together. In fact, it could be argued that their struggles actually strengthen the family unity. It is fitting that the one factor that continually brings the family back together are get-rich schemes and the subsequent legal troubles that ensue. This cycle of recidivism ultimately raises an issue that has sparked debate among psychologists, sociologists, and geneticists for decades: the influence of nature versus nurture on one's personality. Is environment responsible for the overwhelming degenerative behaviors exhibited by the Bluths and Corleones, or is it hereditary, whereby the criminal ethos is passed down from one generation to the next like a dominant gene?

The debate finds its roots in the scientific and philosophical discoveries made hundreds of years ago, in this case centered around two English scholars. Although the term "nature versus nurture" as we know it today was first coined by Francis Galton in his 1875 paper, *The history of twins*, the roots of this debate actually go back much farther. The "nature" argument derives from Charles Darwin (Galton's cousin) and his seminal work *The Origin of Species*. Darwin's research, in part, argues that certain behaviors and characteristics within species, when found to be advantageous, can be genetically passed on through subsequent generations. Conversely, the "nurture" argument stems from, among others, John Locke and his 1689 publication *An Essay Concerning Human Understanding*. In it, Locke puts forth the following proposition: "Let us suppose the mind to be, as we say, white paper, void of all characters, without any ideas; how comes it to be furnished?" (53). Locke's argument, then, asserts that humans are born with a mind that is a blank slate (a *tabula rasa*, as it would come to be known), and that experience, not genetics, is what ultimately shapes a person's mental, physical, and behavioral qualities.

To explore this issue in the world of *Arrested Development*, one needs look no further than Lindsay Bluth-Fünke in order to see the complexity inherent in both the argument and determining an answer. For virtually the entirety of the first three seasons of the show, Lindsay (we are told) is Michael's twin and, like the rest of the family, genetically a Bluth. During this time we see strong evidence to suggest that nature is responsible for her behavior, most noticeable in her interactions with her mother, Lucille. Across numerous scenes, their jab-and-parry banter and their proclivity for hurtful insults suggests that these are innate characteristics in their personalities, and despite living on opposite coasts just prior to the series' premiere episode—and thus having little exposure to one another—each maintains a similar antagonistic, biting tone in their interactions with one another. Lindsay is also a habitual liar, a trait so ingrained in the family's DNA that it is found in every member of the Bluth family, including the most upstanding member, George Michael. As the narrator notes when George Michael first lies to his father and Maeby about his Fakeblock software, "[George Michael] found himself suddenly and effortlessly tapping into a long inbred instinct for lying, a Bluth taking his first steps in deceit" ("It Gets Better" 4:13). However, as season three (and potentially the series) drew to a close, it was revealed that Lindsay was, in fact, adopted, dismissing the idea that her narcissistic personality and compulsive lying were hereditary traits. Instead, we now view Lindsay as a textbook example for the "nurture" argument, having developed these traits as a result of her environment. Instead of being born this way, now it appears that being raised by a sardonic alcoholic has resulted in Lindsay becoming the same. Regardless of her biological lineage, however, Lucille leaves no doubt as to Lindsay's place in the family when she tells Lindsay during the Cinco de Quatro festival, "I'm a Bluth, and so are you" ("Red Hairing" 4:8).

Since Lindsay is both Lucille's biological daughter and adopted daughter at the same time (unbeknownst to the audience), she functions as a sort of personification of Schrödinger's cat, whereby she was a product of nature and nurture simultaneously. This type of duality, as it relates to family relationships, presents itself multiple times over throughout *The Godfather* films and *Arrested Development*. From a psychological standpoint, the juxtaposition of their views on the importance of family and their willingness to hurt family members is the sort of cognitive dissonance that plagues both families. For the Bluths and the Corleones, their proclamations that family is "the most important thing" is in direct conflict with the decisions they make which routinely show that personal attainment (primarily money or power) trumps what is best for the family.

The importance of family in *The Godfather* trilogy is highlighted by a celebration at the opening of each film (Connie's wedding, Anthony's first communion, and Michael being named a Commander of the Order of St. Sebastian), which visually and metaphorically reinforce the theme that "family comes first." However, the festivities in each case are quickly revealed to be camouflage for more important matters: business. To use the original film as an example, even during his daughter's wedding celebration Don Vito sits in his study and coolly listens as supplicants ask for favors. While this may be rooted in tradition and heritage, the requests are, it is safe to assume, predominantly requests for financial assistance, most famously Johnny Fontane's entreaty to help him land a coveted film role. The Corleones continue to pay lip service to the importance of family throughout the film series, but it comes off as superficial when decisions are ultimately made based on what is best for the business, not the family; one would be hard pressed to make a strong case that Michael's decision to have his brother Fredo killed was for the betterment of the family. But when Fredo begins dealing with rival gangster Hyman Roth, Michael handles the situation as he would with any employee who might cross him (Fredo's initial betrayal of the family is a business decision as well, since he decides to work with Roth as a result of being passed over as Vito's successor in lieu of Michael). The combination of the Corleones' criminal activities with the priority of business over family ultimately serves to engulf the family in contempt and mistrust for one another until virtually every relationship has been destroyed. And while the third film does largely deal with Michael's guilt over Fredo's death and the ensuing dissolution of his family, the damage to the family, by that point, is irreparable.

Similar to the opening scenes of each of *The Godfather* films, *Arrested Development*'s pilot episode establishes the Bluths' (or, at least, Michael's) perception of the importance of family almost immediately:

MICHAEL: What comes before anything? What have we always said is the most important thing?
GEORGE MICHAEL: Breakfast.
MICHAEL: Family.
GEORGE MICHAEL: Family, right. I thought you meant of the things you eat.

This exchange can be seen as a microcosm for the larger family issues that permeate the entire series; family *should* be "the most important thing," but oftentimes the Bluths prioritize selfish concerns over secondary issues such as their personal relationships. Even Michael, who the audience is led to believe is above the petty flaws of his parents and siblings, unintentionally causes as much strife within the family as anyone, perhaps best exemplified by engaging in romantic relationships with his brother's girlfriend (Marta) as well as his son's (Rebel). However, Michael does occasionally relish hurting his family, particularly Gob. In the episode "Bringing Up Buster" (1:3), after kicking Gob out of the model home, Michael informs his brother that he can't live in the Bluth Company offices either. Upon hearing the news, Gob asks Michael:

GOB: Is this a business decision, or is it personal? 'Cause if it's business, I'll go away happily. But if it's personal, I'll go away, but I won't be happy.
MICHAEL: It's personal.

Michael Bluth's caustic response to his brother serves as the inverse to Michael Corleone's more pragmatic and indifferent decision to kill drug dealer Virgil Sollozzo and crooked police captain McCluskey, the men responsible for critically shooting his father. When Sonny (ironically) tells Michael to calm down and not to act rashly, Michael coolly responds, "It's not personal Sonny. It's strictly business." In this moment, Michael Corleone transitions from an outsider wanting nothing to do with his family's criminal activities to a vengeful son who will shortly become complexly immersed in the lifestyle he so previously deplored.

Falling from Grace

Michael Corleone initially has no intention of following his father into a life of crime, and makes his position clear in the first film. When Michael is introduced in *The Godfather*, his entire demeanor suggests that he has every intention of foregoing his family's unscrupulous lifestyle to become a law-abiding, model citizen. As Santopietro notes, "With his Ivy League education and military service during World War II, he [Michael] initially reads as the one member of the family who can and will escape the insularity of life within the family compound" (33). Michael even goes so far as to acknowledge his family's illegal behaviors in order to repudiate their actions, as he does when he tells Kay about how his father used intimidation and a death threat to get Johnny Fontane out of a contract. He allays her shock and unease by telling her, "That's my family, Kay. That's not me." This initial dissociation from his family is mirrored by Michael Bluth, who chooses to distance himself from his family's lack of morals with an often skewed perception of events, rationalizing his own immoral behavior as different from his family's. For instance, Michael claims that taking a leather chair from the Bluth Company offices isn't stealing, although George Michael is quick to point out that taking things from the company is why George Sr. is in jail ("Storming the Castle" 1:9). However, just as Michael Corleone is forced to delve into the criminal world inhabited by his late father, so too is Michael Bluth forced to lie, deceive, and prostitute himself for money, as he attempts to do with Lucille Austero in order to defer the repayment of a $700,000 loan ("Flight of the Phoenix" 4:1).

The irony is that in both cases, Vito and George Sr. each actively try to prevent their most promising sons from becoming involved in the illicit empires they have built. After Michael Corleone graduates from college and returns from World War II as a decorated soldier, Vito sees the potential his son has to become a legitimate member of society. At the same time, Vito also recognizes the danger inherent in being a high-ranking member of a mafia family. Rather than encouraging Michael's involvement in crime, Vito expresses his hopes for something more for his son:

> I never wanted this for you. I work my whole life, I don't apologize, to take care of my family. And I refused to be a fool, dancing on the string, held by all those ... big shots. I don't apologize, that's my life, but I thought that when it was your time that you would be the one to hold the strings. Senator Corleone. Governor Corleone, or something...

Similarly, George Sr. wants to keep his son Michael from becoming ensnared in his illegal ventures as well. In the pilot episode of the series, George Sr. announces that his wife Lucille, not Michael, will take over as CEO of the Bluth Company, leaving Michael to question his worth and consider leaving his family for good ("Pilot" 1:1). By the end of the episode, visiting with his father in prison, George Sr. explains to Michael why he wasn't put in charge of the company:

MICHAEL: I was so loyal, I worked so hard. Why didn't you just put me in
 charge?
GEORGE SR.: Michael, listen to me. These guys, the SEC, they've been after me
 for years. I put you in charge, you're going to be wearing one of these orange
 jumpsuits too.
MICHAEL: I could've helped you if you'd told me.
GEORGE SR.: You'd be an accomplice. No, it had to be your mom.

Despite their callous and calculated actions with regard to their business ventures, both Vito and George Sr. are, at heart, fathers who want the best for their sons. They recognize the lives they have chosen are fraught with risk, and enmeshing their sons in those worlds would only serve to cement them into lives they will never be able to escape.

It is, in fact, their wives that offer both of the Michaels the escape they desperately want but ultimately fail to attain. For Michael Corleone, Kay is a non–Italian from New England, giving him a touchstone to a world devoid of his family's criminal empire. For Michael Bluth, his wife Tracey briefly offered him the traditional loving and stable family environment he craves, thereby lessening his dependency on the dysfunctional bonds with the other Bluths. Unfortunately for both men, their wives leave them to the mercy of their family's pull; Kay by divorce, Tracey through death. However, it is through these shortened marriages that both families receive what could be the redeeming factor in resurrecting their family names from the mire of scandals and corruption: grandsons whose purity allow them to transgress beyond the limited scope of the unethical life their families bequeath them.

The grandsons in each family, George Michael and Anthony, are the ones that offer the possibility of redemption for the sins of their parents and grandparents. George Michael's innocence and Anthony's desire for a legitimate career as an opera singer offer the hope that the cyclical nature of their families' corrupt lifestyles can be extinguished. While George Michael does occasionally lie to his father, it is never done for insidious or illegal reasons. For example, during the season four episode "It Gets Better" (4:13), George Michael lies to his father about being stuck in traffic in order to continue his date with Rebel. While certainly a lie, this is the type of behavior we expect from young men trying to break free of their parental bonds, and not the impetus to a life full of illegal behaviors the rest of his family have succumbed to. For Anthony Corleone, it is his decision to abandon law school in favor of a career in opera that allows him to escape the inevitability of his father's life. Presumably, were he to complete law school, it is likely that he would be employed by his father as one of the Corleone family's many lawyers. As Michael says in *The Godfather*

Part III, "I don't need tough guys, I need more lawyers," suggesting that Anthony would have become the legitimate face of an illegitimate organization, like Tom Hagen and B. J. Harrison before him.

Attaining the American Dream

Although the similarities between the two families are striking, in certain ways the Bluths of *Arrested Development* serve as mirror opposites to their Corleone counterparts. Both families aspire to create empires, but where the Corleones largely succeed, the Bluths routinely impede their own success through wanton greed and self-absorption. Both families operate businesses that benefit the entire lineage, even those not directly involved in the day-to-day affairs of the companies. For the Corleones, the legitimate face of their business is as importers of olive oil from Italy, and later, under Michael's leadership, as part of an international real estate company, International Immobiliare. The Bluths, while not nearly as prosperous, also have legitimate business interests in real estate development through the Bluth Company and the more-sentimental-than-profitable banana stand at Newport Beach. This fact alone doesn't mean much, considering that "family business is the most prevalent and pervasive form of business through all of history" (Kenyon-Rouvinez and Ward 1), but it does provide a structure under which both families can conduct their illicit endeavors with a modicum of legitimacy.

This type of legitimate-business camouflage is well known in both fictional and real-life stories of the mafia and their operations, and is one of the many reasons why these organizations are often considered to be, although corrupted, the embodiments of the American Dream. In support of this claim, Martin characterizes "the mob" as "the quintessential American story, a way to talk about both the aspirations and the rot at the nation's core" (63). It certainly doesn't take much imagination to apply that definition to Hurwitz's depiction of the Bluths, perhaps best exemplified by Lindsay and Tobias' extravagant home purchase in season four ("Indian Takes" 4:3). In a flashback to 2006, the couple's "aspirations" include living out the American Dream in a McMansion of their own while at the same time ignoring the "rot" of knowing that without jobs, savings, or any sort of financial plan, they will almost certainly be unable to make any payments on the type of predatory NINJA loan (No Income, No Job, No Assets) that, in the real world, led to the financial collapse of 2007. Tobias' response to extravagant upgrades such as a wine cellar and a double gatehouse ("That way we have it") highlights the absurdity of both the lenders and the borrowers in the bacchanalia of the mid-aughts housing bubble. Tobias and Lindsay have each been insulated from the realities of hard work and the responsibilities of financial planning due to the opulent lifestyle the once prosperous Bluth Company afforded them for so long. In a similar way, this trickle-down version of the American Dream ultimately leads Vito's daughter, Connie, to devolve into a self-centered narcissist and negligent parent. Santopietro notes that as part of her self-indulgent lifestyle, "Connie begins having affairs and pays little or no attention to her own children. The depths to which she has sunk are illustrated by her dalliance with the ill-suited, weak, white-bread Merle Johnson" (186), which is clearly mirrored in Lindsay and her relationship with Marky Bark.

This is all to say that if Don Vito and his family are the quintessential embodiment of the paradigmatic American Dream, then George Sr. and the rest of the Bluths represent a distorted, contemporary version. Whereas the younger Vito takes initiative and works—albeit illegally—in order to provide a better life for his family, the Bluths almost seem to expect that part (the "working") to be taken care of for them. Or, to put it another way, for the Bluths, the American Dream is about *being* wealthy, not achieving wealth, and enjoying the end result without any of the sweat equity that is required.

Conclusion

So what can be taken away from the strong parallels that exist between *Arrested Development* and *The Godfather* films with regard to family and business? Do they serve as cautionary tales about the dangers of greed and avarice? Are they critiques of American culture, suggesting that striving to *attain* the American Dream is better than actually achieving it? At the least, they each seem to send the message to viewers that power (i.e. money) comes at the expense of family. Both the Bluths and Corleones routinely contradict themselves by claiming that family is "the most important thing" while continually causing the family harm in the name of business. Santopietro makes the case that "the corruption of his [Michael Corleone's] business dealings inevitably taints his family" (93), a sentiment that is reflected in *Arrested Development* as Michael Bluth spends most of season four manipulating his family into signing releases for the film he wants to produce about their lives. Despite the fact that the Corleones' power and fortune exponentially increase across the three films, their family surely and irrevocably deteriorates as business takes priority over relationships. Chronologically speaking, from a young Vito Corleone (*née* Andolini) arriving alone at Ellis Island after witnessing his family's murder, to Michael Corleone's multi-million dollar empire, no family has experienced the American Dream as they have, rising from nothing through hard work and determination to earn their place as successful entrepreneurs. However, while serving as the paradigm of success in a business sense, the family is diminished—both in affection for one another and in size as a result of numerous homicides—because of Michael's actions. Contrast this with the steady and constant decline the Bluth Company experiences over the course of the series. From a prosperous home builder to a company mired in suspected illegal activities and financial ruin, the Bluths in many ways represent the antithesis of the American Dream, eschewing hard work for laziness and dependence on others to support them. It is ironic, then, that the family unity and cohesion of both groups can be tracked inversely. In the opening scene of *The Godfather*, Connie's wedding is a resplendent affair with her entire family around her celebrating her new life and supporting her. By the end of *The Godfather Part III*, Michael is alone, longing to atone for his sins while simultaneously being the person most responsible for the dissolution of his family (or in the case of Fredo, the murder of a brother).

By contrast, the Bluths become more united through their deceitful behaviors. In the premiere episode ("Pilot" 1:1), George Michael notes to Maeby that he hasn't seen her or her family in some time, and by the end of the episode, as the SEC boats close in, he laments, "I guess we're going to see you guys even less now." But as the series progresses, the family becomes more intertwined in each other's lives and, in some cases, completely dependent on one another: Who else but his family would bring Pop Pop treats when he's hiding in the attic? Santopietro claims that through *The Godfather*, Coppola demonstrates "the ability to movingly portray intimate, personal concerns within the framework of a sprawling, larger-than-life epic" (112). If this is the case, then the incorporation of the same elements in *Arrested Development* surely makes it a "comedy epic" in a similar way. A comparison between the Bluths of *Arrested Development* and the Corleones of *The Godfather* films underscores the ways that family and business intersect and ultimately influence the characters in these stories. The fact that both are regarded as paradigmatic of their genres (comedic television and dramatic film) suggests that the themes and motifs they exhibit may, to some degree, accurately reflect the human condition.

Works Cited

Greene, Andy. "'Arrested Development' Movie Is Moving Forward." *Rolling Stone*. 26 Aug. 2013. Web. 19 Jan. 2014. http://www.rollingstone.com/movies/news/arrested-develop ment-movie-is-moving-forward-20130826.

Kenyon-Rouvinez, Denise, and John L. Ward. "Introduction and Models." *Family Business Key Issues*. Eds. Denise Kenyon-Rouvinez and John L. Ward. New York: Palgrave MacMillan, 2005. 1–16. Print.

Lebo, Harlan. *The Godfather Legacy: The Untold Story of the Making of the Classic Godfather Trilogy Featuring Never-Before-Published Production Stills*. New York: Simon & Schuster, 2005. Print.

Locke, John. *An Essay Concerning Human Understanding*. 1690. London: W. Tegg, 1849. Print.

Martin, Brett. *Difficult Men: Behind the Scenes of a Creative Revolution*. New York: Penguin, 2013. Print.

Santopietro, Tom. *The Godfather Effect: Changing Hollywood, America, and Me*. New York: St. Martin's Press, 2012. Print.

The Kafkaesque in the Trial of George Bluth

MATTHEW GANNON

There exist unexpected yet strong connections between *Arrested Development* and Franz Kafka's 1925 existentialist novel *The Trial*, which can be read as an extensive allegory concerning the anxieties of human existence and the challenges of forging a self and subjectivity in a world that is simultaneously too social (in that it strips away an authentic sense of individuality through industrialism, social media, and commodification of experience) as well as frustratingly anti-social and alienating (via technological mediation and dehumanizing political superstructures). At the center of this allegory is the endless trial of George Bluth, Sr., which mirrors the endless trial of Josef K. in Kafka's *The Trial*. Both *The Trial* and *Arrested Development* interrogate notoriously slippery concepts of guilt, crime, and punishment through an existential analysis. With *Arrested Development*, it is unclear precisely what George Sr. is even accused of, never mind whether or not he is guilty of anything. Towards the beginning of the series George Sr. is presumed guilty even by his own children, and they take solace in the fact that the legal system is rational and comprehensible. As the series progresses, however, it becomes obvious that the legal system is erratic and irrational, and perhaps George Sr.'s guilt is not entirely certain after all. Nevertheless, as the series progresses it also becomes clear that while George Sr. may not be guilty of specific crimes in a legal sense, his moral and social innocence is thrown into doubt, and the concept of guilt expands into such terrains as the political and the existential.

Existence under modernity (and postmodernity), *Arrested Development* claims, is itself part of an endless crime and punishment feedback loop. In this cycle, human existence is considered a crime, and social alienation and limited consciousness of the political and existential subject are the punishments. *Arrested Development* proposes an overcoming of this imprisonment qua social alienation through the transformative capabilities of the family. In order to bear the brunt of this emancipation, the family itself must be emancipated. The nuclear family is first understood as prison-like, as interactions with the family, fraught with tension and discomfort, serve as a form of punishment. Towards the beginning of *Arrested Development*, we see various characters attempt to liberate themselves from the family in order to gain an illusory sense of freedom. Such acts are futile, however, as without a social foundation no existential emancipation for the self is possible.

Throughout the series the characters slowly discover that liberation *from* the family is an inevitably unsuccessful politico-existential strategy, while the liberation *of* the family is a dire necessity. Such liberation entails a reformulation of social consciousness, renewed familial ties based on empathy and shared-consciousness, and an unflagging commitment to finding individual fulfillment *through* each other rather than *against* each other. Thus familial community structures provide individuals the opportunity to liberate the self, rather than liberate individuals from the self. This existential opportunity is alternately successful and unsuccessful for various characters and the ambiguity in the show is itself reflective of the ambiguity of the self in society. The absurdity of this existential task calls not only for an analysis of Kafka's *The Trial* but also a consideration of several other works by the author in order to see how his protagonists and their subsequent legal and criminal proceeding mirror what the Bluths experience throughout *Arrested Development*.

The Bluths are a uniquely dysfunctional and obscenely wealthy family from Newport Beach, California that run the Bluth Company, a real-estate development firm. The plot of the series features (among other things) the imprisonment and trial of George Sr., the family patriarch and CEO of the Bluth Company. For much of *Arrested Development*, the viewer is under the unalterable impression that George Sr. is guilty. There is a lingering and unresolved question attached to this assertion though: guilty of what? This is never so clear. There are vague hints at some "creative accounting" and other dishonest business practices. The pilot episode asserts that the Securities and Exchange Commission has accused him of using the Bluth Company's funds "as his personal piggy bank" ("Pilot" 1:1). Once in prison, however, the corrupt business practices are overshadowed by what George Sr. himself calls "light treason." This treason plot is picked back up in later seasons, culminating with a trip to Iraq to see firsthand some of the model homes the Bluth Company built there under (the aforementioned treasonous) contract with Saddam Hussein.

Despite all his time in jail and several court appearances, George Sr. suspiciously never seems to be formally charged with his crimes. Nevertheless, the assurance of guilt is partly what makes *Arrested Development* such a comedic success. If George Sr. had been obviously innocent, it would have taken away much of levity from the show. It would have instead looked more like a crime drama, or even similar in tone to *The Trial* itself. However, if George Sr. were too obviously guilty, it also would not have been so humorous either. A guilty man in prison is too straightforward, so the show sought to walk the fine line between guilt and innocence. The guilt of the Bluth patriarch was ambiguous enough to provide the comedic tension needed to drive the show. The irresolvable nature of his situation was partly due to bureaucratic hang-ups, lawyerly missteps, and the running confusion about George Sr.'s guilt. The absurdity of so-called "light treason" symbolizes the overall comedic ambiguity of his situation.

Arrested Development's brilliance thus arises not only out of such common frustrations as fighting through bureaucracy and the difficulty in ascertaining guilt, but also out of its intentional obfuscation of the very concepts guilt and law. It calls into question what it means to be guilty and what it means for justice to be served. As Michael states in the episode "Exit Strategy" (3:12), "these guys will bend the law to enforce the law." The irrationality of law is obviously reflected in the incompetence of Barry Zuckerkorn. This is even more obvious when the family replaces Barry with the superficially lucid but equally nonsensical Bob Loblaw. The homonym with "blah blah blah" emphasizes this: "You don't need double talk. You need Bob Loblaw" ("Forget-Me-Now" 3:3).

Newport Beach Kafkaesque

The central argument here is that *Arrested Development* contains elements that can be referred to as *Kafkaesque*, particularly in that it has similarities to *The Trial*, one of Kafka's best-known and most revered works. Yet the term Kafkaesque is notoriously vague if left undefined, especially as it does not simply mean that something possess traits similar to the works of Kafka. There is a deeper, if more nuanced meaning relating to bureaucratic arbitrariness, perversions of justice, social alienation, and an often futile quest for existential meaning.

The term Kafkaesque has long since passed into public consciousness and is now used by the general populace as often as any other literary buzz-words such as *Orwellian* or *Shakespearian*. However, despite its popularity, its source, Kafka, is often sorely misunderstood and the term misused. An entry to understanding Kafkaesque comes from noted German scholar Harry Steinhauer, who describes Kafka's fiction as "a world seen through a distorting mirror" that captures "the anxiety, suffering, turmoil, the frustrated hope and longing that constitute the human condition" (391). Yet Kafkaesque does not simply connote individual frustrations, but immense and intimidating social and bureaucratic structures. The Kafkaesque has more to do with processes and less to do with individualistic hopes and longings. It is for that reason that the original German title of *The Trial* is *Der Prozess*, hinting at the importance of process and giving an aura of the inhuman and inevitable to the story. The human self is thus trapped in a system beyond understanding and frequently characterized by irrationality. It is for this very reason that Kafka is both a social critic taking on large incomprehensible systems like bureaucracy and the law (or *the Law*, as the capitalized word connotes the formality, authority, and generalized applicability of the concept) as well as an existentialist, charting our uncertain place in the intimidating cosmos. His fiction, Steinhauer notes, operates on three levels, as it portrays "a topsy-turvy world pervaded by anxiety and frustration: individual, social, and cosmic" (391). Rather than upholding goodness and coherence, Kafka is preoccupied with the precise opposite, noting that industrialism and bureaucratization often provide a mere illusion of order to an inherently orderless world. When faced with that realization, waking life becomes a "nightmare" and "irrationality, injustice, cruelty, and despair abound" (Steinhauer 391).

However, the central feature of Kafkaesque is ultimately guilt, where anxiety and frustration fuse with ideology, power, and bureaucracy. This toxic combination is guilt, and while this guilt is, as Steinhauer notes, individual, social, and cosmic, it also more explicitly existential and political. Though it may be often nightmarish and despairing, the idea that the Kafkaesque is inherently dark and dystopian is patently false, however. The Kafkaesque can just as faithfully be captured through comedy, particularly comedy that makes use of the absurd and bizarre aspects of contemporary life. *Arrested Development* is a paradigm of such absurd humor, and approaches the Kafkaesque from the vantage of satire. In a 2002 analysis of Orson Welles's film adaptation of *The Trial*, Jeffrey Adams argues that the Kafkaesque can more readily be understood as a "strange blend of nightmare absurdity and theatrical farce" (141). Adams specifically makes the case for understanding film noir in terms of the Kafkaesque, but in doing so he broadens the field for Kafkaesque: "The

Kafkaesque can be described as a structural code, a transferable set of stylistic and thematic elements that operates in, even infects other texts, not only in literature but in other artistic media as well" (143).

Adams's nuanced version of Kafkaesque opens it up to more diverse interpretations, including one that could easily mark *Arrested Development* as Kafkaesque. He insists that Kafka himself "tends more toward self-conscious irony and comedic playfulness" than the "imprecise and often self-important" imitators who attempt to employ Kafkaesque (143). Self-conscious irony and comedic playfulness are strikingly appropriate ways to describe *Arrested Development*. Furthermore, Adams sums up the plot of *The Trial* as "an innocent man traces a dangerous path through a twisted network of crime and betrayal, only to discover that [in a] well-known existentialist cliché, he has been the victim of an arbitrary fate" (153). Though it might be more comic than tragic or horrific, *Arrested Development* closely matches such a Kafkaesque description. Above all, notions of guilt and the bizarre and arbitrary machinations of powerful bureaucratic institutions of power are paramount in Kafkaesque.

Bluth Metamorphosis

The Kafkaesque nature of *Arrested Development* could alternately derive from some key similarities to Kafka's "The Metamorphosis." Like the novella, *Arrested Development* is preoccupied with a salesman trapped in a toxic household who finds himself at the beck and call of a domineering patriarch and an ungrateful family. Bernofsky argues that Gregor Samsa, the pathetic protagonist of "The Metamorphosis," is transformed into some sort of monstrous insect not by chance, but because he had already, as a man, become a verminous creature at heart. "Gregor is a salesman," she explains, "but what he's sold is himself: his own agency and dignity, making him a sellout through and through" (124).

Arrested Development too is full of sellouts: George Sr. sells out in dealing with the unjust Bush administration. Michael sells out in allowing his good will to be manipulated by his father (and, at times, the rest of the family). Gob sells out in numerous ways, like wasting family resources on his ailing career as a magician and betraying family members in myriad ways by prioritizing his own desires. Lindsay sells out by inevitably abandoning her many philanthropic and idealistic causes, as well as by being unfaithful to her husband. For his part, Tobias sells out through his self-denial and reckless pursuit of a stalled acting career even if it means his family is worse off for it.

Though "selling out" has much to do with social responsibility and existential authenticity, the phrase is not coincidentally rooted in economic terms. Both "The Metamorphosis" and *Arrested Development* are financial farces, tragicomic tales springing from money troubles. "The story is brutally comic in parts," insists Bernofsky, concurring with Adams's interpretation, "and never more so than at the moment when it is revealed that—despite the fact that Gregor has been living more or less as indentured servant to pay off his parents' ancient debts—in fact the family has plenty of money; not enough to allow them to stop working altogether, but a proper little nest egg" (125). This too encapsulates the Bluths, who bemoan their financial state but in reality could be economically secure if they managed to retain a modicum of restraint and tended more towards responsibility rather than focusing on inflating their egos and saving face. Bernofsky writes that "Kafka's tragicomic tale ... is very often hilariously funny," even as readers witness Gregor Samsa's slow and painful deterioration and, ultimately, death (125). Viewers similarly watch with glee and horror at the missteps of the notorious Bluth family.

Shame (a concept closely related to guilt) is a key component of the Kafkaesque, as Kafka's characters are frequently compelled into situations where they degrade and debase themselves in order to alleviate shame, but find themselves steeped in shame nonetheless. Money is a foundation for such shame, because an impossibly degrading and destructive economic system (such as capitalism) traffics in an economy of shame. The concerns of not being financially capable of survival is a motivating anxiety to earn more, but then the social pressure of attaining a certain class status drives further accumulation of wealth and anxiety. The potential for shame only rises as the highest socioeconomic classes desperately strive to maintain their lifestyle and status. The Bluths belong to that upper echelon, but in tune with the cyclical nature of capitalism and the recent economic collapse (notably associated with the housing industry, something the Bluths are all too familiar with), their reputation and wealth oscillates, and they experience the many varied gradations of the American class system. The Bluths' untenable lifestyle and bitter infighting exemplifies an American capitalist decadence that, Siren-like, begets inescapably alluring, yet ultimately disastrous, socioeconomic practices and behaviors. *The Trial* ends with Josef K. lamenting the despicable conditions of his execution, as he is always concerned with the social unacceptability of his guilt. The final line of the novel, as he is executed, is "it was as if the shame of it should outlive him" (165). And yet, *Arrested Development*, through satire, makes the Bluths shame instructive and enjoyable. As George Michael once quipped: "Sometimes shame can be fun" ("Exit Strategy" 3:12).

Deconstructing Guilt

In order to fully comprehend the similarities between *Arrested Development* and *The Trial*, it is necessary to examine the question of whether or not the central characters of each story (George Sr. and Josef K.) are guilty of their respective crimes. It is also necessary to question the very idea of guilt as it is traditionally understood. In doing so it becomes obvious that *Arrested Development* and *The Trial* share key similarities because they both deconstruct the notion guilt and the Law by virtue of their protagonists being simultaneously guilty and not guilty. Through this oddity they reveal that the Law—and the related bureaucracies that enforce it—are ultimately meaningless, despite the fact that they wield vast amounts of power that ingest the individual in its destructive bureaucratic metabolism. This is best illustrated by considering Josef K. and George Sr. separately and locating the similarities in each case.

The Trial is frequently read as the horrifying and tragic story of an innocent man who cannot escape a totalizing bureaucracy in which only injustice is served. Though the stream of conscious novel is not so straightforward as to be taken as a simple parable or moralizing tale, the main point of the story is nevertheless often understood very simplistically. The protagonist, the mysteriously named Josef K., is not only not guilty from the reader's perspective, but he is never even accused of a crime. This is obviously the height of injustice. Despite his initial claim of innocence, Josef K. ultimately admits his guilt and is executed. Although readers are not told why Josef K. confesses, it is a mistake to assume that he is not guilty. At the heart of this perplexity lies the false conclusion that being innocent is the same as being not guilty. Josef K. is *both* innocent and guilty. On the matter of whether or not he has committed a specific crime, he is undoubtedly innocent. Yet what is he guilty of? This is a complicated matter and traditional interpretations that deny Josef K.'s guilt deny Kafka the profound complexity of this novel. Ultimately it has more to do with Kafka's existential notion of guilt than a bourgeois preoccupation with committing particular crimes.

Though Josef K. is not entirely innocent, he admittedly appears wholly free from guilt at the beginning of the novel. In the opening sentence the narrator insists that "someone must have been telling lies about Josef K." for "he had done nothing wrong" (Kafka 1). Yet moments later, when Josef K. questions "And why am I under arrest?" the authorities reply, "That's something we're not allowed to tell you" (Kafka 2). Along the course of *The Trial*, Kafka painstakingly saps away Josef K.'s sense of guilt and innocence. He later confesses his guilt, but not out of some sense of formality or because he has been brainwashed (as Steinhauer suggests), at least not in a traditional sense. He is guilty simply because the law—or rather the Law, to indicate its singular and all-encompassing nature—deems him to be guilty. The Law operates on a tautology: It determines who is guilty and they are then guilty because the Law has judged them to be so. Josef K. does his best to fight against his (never disclosed) charges and wade his way through the protracted trial. Much like George Sr., he is assisted by inept lawyers that seem to do more harm than good. Josef K.'s lawyer, Huld, is even more pathetic than the Bluths' Barry Zuckerkorn. The Bluths, like Josef K., attempt to defend themselves in court, though their often-incompetent legal advisers routinely lead them astray, demonstrating the sprawling complexity and incomprehensibility of the Law.

Arrested Developments

While *The Trial* reveals the horror and grotesquery that lies at the boundaries of rational law (i.e. the Law), *Arrested Development* delights in it as farce. Furthermore, while *The Trial* begins with Josef K.'s presumed innocence and ultimate guilt, *Arrested Development* operates in the reverse. George Sr. is first presumed guilty but later revealed to be innocent. While this may position *Arrested Development* as more optimistic than *The Trial*, it is a mistake to accept such a superficial reading. *The Trial* and *Arrested Development* are both hopeful and despairing about the prospect of freedom from guilt. Max Brod declared that Kafka's work "is a mixture of nine elements of despair and one of hope" (Steinhauer 394). In this way we can comprehend a mixture of hope in despair, particularly the seemingly despairing ending of *Arrested Development*'s fourth season, which represented a marked change in tone for the show.

Despite the fact that *Arrested Development*'s fourth season ends somewhat myopically, leaving the Bluths unsettled and with an insecure future (both within the fictional world and for the series itself), it provides limitless opportunity for future hope that can ultimately overcome that despair. Brod also rhapsodized that Kafka's personality was "a mixture of hopelessness and constructive will" and in Kafka, "these two opposites did not cancel each other out but elevated each other into infinitely complicated structures" (Steinhauer 392). As Heinz Politzer states, "Kafka is the parabolical writer of helplessness, who poses desperate questions to which we are given no answers" (Steinhauer 394). *Arrested Development* similarly resists patronizing simplicity and encourages viewers to bask in their desperate helplessness so that they may understand their human condition. Ambiguity is thus treated as a virtue. Camus, recognizing this, once said of *The Trial*: "It is the fate and perhaps the greatness of his work that it offers every possibility but confirms none" (Steinhauer 395).

This ambiguity may be best exemplified in the episode "Beef Consommé" (1:13) when, more than halfway through the first season, George Sr. finally gets the chance to hear the charges against him. As always, it is unclear what exactly he is on trial for, but at this point the show has hinted at business corruption and treason, two choices that are so vastly different that they effectively disrupt any clear perception of guilt and depict the justice system as unpredictable. George Sr. may have taken advantage of his company financially or betrayed the country, or some combination of the two. It's hard to get a handle on guilt in such a scenario. They often discuss the upcoming court case, but they often fail to mention any specifics. When presented with a plea deal, everyone, including the lawyer, fails to read it.

When George Sr. actually has his arraignment hearing, the camera is suspiciously and conspicuously turned off. The mockumentary-style precludes directly viewing the hearing because, as the show implicitly suggests, the Law is never something that can be directly observed and comprehended. It exists outside the command of rationality. Nevertheless, from outside the courtroom, viewers can hear the charges being read. They are so numerous that even the incompetent lawyer Barry Zuckerkorn is taken aback. George Sr. himself, claims the narrator, has never heard his charges listed consecutively. Yet this list does not even include some of the main charges the show had hinted at, especially that "light treason" so casually mentioned earlier. George Sr., and all the Bluths, are guilty of so many things it is beyond comprehension. They, like Josef K., seem simultaneously very guilty and, in a way, not really guilty at all. George Sr. is, after all, eventually exonerated

It is in this sense that *Arrested Development* comes to resemble *The Trial* in that both critically explore crime and punishment with an aim of uncovering their social conditions and existential implications. These issues first appear within *Arrested Development* at the beginning of the series when it made to seem as if George Sr. is unquestionably guilty. This false clarity creates the conditions for future disillusionment. Take, for example, George Michael, grandson of the imprisoned George Sr. Imbued with a doe-like innocence, George Michael, upon visiting his grandfather in prison, comes to realize the ambiguity of guilt and justice. In this meeting, George Sr. vehemently asserts his innocence to his grandson, which causes George Michael to contemplate whether anybody can find themselves wrongfully imprisoned. The idea that the machinations of justice are so arbitrary is frightening to him. His father, Michael, comforts him by assuring him of George Sr.'s guilt: "I got news. He's guilty... Incredibly guilty" ("Visiting Ours" 1:5). It turns out that this self-assurance in the straightforward simplicity of guilt and innocence is severely misguided. Viewers discover by the end of the third season that the Bluth patriarch is in fact *not* guilty. At least not of the crimes he is formally accused of. Michael doesn't know that during the episode in which he assures his son of his own father's guilt—and the show's writers may not have yet worked that out either. George Sr.'s legal liminality may have served as a plot device for much of the series, but it eventually evolved into something much more profound and even Kafkaesque.

Complicating the guilt or innocence of George Sr. is not trivial. That is, it does more than just provide comedic tension during George Sr.'s prison experience and drive plots through a long multi-season story arc. Instead *Arrested Development* indicts us all for our own guilt, unsettling long-held complacent notions of crime and punishment. In doing so it uncovers deeper forms of crime and guilt that arise from political apathy and existential angst. As such, *Arrested Development* is, in its own comedic way, poignantly political and irreverently metaphysical. Through this the show lambasts the post–Cold War American cultural malaise from the military-industrial complex and the ideologies of so-called American exceptionalism, to the exploitative financiers of late capitalism. Our collective participation in such destructive behaviors and beliefs, or our apathetic tolerance of them, reveals contemporary life to be a Kafkaesque farce for the twenty-first century. It is through these macroscopic and collective issues that *Arrested Development* finds genuine crime and guilt. Once again George Sr. is a prime example. He is, as is suggested in the first season, supposedly guilty of dealing with Saddam Hussein by building homes in Iraq against American sanctions. However, in the final episodes of the third season it is revealed that the home building project was actually a covert mission carried out under the aegis of the CIA ("Exit Strategy" 3:12). Quite ironically, this "light treason" of dealing with Iraq was, in an unexpected way, an act of patriotism, as the Bluth Company carried out covert work for the U.S. government.

Yet while George Sr. is formally absolved of his legal guilt when the true nature of his work in Iraq is discovered, for viewers who are attuned to politics and foreign affairs, his collaboration with the U.S. government makes him even guiltier. The American invasion and occupation of Iraq (and Afghanistan) was, and remains, deeply unsettling as it was predicated upon faulty intelligence, malicious deceptions in the highest ranks of government, manipulation of the media, American business interests, and more. The entire so-called War on Terror has become deeply unpopular and, for many, symbolizes rash actions taken out of paranoia and ungrounded fears. Many of *Arrested Development*'s undeniably left-leaning viewers see American foreign policy in the early twenty-first century to be wholly disastrous, and even conservatives concede that the Iraq and Afghanistan invasions largely tarnished the legacy of George W. Bush and America's overseas reputation. No matter how viewers see it, it is clear that the show, which is unabashedly left of center on fiscal and social issues throughout the series, finds George Sr. guilty, even if the (fictional) courts cannot.

Throughout *Arrested Development*, while George Sr. fends off treason charges, the rest of the Bluth family can be seen habitually engaging in other crimes such as shoplifting, skimming profits, amateur drug dealing, breaking and entering, and illegally filing documents. Though such crimes are often petty and insignificant, they demonstrate a point as important as that of George Sr.'s story: the Law creates unsustainable and insurmountable expectations. Furthermore, following the Law is often immoral or politically inappropriate since the Law so often represents injustice itself. It is far more worthy to create your own ethical code based on common goodness and your own understanding of the good life. A humorous example of this is found in the one character that is largely free from guilt: Buster. The eternally innocent Buster is only free from crime because of his simplicity and naivety, not his moral rigor. He stands in direct opposition to Michael, the strongest and most independent Bluth. Attached to his mother in Oedipal fashion, Buster is not the Bluth viewers should aspire to emulate (not that viewers should emulate any Bluths). Nevertheless, Buster's prelapsarian purity is not enticing. His blank slate of moral and legal purity comes at the expense of authentic justice and goodness. Michael (at least in the first three seasons), in contrast to Buster, demonstrates that even the upstanding members of society inevitably make mistakes in their attempts to act honorably. George Michael, stumbling his way through young adulthood, exemplifies this inevitability throughout the fourth season. The increasingly complex web of lies he presents to his father, friends, cousin Maeby, and girlfriend Rebel Alley may be minor transgressions, but his misleading statements about the true nature of Fakeblock undoubtedly place him in legal jeopardy after he attracts so many investors for what is an unintentional scam.

Such counterproductive struggles for honesty and goodness demonstrate that if the road to hell is paved with good intentions, the road out of it comes with moral missteps, petty crime, and occasional betrayals. Regardless, adherence to the Law is often impossible and unrelated to the common good of *Arrested Development*'s characters. Adhering to the Law merely replicates the amusingly abusive "lessons" they try and teach each other through the dubious methods of the one-armed J. Walter Weatherman. It is not coincidence, then, that such lessons commonly backfire. Like the Law, the lessons represent a counter-productive and Kafkaesque authoritarian style of demanding obedience, rather than instilling morality or promoting goodness.

The fourth season doubles down on this farcical absurdity of law and, in particular, punishment. Though George Sr. is freed, his wife, Lucille, is on trial under the aegis of the little-understood maritime law. Maritime law, an obvious parody of regular law, is completely absurd. The corruption and commodification of law is evident as the trial is set in a nautically-themed chain seafood restaurant. Lucille is then punished by being sent to a resort-like prison where she stars in a reality TV series and engages in comically-overblown "gang" feuds. Tobias also runs afoul of the law, first for unwittingly engaging in copyright violations and then being mistakenly taken for a sexual predator. His sexual predations are caught on camera as part of a "To Catch a Predator" series. That both he and Lucille star as part of reality TV series illustrates the entertainment value invested in law, revealing it as pageantry in a culture focused more on profit rather than anything close to actual justice. Topping it off, Tobias and Lucille are reunited in a rehabilitation center where they are somehow allowed to throw a woefully overwrought garish musical. This pageantry is sufficient for their punishment. That it partners them with addicts and an exhausted pop star reveals that they are misfits from the Law.

Free at Last

Kafka's use of the Law dramatizes humanity's uncertain place in the universe and the search for meaning in what appears to be a meaningless cosmos. If there is no inherent meaning to existence, then the best that can be hoped for is structure, and systems or bureaucracies provide secure meaning, albeit at the expense of freedom. On the other hand, abandoning structures and bureaucracies provides an almost intolerable amount of freedom, something akin to nihilism. Humans are forever negotiating these two poles of authoritarian meaning and nihilistic meaninglessness. Yet what is truly frightening is when systems of structuration begin to display symptoms of creeping meaningless, and it is revealed that only through there being a structure as such can they derive meaning. The structure is revealed to be a façade, reveling sheer meaningless and cruel power. This is noticeable when, as in *The Trial*, a supposedly coherent and rational system becomes erratic and irrational, and those subjected to its whim are swept along into a cycle of fear, anxiety, and despair.

In such cases there are times when freedom—political or existential—is not even desired. Imprisonment carries its own appeal. In situations in which the state or authority persistently engages in institutionalized terrorism, imprisonment becomes enticing. This is found in both *The Trial* and *Arrested Development*. In these cases the authority has become so all-encompassing that it provides relief from itself. This is not only true in *The Trial*, but also in another famous dystopian novel, *Nineteen Eighty-Four*. Orwell's protagonist Winston Smith is so tortured and molested by "Big Brother" that, through his intensive reeducation, he comes to love it (311). The infantilized character has become a dependent of the authority, which was the authority's original goal. In *The Trial* and *Arrested Development*, the Law is also pervasive to a similar extent. It is abusive and that abuse, when internalized, creates dependence. The irrationality and abuse of the system is not contrary to its rationality, but rather inherent and entirely necessary.

Josef K. laments that "it is often better to be in chains than to be free" (Kafka 136). This is also true for George Sr., who spends much of his time in prison debating whether he wants to leave, and insists that he might just plead guilty to the charges (whatever they are). When he finally goes home under house arrest he finds his newfound "freedom" suffocating, so accustomed is he to the confines of prison ("Mr. F" 3:5). Meanwhile Gob finds himself in a similar scenario when he is imprisoned in Iraq. In a ploy to trick Gob into leading the CIA to the Iraqi Bluth model homes, his jailors constantly attempt to let him escape. Yet Gob always returns himself to his cell voluntarily ("Exit Strategy" 3:12).

Freedom is fickle for *The Trial* and *Arrested Development*. How does one gain a sense of genuine freedom when the weight of the Law is always looming? What is there to do when guilt is metaphysical and moral concept not easily shaken off? Perhaps Camus's "The Myth of Sisyphus" sheds light on the topic of freedom in an impossibly unfree condition. Camus describes Sisyphus as an absurd hero whose tragic fate is a cruel punishment for attempting to elude Death. He is condemned to eternally roll a rock to the top of a mountain, whereupon it always rolls back down and he is forced to repeat the task *ad infinitum*. Yet for Camus, Sisyphus is a hero, if an absurd one. His continuation of his fruitless task in the face of its meaninglessness and pointlessness is, paradoxically, what gives it meaning. Josef K.'s struggle against the Law, even though there is no chance of escaping its inevitability, makes him an aspiring absurd hero, even if he ultimately fails and caves to despair. The Bluths, charting their own farcical course through the delightfully ridiculous and tragically destructive neoliberal era, are equally absurd. Sisyphus's descent to the bottom of the mountain to collect his rock can be performed in sorrow, admits Camus, "but it can also take place in joy" (121). When performed in joy, the descent is "the hour of consciousness" and "he is superior to his fate" (121).

"There is no sun without shadow, and it is essential to know the night," remarks Camus (123). Viewers would do well to remind themselves of this when considering *Arrested Development*'s fourth season, which was largely considered to be much darker and pessimistic than the first three seasons. Peter Queck and Bhaskar Sunkara at *The Washington Post* go so far as to claim that the original three seasons were a "communist utopia, and season four ruined it." However, *Arrested Development*'s apparent myopia at the end of the fourth season may make it more Kafkaesque, and hopeful, than ever. Brod, after all, noted the elevating "mixture of hopelessness and constructive will" in Kafka (Steinhauer 392). *Arrested Development* shows signs of such a mixture. This supports an absurdist reading of the show, particularly the fourth season, which depicts the Bluths intensifying their painstaking task of constantly rolling their comedy rock back up the mountain. Despite his eternally futile laboring, Camus concludes that "one must imagine Sisyphus happy" (123). So too must one imagine the Bluths. That will be their ultimate freedom, even as they wend their way through the entertainingly byzantine legal system.

Family Love Michael

The quest for justice and the quest for meaning are the same in Kafka's bureaucratized and industrialized society. In a world that is "abandoned by God," as Lukács once described it, we look to other sources of authority for meaning (88). This leads to a misplaced faith in institutions of power and putative justice, such as the Law. However, the erratic and illogical nature of such institutions reveals a fundamental nihilism that generates anxiety. As Lukács writes, "the God-forsakenness of the world reveals itself as a lack of substance, as an irrational mixture of density and permeability" (90). Lukács possesses a keen Kafkaesque sensibility for the frustrating futility of modern life and the powerful institutions that evade easy identification yet still contain and thwart us. If a God-forsaken world is plagued by a "lack of substance," then it is secular institutions that must fill the void with their authority. This is what leads to the Kafkaesque, in which institutions attempt to exert power partly for the sake of maintaining authority but also partly to mask the anxious nothingness it shrouds. It is thus only through authority that a sense of meaning can be made. Yet if the Law is proven to be insufficient and abusive, we must look elsewhere. In the cases of Kafka and *Arrested Development*, community (sometimes realized as family) and the uncompromised self are what provide authentic meaning and freedom from metaphysical-moral guilt without leading to abuse of power.

Kafka and *Arrested Development* locate the family as both the root problem of their characters angst, as well as the key to their liberation. In Kafka, domineering patriarchal figures often drive young male characters to madness and despair, as in "The Metamorphosis" or "The Judgment." *Arrested Development* has similar issues with the patriarch, though it even further explores the complex feuding among many family members. In *The Trial*, Joseph K. is plagued by the lack of comradeship from his family or peers. As Josef K. learns, the accused are "forced to spend all their time, day and night, with their laws, and so they don't have the right feel for human relationships" (Kafka 86). Those surrounding him display "neither comradeship nor humaneness" during his trial (Kafka 96). This is because "there's nothing you can do as a group where the court's concerned," explains a character on trial much like Josef K., "so there's no sense of togetherness" (126). It is the Law that drives characters apart and forestalls community.

In *Arrested Development* it is also the Law that drives the family apart, when the fact is that they can only overcome the Law through togetherness. In the second season, the prosecution challenges Michael: "Come on, Bluth. What's it going to be? Your father or your freedom?" ("Sad Sack" 2:5). Family represents contradiction for the Bluths. It was family that had gotten them in trouble in the first place, and so the corrupt and self-interested Bluths were finally getting their due. Yet in order to achieve justice and find meaning, it is only family that can save them. Family, which represents community, is both a downfall and an opportunity for redemption. This contradiction is expressed through dysfunctionality. In this the Bluths stand in for a fractious and bitterly divided contemporary society, with countless social and political tensions preventing cohesion and harmony. The Bluths represent the diversity of American experience because they are a mess of genetic confusion, undisclosed adoptions, and even a little "light incest."

Family, understood as complexly as the Bluths' complicated family, offers freedom and prevents despair because the self is a social self. Kierkegaard described the self as a "relation" and the human being a "synthesis" (43). So too is the social self. What are the fundamental relations of the social self and what is the social human a synthesis of? It is a synthesis of individual and collective social desires that must be balanced, lest the social self fall into despair. The individual and the community must not destroy each other, but work in tandem. Only this will alleviate the guilt and shame associated with modern life. This is tragically demonstrated in the episode "Forget-Me-Now" (3:3) in which the Bluths attempt to give Michael a pleasant surprise but accidentally kidnap, concuss, and drug Michael's girlfriend. All this is so Michael will not be ashamed of his family, but of course, due to their missteps, he is. The banner they present to him at the impromptu party that follows says it all: "Family Love Michael." This simplicity is both urgent and naïve: family is crucial yet cannot be reduced to a party slogan.

The politics of the family are paramount in *Arrested Development*, and this ultimately comes to bear with regard to crime, punishment, guilt, and freedom. In *The Dialectic of Sex*, a seminal 1970 work of second-wave feminism, Shulamith Firestone outlines the contours of power, sexuality, gender identity, and the family in American society:

> Marx was on to something more profound than he knew when he observed that the family contained within itself in embryo all the antagonisms that later develop on a wide scale within the society and the state. For unless revolution uproots the basic social organization, the biological family—the vinculum through which the psychology of power can always be smuggled—the tapeworm of exploitation will never be annihilated [12].

The family unit is stifling, restrictive, and even incestuous. After watching four seasons of Bluth foibles and resurrections, what is needed is not freedom from the family, but freedom of the family as Firestone describes. The traditional family, rooted in the patriarchal, is hierarchal in nature and an institution of authoritarianism aligned with the Law. Family itself must be emancipated from its stifling bonds of infighting and self-centeredness and become about community, progress, and liberation. Michael Bluth's endless attempts to leave his family always end with him returning, precisely because he knows this.

Kafka was familiar with family problems, and not only in his fictions. In a letter to a friend Kafka wrote the following:

> I live in the midst of my family—the best, most loving people—more estranged than a stranger. In the last few years I have spoken on the average of less than twenty words per day with my mother; with my father I have hardly ever exchanged more than a greeting. With my married sisters and brothers-in-law I am not on speaking terms, though I feel no anger toward them. I lack all sense of synchronous living with my family [Steinhauer 392].

Ultimately, the goal must be synchronous living with family in nontraditional forms that espouse a progressive community that subverts the Law, rather than reifies it. The inability of Kafka and many of his characters to accomplish this speaks to Kafka's understanding of its dire necessity. That most of Kafka's relatives died in concentration camps—the horrifying historical embodiment of the tyranny of the Law—conveys the urgent need for community to contend with and overcome the Law.

Works Cited

Adams, Jeffrey. "Orson Welles's *The Trial*: Film Noir and the Kafkaesque." *College Literature* 29.3 (2002): 140–157. Print.

Bernofsky, Susan. "Afterword: The Death of a Salesman." *The Metamorphosis*. Franz Kafka, Trans. Susan Bernofsky. New York: W.W. Norton & Company, 2014. 119–125. Print.

Camus, Albert. *The Myth of Sisyphus and Other Essays*. New York: Vintage International, 1983. Print.

Firestone, Shulamith. *The Dialectic of Sex: The Case for Feminist Revolution*. New York: Farrar, Straus and Giroux, 2003. Print.

Kafka, Franz. *The Trial*. Trans. David Wyllie. New York: Dover, 2003. Print.

Kierkegaard, Søren. *The Sickness Unto Death*. Trans. Alastair Hannay. London: Penguin Group, 2004. Print.

Lukács, Georg. *The Theory of the Novel: A Historico-Philosophical Essay on the Forms of Great Epic Literature*. Trans. Anna Bostock. Cambridge: The MIT Press, 1971. Print.

Orwell, George. *Nineteen Eighty-Four*. New York: Everyman's Library, 1992.

Queck, Peter, and Bhaskar Sunkara. "'Arrested Development' Was a Communist Utopia and Season Four Ruined It." *Washington Post*. 28 May 2013. Web. 14 Mar. 2014 http://www.washingtonpost.com/blogs/wonkblog/wp/2013/05/28/arrested-development-was-a-communist-utopia-and-season-four-ruined-it/.

Steinhauer, Harry. "Franz Kafka: A World Built on a Lie." *The Antioch Review* 41.4 (1983): 390–408. Print.

IT'S NOT TV. IT'S
ARRESTED DEVELOPMENT.

"I swore I'd not go reality"
The Bluths Through the Lens of Genre

PATRICK ALASDAIR GILL

In "Out on a Limb" (2:11), Michael meets Sally Sitwell for brunch at Skip Church's Bistro, a place famous for one particular delicacy: the "Skip's Scramble," an omelet containing every item on the restaurant's menu. The show's narrator has one piece of advice to offer on this culinary challenge: "Don't order the Skip's Scramble." The implication is that any omelet containing all the ingredients of the other dishes listed on the menu will turn out to be neither satisfying nor particularly wholesome. You can, it seems, only mix so much and still come out with a palatable result.

While viewers of *Arrested Development* will hardly feel tempted to try such an overly rich culinary delicacy as Skip's Scramble, and are mercifully warned of its dangers by the show's narrator, they are at the same time indulging in a comparably rich hotchpotch of a televisual kind: the show itself. After all, rather than the usual multiple-camera sitcom format with canned laughter and stereotypical characters in predictable yet still entirely unlikely situations, *Arrested Development* features a highly unusual mixture of techniques and properties found in a host of different TV genres. Simply listing them would probably come close to exhausting the space available here (as well as readers of the present essay), but unlike in the case of Skip's Scramble, the importance of genre to this show depends on the specific way in which ingredients are combined. So it is the qualitative rather than the quantitative analysis of genre in *Arrested Development* that is at the heart of this essay.

197

Before engaging directly with Mitchell Hurwitz's creation, however, a few remarks on the relation between television and genre may be in order.

Anyone habitually watching TV in their leisure time may feel that an abstract discussion of the shows they watch is unlikely to make them any more interesting or relevant. Genre is commonly held to be a blunt instrument, a generalization unable to do justice to the tremendous variety of formats that make up modern television. What difference does it make which category a particular show is put into, what label it is given? This common notion is countered by the literary critic Alastair Fowler when he states that genre "is an instrument not of classification or prescription, but of meaning" (22). To Fowler, then, genre is not something that academics determine after the fact in order to write histories or postulate theories: the genre of any given literary text—and by extension of any product of artistic creation—is an active force in the creation of meaning on the part of its reader, listener, spectator, and so on. In fact, as Fowler goes on to state, genre forms "the basis of the conventions that make literary communication possible" (36). Aside from the general importance of genre for artistic communication, Fowler particularly emphasizes its dynamic nature. Any artistic artifact will "relate to existing genres—by conformity, variation, innovation, or antagonism" (23). And in doing so it will help to bring about a change within the genres it refers to. This change may be gradual, too slow to be observed in our contemporary culture (221), but with the benefit of hindsight we may be able to see it hard at work in both high art and popular entertainment. While genre can thus be seen as a framework central in deriving meaning from the enjoyment of any cultural artifact in general, it gains a more immediate and concrete significance within the context of American television. So great is the role played by genre in the world of American television that Laura Stempel Mumford calls the industry "uniquely genre-driven" (20). As she goes on to say:

> However malleable TV formats may seem, industry self-promotion and trade publications make it clear that programmers rely heavily on viewers' realization that specific programs belong to specific genres. Even industry discussions of programming innovations demonstrate the importance of a basic genre stability, and most new shows are designed to be immediately recognizable in terms of familiar existing genres, whether as traditional members or as new variations on them. This process is a self-perpetuating one: Programs that viewers find impossible to understand in familiar genre terms tend to be interpreted as mocking audience expectations—as indeed they are, since audiences have been led to expect that new programs will conform to old patterns [Mumford 20].

In shaping viewers' expectations of the television programs they see and in thus predefining viewers' reactions to these programs, genre seems to be eerily effective, even if its efficacy often goes unnoticed or unremarked (Fry 5–9). How *Arrested Development* engages with this potential of genre to establish, manipulate, and frustrate viewers' expectations will be discussed in the following.

Mockumentary

Those who caught the first few episodes of *Arrested Development* during its initial run in the winter of 2003–2004 would no doubt have been struck by its unconventional aesthetics, particularly in contrast to the more traditional-looking sitcoms that continued to populate network and cable programming at that time. What they witnessed was "a new kind of sitcom: one using a character narrator and an unlocked, hand-held camera, and one without a laugh track" (Hart-Gunn 14). In addition to its sparse use of lighting, it is the unsteady single camera and the voiceover narration that give *Arrested Development* its unique feel of semi-authenticity. The role of the narrator, who does indeed make himself conspicuous by means of a number of obtrusive references, is largely restricted to providing orientation and additional texture to the stories being played out in front of the audience. Switching as it does between an unusual number of settings, *Arrested Development* has a greater need than most other shows for a continuity announcer, which the role of the narrator provides. In addition, the documentary format in general, and the use of a narrator in particular, provides plenty of opportunities to fill viewers in with background knowledge.

Strange as it may seem, the mockumentary aspect in *Arrested Development* is played down rather than up. Camera equipment and microphone booms rarely enter the frame and against the general norm of the mockumentary genre (Savorelli 65) the fourth wall is hardly ever broken. Instead, the characters are simply shown behaving quite naturally with no particular awareness of the camera. Their narcissism, it is suggested, is all their own rather than a result of the presence of the camera. While it is likely the makers of *Arrested Development* could have produced some truly hilarious episodes intent on providing a scathing commentary on the reality TV craze, these episodes would have been less likely to engage viewers in characters' storylines. As a mere satire on the reality form, *Arrested Development* would certainly have had laughter on its side in the short run, but it would have been a much more one-dimensional affair. And while it clearly is a comedy program, *Arrested Development* has enough riding on the development and interrelationship of its characters to make it shy away from a merciless exploitation of the documentary form at the expense of character development.

Rather than using the outward trappings of the reality format for their own sake, then, *Arrested Development* actually turns things on their head by foregrounding the documentary aspects in exactly those situations where they can provide depth and substance—an additional dimension to what is already a fairly dense mixture, given the action being played out by the characters and the voiceover commentary. Cutting to home video footage of the Bluth boys growing up or to infomercial footage of George Sr. selling the Cornballer helps establish elaborate backgrounds in front of which the current lives of members of the Bluth family are played out. There certainly are those instances in which the sheer playfulness of adding a sign of supposed authenticity to proceedings outweighs the strict narrative need for background information. This is clearly the case when documents are shown on screen with their actual details such as names and telephone numbers blurred to preserve anonymity (even though the audience is very familiar indeed with the person in question) or when the audience is shown security camera footage of an illicit act perpetrated by one of the characters, as when George Sr. runs a red light in the stair car ("The One Where Michael Leaves" 2:1). The camera itself is even acknowledged (against common practice elsewhere on the show) when, for instance, it cuts to static as a result of a car accident ("My Mother, the Car" 1:7) and is covered by a hand when Kitty once again flashes Michael ("Spring Breakout" 2:17).

In all, though, these are the decorative trimmings of the documentary form that—for all its potential to create entertaining meta-references—is substantially used to give texture and depth to the characters in *Arrested Development*. Those may not necessarily be qualities immediately associated with the mockumentary or even with the sitcom format, but they certainly come into their own in television drama.

Drama

With regard to contemporary television, the term "drama" has come to occupy a space in between other designations: drama is not factual TV, it is not comedy, nor is it soap or telenovela. Depending on the direction one chooses to approach it from, drama is either a "macro-genre," as Savorelli has it (173), or it is simply an unmarked case, the mainstream genre that requires no further designation, since it fulfills average viewers' expectations of televisual storytelling to such a degree that no further explanation is required. Any attempt at defining drama more closely as a genre is complicated by developments over recent decades that have seen an increase in the inclusion of comedic elements into supposedly dramatic shows and vice versa. The inclusion of humor, then, can hardly be deemed a determining feature when it comes to distinguishing between drama and other genres.

There are other factors that lend themselves more readily to a definition or demarcation of the dramatic genre. Some, such as the common rule that drama episodes last "about forty minutes versus comedy's twenty" (Savorelli 173) predominantly concern extradiegetic factors, i.e. they do not immediately occur in and affect the storyworld. As such they are on the one hand useful for constituting categorical differences, on the other they may be deemed relatively superficial, not adequately concerned with the substance of the narratives themselves. One aspect in operation within a drama, particularly when compared with comedy, is a feeling of actual jeopardy. When, for instance, deputy communications director Sam Seaborn consorts with a prostitute in the pilot episode of *The West Wing* (1999–2006), there is a sense that this minor moral failing could have far-reaching consequences, endangering not only the career of Sam himself, but the credibility of the entire Bartlet administration. Conversely, when Homer once again causes trouble at the Springfield Nuclear Power Plant (as he does in "Homer Goes to College" [5:3], among other episodes) in *The Simpsons* (1989–present), any feeling of jeopardy on the part of the viewer is firmly held in check by generic conventions: *The Simpsons* is, after all, a comedy program, so we can rest assured that—very few exceptions aside—nothing bad of any lasting influence will happen.

With regard to the Bluths, the question of jeopardy is a complicated one, not as easily answered as on *The West Wing*, let alone *The Simpsons*. In some respects, the Bluths are constantly in danger of being permanently adversely affected by goings-on in the show, so that there is indeed a notional sense of jeopardy. After all, the entire show is based on the considerable downfall of George Sr., so the audience knows that things can indeed go badly for the family. And yet the sense of jeopardy on the part of the audience is held in check as the audience is prepared for the characters to take almost unlimited amounts of punishment without pity. This strange mixture of a feature that should be an integral part of a television drama (jeopardy) and one that is essential to the sitcom (strictly limited pity and a sense that nothing too awful will happen) is also reflected in another balancing act *Arrested Development* undertakes between dramatic and comedic storytelling. Complex narration has been the watchword for television shows espousing popular as well as critical acclaim since the beginning of the 21st century. By emphasizing aspects of serial narration (i.e., representing a long narration in continuous installments), over those of episodic closure (as in traditional procedural dramas, where one case is solved in every episode with little or no connection between episodes and/or seasons), television dramas have become more challenging viewing and have tended to differentiate themselves further from sitcoms, which have by and large stuck with the episodic format. As Mittell elaborates, though, *Arrested Development* is a sitcom only too happy to bridge this traditional divide:

> [C]omedies like ... *Arrested Development* use television's episodic form to under-cut conventional assumptions of returning to equilibrium and situational conti-nuity while embracing conditional seriality—some story lines do in fact continue, while others are never referred to again. *Arrested Development*, a more explicitly serialized comedy, subverts these conventions even more, as most episodes end with a "next week on [*sic*] *Arrested Development*" teaser, showing scenes continuing that episode's stories. However, regular viewers soon learn that future episodes will not show these scenes, nor will they have actually occurred within the ongoing storyworld (although in the second season the show varies this norm by allowing some of the teaser material to occur diegetically) [34].

As a "more explicitly serialized comedy," then, *Arrested Development* goes out of its way to shed some of the expectations associated with traditional comedy shows, instead embracing narrative strategies that have become increasingly central to TV dramas. In contrast to the gradual development of seriality in drama shows, however, it has taken on this new guise from a standing start, not really giving viewers time to acclimatize to new ideas of continuity and seriality, presenting a challenge to the viewer's ability to integrate this new treatment of the genre's rules. But while it clearly poses a challenge to viewers' habits and expectations, what this new treatment does is to allow for more complex storylines, more depth of character, and a more elaborate idea of the interdependency of characters' stories beyond the mere set-up of a punch line: "Rejecting the need for plot closure within every episode that typifies conventional episodic form, narrative complexity foregrounds ongoing stories across a range of genres" (Mittell 32). And the genre of which this level of narrative complexity and continuity beyond single episodes and even seasons is reminiscent is not the sitcom but rather the quality drama of recent decades. *Arrested Development* has thus been shown to feature a number of characteristics typical of television drama, even though they tend to be balanced with features typical of other genres to stop the show from permanently taking up residence in the domain of drama.

Sitcom

For all its tongue-in-cheek exploration of the reality angle and its unusual focus on serial storytelling, *Arrested Development* clearly belongs to the sitcom genre as it displays a number of crucial properties typical of the form, such as its relatively restricted episode length of 22 minutes (at least in its first three seasons). Lest in the absence of a laugh track the audience lose sight of this plain and simple fact of the show's genre designation, *Arrested Development* is sprinkled with other archetypal sitcom features. Take, for instance, the show's use of catchphrases and recurring jokes. So dominant a feature are they on the show that they have even spawned a dedicated web site, recurringdevelopments.com, on which recurring *Arrested Development* jokes are not only listed but indexed to give the specific episodes in which they occur.

Such recurring jokes in general and catchphrases in particular constitute a throwback to much earlier days of comedy, when catchphrases deployed in radio comedy "provided predictable recognition points for audiences ... as television moved away from stand-up towards situation-based comedy drama, catchphrases tended to be linked more with fictional characters than with real performers" (Ayto viii). While catchphrases thus originate from a need for recognition and familiarity, their conspicuous use in *Arrested Development* seems to go almost the opposite way: recurring lines are used so frequently and by such a wealth of characters that they become almost entirely unpredictable, and instead of being associated with a specific character, they appear to point at shared ways of thinking and communicating among the Bluths. It is interesting to note in this context that characters do not simply start out with a catchphrase or two but that the catchphrases used in the show gradually accrue, giving viewers a chance to first become familiar with the phenomenon before it is employed to maximum quantitative and qualitative effect over the course of four seasons. The stereotypical function of catchphrases on sitcoms is thus undermined by their concrete use on *Arrested Development*.

Another trait typical of the classic sitcom consists of the careful manipulation of individual characters' knowledge or insight in relation to the viewer's. The type of laughter engendered from a situation in which the audience knows more than a particular character is a staple of the traditional sitcom (although other forms of laughter exist). Where this occurs in *Arrested Development*, though, it is not a case of a momentary ignorance or a charming naivety on the part of the character in question: when viewers are given to understand that their knowledge is superior to that of a character, it is a permanent and categorical superiority. Any so-called "insight" gained by characters like Gob, Buster, Tobias, or Lindsay will not only come long after viewers have drawn their own conclusions, but even when it finally comes, it will still be a wrong-headed and entirely inadequate response to the problems facing the Bluths.

As has been pointed out in the discussion of *Arrested Development*'s relation to the form of television drama, the show features seemingly progressive story arcs often extending beyond the limits of a single episode or season, even. This may indeed be uncharacteristic of traditional sitcoms which have typically favored episodic storytelling. It must be said, though, that the very concept of serial narration is hardly best served by a television series whose very title implies stasis. Thus the ventures outlined in *Arrested Development* have a habit of turning back on themselves (though not necessarily within a single episode), creating a deep-seated sense of stasis and paralysis. Whatever they do, the Bluths can't seem to get anywhere.

In all, it can be said that *Arrested Development* is fairly selective in its use of traditional sitcom components. There are no punch lines requiring elaborate setups, just as there is no laugh track, since the show eschews the typical rhythms of the three-camera sitcom filmed in front of a live audience. Where *Arrested Development* decides to fulfill clichéd notions of the sitcom genre, however, it does so wholeheartedly, embracing supposedly outdated conventions such as catchphrases with such fervor that their original function and thus their utility within the sitcom genre is turned on its head.

Now that *Arrested Development*'s relation to the genre of the sitcom has been established, another concept expressed by the term "comedy" ought to be explored. This is "comedy" in the wider sense of a narrative featuring a certain shape of story arc in which the hero has to overcome various obstacles to emerge triumphant in the end (Frye 164). How do the story arcs of individual episodes and even entire seasons of *Arrested Development* relate to this concept of a comic mode? The traditional assumption on sitcoms is—as has been pointed out—that they tend toward episodic storytelling, i.e., narratives in which the original state of affairs is restored at the end of each episode. Once the original state of affairs that the Bluths are restored to at the ends of story arcs (which rarely happen to coincide with the length of exactly one episode) is considered, the concept of the comic mode of storytelling becomes doubtful. As the show's title indicates, *Arrested Development*—while filled with incidents and decisions on the small scale of its characters' individual lives—is primarily shaped by the concept of stasis on the bigger scale of the family's fortunes. Identifying a comic shape to its story arcs in the sense of virtue rewarded, difficulties overcome, and happy endings achieved thus becomes problematic. The very idea of normality restored holds no promise when that normality includes incarceration, "light treason" ("Let 'Em Eat Cake" 1:22) and allusions to potentially incestuous feelings (between, among others, George Michael and Maeby as well as Buster and Lucille).

Rather than the story arc traditionally described by texts composed within this tradition of comedy, it may perhaps be more useful to look at another defining feature of this comic mode: the position of the hero vis-à-vis society. It is here that Northrop Frye offers the useful distinction of "[t]he theme of the comic" as "incorporating a central character into [society]" (43) as opposed to the tragic mode, which revolves around "the exclusion of an individual on our own level from a social group to which he is trying to belong" (39). In that sense, Michael's comic attempts at reintegrating the Bluths (by means of business ventures and even a PR campaign) are constantly thwarted by other family members' actions. So dominant is this theme of exclusion that it can be discerned in every single one of the Bluths, from Gob's expulsion from the Magicians' Alliance to Tobias's hopeless quest to join the Blue Man Group. Pariahs all, they inhabit a space that, in terms of narrative modes, can perhaps best be described as post-tragic: after their fall, they are excluded from society and their attempts at reintegration are forever doomed to fail.

In this respect, then, *Arrested Development* is clearly not a comic story: It withholds success, reconciliation, and resolution based on a reintegration into society from its principal characters, even though it may at times appear to set them up for these things in the eyes of a traditional sitcom audience. After all, having plunged them deep into adversity at the start of a show that is clearly marketed as a sitcom and has the running time of a sitcom, *Arrested Development* would appear to provide the perfect springboard for characters to overcome difficulty, persevere, and win out in the end. Instead, it never allows its characters to achieve any lasting release from their predicaments, thus setting up its audience—just like its characters—for a series of frustrated expectations. In so doing, it also clearly frustrates viewers' expectations of the strict episodicity traditionally associated with the sitcom form.

Other Genres

As has been pointed out, *Arrested Development* benefits from a finely balanced mixture of television genres, from the aesthetics of reality TV to "the dual demands of serial and episodic pleasures" (Mittell 33) typically associated with drama and sitcom respectively. These structural foundations, which determine how the show functions as well as the expectations and assumptions with which first-time viewers encounter it, may be less obvious than their actual importance for the show might suggest. If they remain largely undetected by viewers, it is in no small part thanks to the many other, more open references that are made to diverse television formats throughout *Arrested Development*. There is a long list of fictional films and television programs that make an appearance on the show, from soap opera *El Amor Prohibido*, to home video collection *Boyfights*, to monster flick *Gangie*, courtroom show *Mock Trial with J. Reinhold* and documentary-within-the-documentary *Scandalmakers*. Where the influence of these goes beyond the mere meta-reference, it is, broadly speaking, in line with the use of comedy and drama as discussed above: viewer expectations may be raised by the inclusion of clues from a particular genre but in the end the Bluths' story will not have been advanced substantially. A fine example of this could be found in *El Amor Prohibido*, which introduces a note of the soap opera into the first season when first Michael and then Buster fall in love with Marta, Gob's girlfriend, who happens to be part of the cast of a Spanish-language soap. Having gone through all the confusion and confrontation imaginable in that particular televisual context, the three Bluth boys will in the end continue their lives largely unaffected by the character of Marta.

A similar inclusion of a familiar genre can be detected in season three, when Michael starts dating Englishwoman Rita and is repeatedly warned off her by a mysterious man (who is later revealed to be her uncle). Continuing over five episodes, this story arc—by means of musical clues, episode titles, and intradiegetic allusions—establishes ideas of secret agents and mysterious abbreviations, making the viewer wonder what great conspiracy Michael may have stumbled upon. Needless to say, though, the inclusion of Rita does not turn season three into a spy thriller.

In terms of meta-references in general, "*Arrested Development*'s winking acknowledgment of television techniques like product placement, stunt casting, and voice-over narration" (Mittell 35) are the viewers' constant companions. This includes (but is clearly not limited to) casting actors to play real-life versions of themselves, as, for instance, Andy Richter, Carl Weathers and Ron Howard all do; or to play fictional characters with explicit references to their best-remembered roles, as in the case of Henry Winkler and Scott Baio and *Happy Days* (1974–1984), or Charlize Theron and *Monster* (2003); nor does it stop short of unsubtly praising the qualities of consumer brands in cringe-inducing takes on product placement, as in Tobias's praise of Burger King in "Motherboy XXX" (2:13); or of having characters compare story arcs within the show with ones in other shows or formats only to be contradicted by the narrator, as when Tobias remarks: "If this were a Lifetime Moment of Truth movie, this would be our ad break," only for the narrator to respond: "But it wasn't" ("Motherboy XXX" 2:13). The list of occasionally obscure references and in-jokes is positively byzantine and adds greatly to the overall "rewatchability" (Mittell 31) of *Arrested Development*. In addition to this, the show also highlights the performative aspects of almost everything its characters do. From Lindsay wanting (but being unable) to cry to Gob's magic shows; from Steve Holt's constantly having to celebrate his own name to Lucille's hopeless efforts at winking; from Kitty's compulsive flashing to the appearance of Mrs. Featherbottom; from Maeby's fraudulent assumption of new identities to George Sr.'s fraudulent assumption of his twin brother's identity—the show constantly entertains viewers with ideas and failures of performance.

But there is a more serious function of these cameos, allusions, and minor transgressions: they all draw the viewer's attention to questions of the production and creation of seasons and episodes. Mittell suggests that "[a]s programs become established in their own complex conventions we also marvel at how far creators can push the boundaries of complexity, offering baroque variations on themes and norms" (35). By encouraging the audience to keep in mind extradiegetic as well as intradiegetic processes, the show creates a more complete viewing experience and makes viewers more critically aware of the product they are consuming. It also goes out of its way to establish and manipulate genre expectations and to flag the fact that questions of genre are being negotiated before the viewer's very eyes. The viewer is thus made aware that the first three seasons of *Arrested Development* achieve a fine balance between genres that incorporates the complexity, continuity, and in-depth characterization of a quality drama while at the same time making sure that despite a wealth of goings-on in the storyworld, the show's underlying concept of stasis (as expressed in its title) would not be threatened by any conclusive or decisive progression. This would make *Arrested Development* one of the most layered television narratives ever produced.

In terms of critical acclaim, the recipe underlying the first three seasons of *Arrested Development* was an unqualified success, and the influence of the show as a sitcom embracing genre blending and narrative complexity should not be underestimated. Obvious admirers and emulators like *30 Rock* (2006–2013) and *Parks and Recreation* (2009–2015) aside, the habit of serial storytelling, even in sitcoms, has become so ingrained that in the past decade few successful sitcoms have launched that have not at least tried to convince the audience that they were about extensive story arcs rather than purely episodic narration.

As "critically beloved" as it may have been, *Arrested Development* remained "ratings-challenged" (Mittell 29) and was finally canceled for its failure to find a large enough following (Hart-Gunn 17). *Arrested Development* had not managed to translate critical success into ratings success, and if it was ever to contemplate a comeback, it had to be assumed that it would need to go out of its way to find a new audience elsewhere.

Season Four

When Netflix announced the commissioning of season four of *Arrested Development*, fans of the original three seasons could be forgiven for having mixed feelings about this new venture. Surely, having failed to attract a sufficient audience once, the show would now be made compatible with traditional viewer expectations to such an extent that its dyed-in-the-wool fans, those in the know, could no longer enjoy it. *Arrested Development* would be stripped of its complexity and in-jokes in order to broaden its appeal. What else could its makers do? Traditional wisdom holds that in order to be successful, sitcoms need to "establish complicity with the audience and its knowledge frames" (Curtis 7). Surely this time around *Arrested Development* would try to meet its intended audience more than halfway.

The makers of the show were undeterred, however. They continued exactly where they had left off but this time—whether by necessity or design—went a whole lot further in deviating from genre norms. For one thing, the fourth season of *Arrested Development* varies in the length of its episodes. This once surefire way of establishing a show's genre credentials is thus under threat simply because without the need to fit into strictly defined slots in a broadcaster's schedule, episodes distributed by video on demand and/or subscription can be as long as they need to be to tell the story they are supposed to tell. Admittedly, the variation in season four episodes is relatively slight, stretching as they do from 28 to 37 minutes. But in this as in other aspects, the variations put into practice by *Arrested Development* will no doubt be taken up by creators of other shows.

Beyond the question of episode lengths, though, it needs to be asked where the show's fourth season can go if the effect achieved in seasons one through three of *Arrested Development* can be adumbrated as narrative complexity through a careful manipulation of genre expectation. After all, narrative complexity can only go so far, it seems: "*Arrested Development* expands the number of coinciding plots per episode, with often six or more story lines bouncing off one another, resulting in unlikely coincidences, twists, and ironic repercussions, some of which may not become evident until subsequent episodes or seasons" (Mittell 34). Simply adding to the quantity of storylines and the number of genres combined, negated, or simply spoofed, would not constitute a categorical change.

Instead of combining a number of extant genres in season four, the makers of *Arrested Development* have given the title of their show a new meaning while at the same time forging an entirely new approach to the writing of televisual storytelling. The basic strategy deployed here is that of "retelling the same story from multiple perspectives, often called the '*Rashomon* effect' after the landmark Kurosawa film" (Mittell 37). Throughout season four of *Arrested Development* the same series of events is recounted by different characters with very different (and perpetually evolving) takes on what constitutes the truth. This has been used to great effect in a number of sitcoms already, but always restricted to both a single episode and a limited cast. In season four of *Arrested Development*, this phenomenon extends over 15 episodes told from the limited viewpoints of nine different characters. It may indeed have been done out of the sheer necessity of agreeing on a shooting schedule with actors who were all otherwise engaged at the time, but it has resulted in a storyline that tells—layer upon layer—of the complex entanglements of a huge ensemble cast.

If genre is created not only by the makers of television but also by the habits and expectations of those who watch television, then season four of *Arrested Development* is an entirely new departure. A model of generic experimentation before, the show has now become not a variation on a theme but, for the time being, *sui generis*. Where other successful shows may have encouraged binge viewing by means of complex narratives interrupted by cliffhangers, season four of *Arrested Development* positively necessitates binge watching to be comprehended. This is also reflected by the form in which its episodes were made available simultaneously on Netflix. Where other complex narratives have rewarded a second viewing with the discovery of a detail originally overlooked or a new perspective gained through better knowledge of the story-world, as in a whole range of shows from *The Wire* (2002–2008) to *Lost* (2004–2010) and *Breaking Bad* (2008–2013), season four of *Arrested Development* presents itself to the first-time viewer with more than just the promise of rewatchability—it may well necessitate a second viewing.

Through its four seasons, *Arrested Development* has been one among a select few programs that have helped establish new forms of entertainment, and it is one of an even more select band of sitcoms to have done so. In its first incarnation it went against "[t]raditional industry logic" which said that "audiences lacked the weekly consistency to allow for serialized narratives" (Mittell 31), particularly in sitcoms, whose strength never lay in serial storytelling to begin with. It also challenged the primacy of "a basic genre stability" (Mumford

20) as well as the orthodoxy that "the audience and its knowledge frames" (Curtis 7) needed to be handled with particular caution by the sitcom genre. Having been a critical—though admittedly not a popular—success in the burgeoning age of complex serial narration in drama, it has helped to establish new variations on the sitcom genre which all foreground seriality.

In its second incarnation, the fourth season produced for Netflix rather than any broadcaster, *Arrested Development* has decided to look not at new ways of combining traditional genres but at the optimum way of adjusting the traditional content of complex narratives to the new ways in which content is transmitted and consumed today. On-demand services as well as sales of DVD box sets mean that binge watching is not only technically possible but can be actively encouraged by the nature of the content. The same goes for multiple viewings of the same content. That viewers' habits are formed gradually is a fact borne out by the very tenacity of genre stability outlined by Mumford above. As far as the development of television genres is concerned, *Arrested Development* has been ahead of the curve every step of the way. That has been both the secret of its critical success and the reason for its mixed reception among viewers.

Works Cited

Ayto, John. "Introduction." *The Oxford Dictionary of Catchphrases.* Ed. Anna Farkas. Oxford, New York: Oxford University Press, 2002. vii-ix. Print.
Curtis, Barry. "Aspects of Sitcom." *Television Sitcom.* BFI Dossier 17. Ed. Jim Cook. London: British Film Institute, 1982. 4–12. Print.
Fowler, Alastair. *Kinds of Literature: An Introduction to the Theory of Genres and Modes.* Oxford: Oxford University Press, 1982. Print.
Frye, Northrop. *Anatomy of Criticism: Four Essays.* Princeton: Princeton University Press, 1957. Print.
Hart-Gunn, Lesley. "*Arrested Development* and the Theatre of the Absurd." *Velox: Critical Approaches to Contemporary Film* 2:1 (2008). 14–20. Print.
Mittell, Jason. "Narrative Complexity in Contemporary American Television." *The Velvet Light Trap* 58 (2006). 29–40. Print.
Mumford, Laura Stempel. *Love and Ideology in the Afternoon: Soap Opera, Women, and Television Genre.* Bloomington: Indiana University Press, 1995. Print.
Savorelli, Antonio. *Beyond Sitcom: New Directions in American Television Comedy.* Jefferson: McFarland, 2010. Print.

Saving Our Bluths

Why the Smartest Comedy on Television Struggled to Find an Audience

Kristin M. Barton

To a significant degree, there seems to exist a disconnect in the twenty-first century between the television shows that viewers consume *en masse* and those shows that are generally regarded as paradigms of what the medium is capable of (and should be) producing. Take, for example, the 1970s, a decade that found critically applauded programming such as *M*A*S*H* (1972–1983) and the miniseries *Roots* (1977) dominating the Nielsen ratings. Compare this to the contemporary programming that has been dominant since the early 2000s: reality TV and serialized crime procedurals. This isn't to suggest that *Survivor* (2000–present) and *American Idol* (2002–present) aren't entertaining products, or that *CSI* (2000–present) and *NCIS* (2003–present) don't employ a talented group of writers, but these programs generally place an emphasis on style and spectacle rather than substance. Certainly, there exists programming that overcomes this divide, such as AMC's critically acclaimed series *Breaking Bad* (2008–2013), which drew in 10.28 million viewers for its series finale in September of 2013. As impressive as that number is, however, *Breaking Bad*'s popularity is put in perspective when compared to A&E's controversial reality series *Duck Dynasty* (2012–present), which, just a month prior in August 2013, had 11.77 million people tune in to its fourth season premiere, eclipsing *Breaking Bad*'s highest-rated episode by over a million viewers. This is all to suggest that while high-quality programming can and does perform

211

well on television, more often than not commercial success falls to more prominent and mainstream shows that carry broad appeal.

It was within this dichotomy of critical-versus-commercial success where *Arrested Development* seemed destined to be too smart for its own good. While not all critics loved the series when it premiered, virtually all recognized the high quality writing and nuanced storylines that made the show exceptional. Indeed, some critics cited the complicated storylines as the principal reason the show failed to appeal to them. Tim Goodman, columnist for the *San Francisco Chronicle*'s online sister-site *SFGate.com*, may have summed up *Arrested Development*'s tenuous situation best in 2003 when he wrote of the freshman series, "There's a reason so many of Fox's most daringly original series are now cancelled gems. Quirky is great, but broad is what sustains comedy on American television in 90 percent of the cases." Citing similarly innovative "cancelled gems" such as *Andy Richter Controls the Universe* (2002–2003), Goodman correctly foresaw the troubles that *Arrested Development* would have at Fox, a network which he describes as "an advertiser-supported channel beholden to the Nielsen numbers" (Goodman).

That's not to say that there weren't other networks initially interested in keeping *Arrested Development* on the air when Fox cancelled the series in 2006, but it appeared that every offer for the show's continuation carried with it stipulations that would inherently and irrevocably alter what made the series special in the first place. Following the show's cancellation, creator Mitchell Hurwitz received one such offer from Showtime to continue the series, but only if he could reduce the cost, which would translate to cutting at least some of the nine primary cast members. As Hurwitz states, "The Showtime offer, as it was presented to me, was half the money for half the show. I was not interested, at that point, in doing a smaller cast and a more simplified *Arrested Development*" (Evans).

But *Arrested Development*'s rabid fan support in the wake of its cancellation and its popularity on Netflix suggest that smart comedies *do* have a place on television. The question, then, becomes whom to blame for the untimely demise of the series: the audience that recognized the show's brilliance only after it was cancelled, the show itself for being too ambitious and not bending to industry standards, or the network that, by all appearances, failed to give the show the support it needed to succeed? The blame, to some degree, rests with all three. With that in mind, what follows is an examination of the ways in which these three primary stakeholders (the fans, the show itself, and Fox) helped make *Arrested Development* one of the most groundbreaking comedies of all time while simultaneously bringing about its premature cancellation.

The Fan Inside Me

> In the first three seasons, oftentimes the fans hated the shows when
> we put them out that night. Their first reaction was always, "Oh, I
> hate this one. Why Annyong? They've ruined the show." Then they
> would kind of grow to like it. Then they'd say, "I hate this now.
> Why'd they do this Motherboy thing? I hate it."
> —Mitchell Hurwitz (qtd. in Greene).

Fans can be a television show's most ardent supporters and its harshest
critics, often at the same time. In looking back today, it is unsurprising that
Arrested Development earned a dedicated and loyal fan following given the
way the series unfolded, but some viewers had initial difficulty in reconciling
the unusual approach to comedy. When *Entertainment Weekly* published the
article "Do You Hate a TV Show That Other People Love?" on their website
in 2010, a number of posts specifically cited *Arrested Development* in the comments section, including "Sarah" who said, "I've tried really hard to like
Arrested Development, but I just don't get it" and "MCS" who commented
that the show was "scattered" and "perplexingly odd" (Franich). These types
of comments were fairly indicative of other critical responses to the unusual
approach the series took in structuring television comedy, but as viewers
became more immersed in the lives of the Bluths and better attuned to the
unique style of storytelling, many came to appreciate the elements that they
originally disparaged. As Hurwitz himself confirms in the quote above, some
fans' early inclinations were to dislike elements of the show they didn't understand, only to come to appreciate them more fully once they could see how
these elements fit into the overall story. As the series progressed and DVDs
allowed for repeated viewings, appreciation for the series continued to increase
as viewers now began recognizing the level of sophistication that was woven
into the series' running jokes. In this way, *Arrested Development* presented
viewers with a sort of time-delayed comedy that didn't fully resound with audiences until they had time to properly reflect on the creativity and originality
of what they had seen and heard. While this may be extremely satisfying for
fans who stuck with the series, it served to disenfranchise those who lacked
the patience or willingness to allow the comedy to fully develop.

Some of *Arrested Development*'s difficulties in finding an audience may
have also stemmed from its early categorization as a "cult" series, a moniker
that has a tendency to discourage neophyte viewers or late-comers from watching. In its 2012 list of the "25 Best Cult TV Shows from the Past 25 Years,"
Entertainment Weekly included *Arrested Development* at #2 on the list, and
while the article never specifically indicates that the list is a ranking of the

shows, many of the more popular and well-known series like *Buffy the Vampire Slayer* (1997–2003) and *The X-Files* (1993–2002) appear at the beginning of the list while the more obscure shows such as *Wonder Showzen* (2005–2006) and *Popular* (1999–2001) appear near the bottom (Franich et al.). But the trouble that can arise from using the term "cult" in connection with a television series is that it has the potential to label the show as something that will appeal to a small and particular segment of the viewing population. Cult shows often bring to mind series such as *Doctor Who* (1963–1989, 2005–present) and *Dark Shadows* (1966–1971), which boast small but dedicated fandoms, and for which casual viewers are virtually non-existent. Because of the niche and genre-specific type of shows that are usually labeled as "cult," the stigma attached to being a fan of these shows is that it implies a level of "nerdiness" that many look to avoid, at least publicly.

However, renowned fandom scholar Matt Hills offers a different view on what "cult" means in this context. According to Hills, "cult" (and "cult fans") simply refers to a fandom that *"relates not to the intensity, social organization or semiotic/material productivity of the fandom concerned, but rather to its duration, especially in the absence of 'new' or official material in the originating medium"* (x; italics in original). In lay terms, this means that regular fans make the transition to "cult fans" once new content (i.e. episodes) is no longer forthcoming. Without new content, fandoms generally decline, and only the most dedicated and die-hard fans remain highly engaged with the property, usually to promote the show to new viewers and contribute to online ventures such as message boards or Facebook pages. But for a select number of media properties, including *Arrested Development*, these dedicated fans and their efforts to raise awareness sometimes succeed spectacularly, bringing forth a host of new fans who may not have known about the shows during their original television runs. Netflix's chief content officer Ted Sarandos acknowledged the impact fans were having, saying that the decision to bring back *Arrested Development* for a fourth season was at least partially based on the fact that, "Television cult fan bases typically get smaller and more intense. The *Arrested* fan base has gotten bigger and more intense" (Snierson 30). So while the "cult" label may have turned some viewers off, it also help revive the show via Netflix seven years later.

The Show "Blue" Itself

By now most people are aware of the numerous awards *Arrested Development* won during its initial three seasons on the Fox Network, many of which it earned due to the smart and intricate writing for which the show has become famous. But despite being hailed as a modern classic by fans and critics alike, the series was unable to garner an audience sizable enough to satisfy Fox. Dan Snierson, noting the challenges faced by the series, states that "*Arrested* filmed much of its 2003–06 run with the noose of cancellation slowly tightening around its neck" (30). Despite this uncertainty permeating every facet of the series, the show's writers increasingly raised the bar on the quality and sophistication of the show's humor, incorporating subtle background puns (such as the "Blendin" vehicles used by numerous government agencies throughout the series) and "labyrinthine meta-plots" (Snierson 29) that took weeks (or years) to pay off, a tactic that seems almost counterintuitive when the creators were desperately trying to retain and cultivate an audience in the present. With almost nothing to lose, breaking away from traditional sitcom tropes and audience expectations could hardly be viewed as a risky endeavor for the show. However, some saw this convention-defying approach as yet another detriment to the show's longevity. As *TV Guide*'s Michael Schneider observes, "for some reason, at least in broadcast primetime, 'smart' plus 'sophisticated' usually equals 'low-rated.'" The show's long-range comedic payoffs, it can be argued, alienated new viewers and served as a detriment to enticing casual viewers to give the show a chance. It appears that the broad comedy strokes of series like *The King of Queens* (1998–2007) may have a greater appeal for audience members looking for instant gratification in their comedy as compared to more cerebral and layered humor.

But fortunately for the show and its fans, this telescopic approach to humor and the diligence on the part of the viewers in allowing the jokes to develop were two of the factors that made the show's overlapping and elaborate storylines in the fourth season possible. While part of the decision to focus on individual characters in season four was the result of difficulties in scheduling the main cast and their limited availabilities, adopting an anthologized format was conceivable only as a result of the style of writing that had become a hallmark of the first three seasons. What had always worked so well for the series and had made it such a creative and unique television experience from the very beginning were the multiple storylines that crossed and intersected throughout not just each season, but the entire series. This style of writing emerged during Hurwitz's time as a writer on *The Golden Girls* (1985–1992), of which he notes, "When I was doing that show, I didn't think of myself as a hard joke writer," suggesting he intentionally avoided the standard broad-appeal punch line formula sitcoms had become (in)famous for (Robinson). He continues, "My style became more intricate storylines, callbacks to references earlier in the script, tying things together in unusual ways, all covering up what, at the time, I thought was a deficit at writing hard jokes."

As a result of this atypical approach to writing for sitcoms, one particular argument that is often levied against *Arrested Development* is that the multiple gags and inside jokes can only really be appreciated by long-time viewers. For example, when George Sr. confesses to Michael why he made Lucille the new president of the Bluth Company in the pilot episode, he claims it is because "you cannot arrest a husband and wife for the same crime" ("Pilot" 1:1). That scene originally aired in November of 2003, and almost ten years later, in May of 2013, a flashback during the show's fourth season references this bit of ill-advised legal counsel when a young Barry Zuckerkorn, fresh out of law school, brazenly states to George Sr. and Lucille, "you can't try a husband and wife for the same crime" ("Borderline Personalities" 4:2). During its initial run on Fox, some critics argued that this sort of long-term approach to comedy may pay off for dedicated fans of the series, but not the casual viewer just looking to be entertained or those considering picking up the show in mid-season. Despite giving the show a 10/10 rating, *IGN*'s Michael Drucker concedes that:

> It's hard to blame America for missing the boat with *Arrested Development*. It's a quirky show without a laugh track, precocious child, or quirky neighbor. There's no celebrity starring in the show and, on paper, a sitcom about a wealthy family dealing with their father's corrupt business sounds pretty dry. In fact, with its running jokes and self-referential humor, *Arrested Development* had the rare television problem of being too smart for its own good.

This certainly isn't to say that Hurwitz and the writers should feel responsible for the show's small audience; indeed, if anything, they deserve to be commended for deviating from the formulaic sitcom style of the time. What this does suggest, though, is that like other trailblazing shows before it, the public was unaware what it wanted (or needed) until someone showed it to them. As industrialist Henry Ford said, "If I had asked people what they wanted, they would have said faster horses." In this same way that Ford envisioned a better means of transportation, visionary sitcoms like *Seinfeld* (1989–1998) and *Arrested Development* broke through traditional expectations of what worked on television, surprising audiences and perhaps even catching them off guard. Extending Ford's adage, if asked what they wanted in a sitcom, viewers may very well have provided the structure for history's most popular sitcoms to date such as *All in the Family* (1971–1979), *The Cosby Show* (1984–1992) and *Home Improvement* (1991–1999). They likely would have indicated that a sitcom should be centered around a nuclear family, with a father who is a fallible but good-hearted breadwinner, a mother who serves as the emotional core of the family, and where each week emotionally-charged situations are diffused by the episode's end, thereby reestablishing the status quo in time to start it all over again the next week.

Arrested Development parodied these traditional expectations in the episode "S.O.B.s" (3:9), in which Michael hopes his family is becoming more "sympathetic and relatable" through Gob and Lindsay engaging in more traditional sitcom roles as a waiter and housewife. But as one might expect from the show, the narrator quickly shatters the illusion of the Bluths-*cum*-Cleavers (as well as the fourth wall) to supplicate "please tell your friends about this show" ("S.O.B.s" 3:9). In looking back now, it is clear that *Arrested Development* helped lay the groundwork for a new breed of television comedies, and as a result it serves as the model for original and cutting edge sitcoms. *The Guardian's* James Donaghy specifically cites *30 Rock* (2006–2013), *Archer* (2010–present), and *Community* (2009–present) as owing a debt to *Arrested Development* for paving the way for their particular brands of irreverent and quirky comedy.

Arrested Development's novel approach to creating narratives also stood opposed to decades of cyclical conditioning in which viewers had come to expect certain story elements from writers and writers had obliged them by spoon-feeding viewers the story elements they were expecting. Even as far back as the late 1970s, television scholars noted the repetitive and formulaic approach to serialized programming and argued its monotony was doing a disservice to both the viewers and the industry. As Todd Gitlin notes of this hegemonic approach to television, "This week-to-weekness ... obstructed the development of characters," further arguing that "Perry Mason was Perry Mason, once and for all; if you watched the reruns, you couldn't know from character or set whether you were watching the first or last [episode] in the series" (Gitlin 254). Decades after Gitlin's analysis, Brett Martin offers the same critique of mainstream programming, observing that "procedural franchises" like the *CSI* and *Law & Order* series were intentionally designed to feature "stand-alone episodes that could be easily rearranged and sold into syndication" (6). In these cases, character development, story arcs, and the verisimilitude of real life would only serve to hinder viewer enjoyment by making the shows more complicated than their hour-long windows would allow. The key to preventing this stagnation, as Martin sees it, is through the forward progress of storylines. Just as events in the real world rarely have tidy endings and continue to impact our future actions and decisions, so too should the events on television affect the characters in a substantive way. For a police officer to be shot or otherwise wounded in the line of duty, only to appear in the next episode with a "business as usual" attitude, detracts from the realism those types of events would have on a person.

According to Steven Johnson, author of *Everything Bad Is Good for You*, this is exactly what television has been building towards since the 1980s. In looking at the evolution of television dramas, Johnson notes that older series such as *Dragnet* (1951–1959) were unwaveringly linear in their storytelling, rarely (if ever) allowing the action to abandon the lead characters. Then in the early 1980s with the debut of *Hill Street Blues* (1981–1987), a new approach to storytelling emerged that led to "multithreaded dramas" (Johnson 71) where individual characters and plotlines intersected as the stories warranted. This type of structure was based on the episode construction utilized by soap operas, with the key difference being that *Hill Street* combined "complex narrative structure with complex subject matter" (Johnson 68). So while this style may have dissuaded tracts of viewers from tuning it due to unusually complex narratives, it also served as a starting point for a new approach to televisual storytelling. And just as *Hill Street Blues* set the standard for more realistic dramas, *Arrested Development* should similarly be viewed as one of the pioneers in the current era of smart comedies, an era that defies the formulaic approach to story and structure. As Hurwitz laments, "*Everybody Loves Raymond* goes on for eight years with the same 'She doesn't like the wife,' and it's successful and that's what makes great TV," essentially giving audience members a story where they already know how it will end (Heisler). Revealing his preferred story structure, Hurwitz adds, "then there are shows like *The Sopranos* where you tune in because you have *no* idea what's going to happen."

This element of unpredictability that is embodied by *The Sopranos* and *Arrested Development* (as well as other shows that feature elaborate and interwoven storylines), requires what Martin calls "institutional memory" on the part of the writers, whereby everyone in the writers' room must be familiar with the series' storylines and evolution up to that point (30). Failure for any writer to remember or incorporate what another writer may have previously penned would almost assuredly result in plot holes or breaks in character development. This attention to detail and narrative complexity, to return to Johnson's argument, ultimately serves to enhance viewer enjoyment through requiring them to "earn" the enjoyment they receive. Or, from another perspective, it is not unlike those who stare at a particularly challenging Sudoku puzzle for an extended period of time only to have their consternation rewarded when the last box is successfully filled in. The payoff, in both cases, is usually worth the investment. To facilitate this institutional memory, more and more television series have come to rely on showrunners who map out the overarching season/series narratives and act as the guardians of storylines. If the director's vision of a story is what ultimately comes across in film, then it is the showrunner's vision that shapes television.

The drawback of this approach to television storytelling is that this idea of institutional memory is then required of the audience as well, who must also be aware of background, character development, and story evolution in order to fully appreciate each episode, as well as the series as a whole. Requiring that viewers pay careful attention can bring to mind classroom lectures in school, where students are compelled to take copious notes in order to ensure they don't miss something important they will need to know for a future test. In a similar way, viewers of complexly-written series such as *Arrested Development* or *The Sopranos* have learned that every detail, whether a passing glance or a seemingly trivial line of dialogue, can have a tremendous impact on the story. Perhaps nowhere in contemporary television was this better seen than on *Lost* (2004–2010), which intentionally included subtle references and foreshadowed events in order to specifically challenge viewers to remain vigilant in watching. For these shows to ask so much of their audiences—particularly when many viewers watch television for relaxation and escapism—requires that viewers seriously consider whether they are willing to invest their time and energy into a series. Communication scholar Wilbur Schramm identified this dilemma as it relates to media when he developed his "fraction of selection" concept in 1954, which proposes that we weigh our level of reward expected from media content against the effort required on the part of the consumer in obtaining that reward. This is all to say, then, that crafting complicated storylines is akin to a gamble on the part of these shows, ostensibly betting that the audience will see the long-term benefits of sticking with their complex storylines.

Ready, Aim, Cancel Me

> [Television] is an industry, it's a business. We exist to make money. We exist to put commercials on the air. The programming that is put on between those commercials is simply the bait we put in the mousetrap.
>
> —Ted Koppel (qtd. in Kurtz)

The preceding quote from news anchor Ted Koppel hits at the heart of the antagonism that often exists between fans and networks. Without question, television networks (as with all businesses) are designed to turn a profit. In the case of television, that profit is the result of advertising revenue that increases in proportion to the size of the viewing audience. To that end, catering to the demands of the audience and attempting to rehash tried-and-true premises seems the safer financial route than engaging in experimental television that has a greater potential to fail. To its credit, though, Fox has taken risks on shows that stand outside the mainstream of what one might traditionally expect from situation comedies. As Goodman notes, "That Fox keeps banging its head on the wall with all of these risky, aggressively challenging comedies is admirable." In addition to the aforementioned *Andy Richter Controls the Universe,* Fox has experienced various levels of success with many of its other innovative comedy programs, including *Ally McBeal* (1997–2002) and *Married ... with Children* (1987–1997). Even Fox's biggest moneymaker, *The Simpsons* (1989–present), was a risky endeavor when first proposed, given that it was developed from the crudely-drawn cartoon bumpers inserted in *The Tracy Ullman Show* (1987–1990) and that cartoons had been virtually nonexistent on primetime since *The Flintstones* (1960–1966). So to say that Fox is unwilling to gamble on avant-garde programming would be untrue, but at the same time the network also seems readily prepared to cancel a series with little hesitation. The fact that *Arrested Development* engendered such fervent fan support and found a home on Netflix after a seven-year hiatus clearly suggests that, had it been properly nurtured, it could have been tremendously lucrative for Fox.

It is worth mentioning that this is by no means the first time a cancelled Fox series has been brought back to life by rabid fan support. Joss Whedon's *Firefly* (2002) was maligned by the network, which aired many episodes out of order and preempted the series with baseball playoffs. The characters from the series were brought back three years later in the film *Serenity* (2005) following unexpectedly high DVD sales and fervent fan support for the series. *Family Guy* (1999–2002, 2005–present) was cancelled by Fox following its third season in 2002, but returned in 2005 as a result of DVD sales and the popularity of the reruns airing nightly on Cartoon Network's Adult Swim. *The Simpsons* creator Matt Groening's second primetime cartoon series *Futurama* (1999–2003, 2010–2013) aired on Fox from 1999 until 2003 when the network cancelled it. But once again, following a strong showing on Cartoon Network's Adult Swim programming block and four direct-to-DVD films that were released between 2008 and 2009, the series was back on television by 2010, this time with the show's final two seasons airing on Comedy Central. While each of these shows enjoyed a growing popularity in the times leading up to their cancellations, the relatively modest number of total viewers negated the passion of these small though highly-dedicated groups of fans.

But *Arrested Development* certainly isn't the only progressive sitcom to experience the critical-vs.-ratings dilemma. Other half-hour comedies that have gone for subtler, connective comedy have faced similar challenges. *Community*, *30 Rock*, *Parks and Recreation* (2009–2015), and *Happy Endings* (2011–2013) each danced on the razor's edge of cancellation more than once. Even the more successful comedies in this vein, such as CBS's *How I Met Your Mother* (2005–2014), which routinely featured flashbacks, time-jumps, and even occasionally broke the fourth wall, finished its first season outside of the Nielsen top 50, coming in behind epic programming failures such as Fox's solitary season of *Skating with Celebrities* (2006) (Goldblatt 30). And while *How I Met Your Mother* conforms to some standard sitcom tropes (The "will they/won't they" dynamic between Ted and Robin; Barney's multitude of catchphrases), it also rewards its longtime viewers with subtle jokes that casual viewers may miss, as well as season-spanning plotlines such as The Slap Bet that Marshal and Barney make in season two (2006), which is not fully paid off until the show's final season in 2014. What this suggests is that when given time to mature, innovative storytelling and authentic character development can be a profitable endeavor for networks. However, as Fox has repeatedly shown (again, referencing *Family Guy* and *Futurama*), it, like traditional sitcom audiences, appears to prefer instant gratification from its programming. In the end, shows that require time to mature initially earn smaller ratings during the critical time when networks must decide whether or not a series has the potential to draw in more viewers or if it will continue to pull in mediocre ratings.

For *Arrested Development*, surviving the first season did little to garner more support from the network, which increasingly frustrated the cast and crew. In one instance, following Charlize Theron's appearance on the show for a six-episode arc during the third season, Hurwitz remembers:

> It was a great fortune to have gotten this gorgeous, Academy Award-winning actress, Charlize Theron, to star in six episodes. You just don't get that on a weekly TV show, and certainly not one with low ratings like that. I was like, "OK, they aren't going to be able to ignore this." And they ignored it. There was not a single ad. I was so embarrassed for her [Greene].

To add insult to injury, as the show approached the end of the third season (with cancellation already determined), Fox decided to air the show's final four episodes opposite the opening ceremonies of the 2006 Winter Olympics, a strategy that assured smaller ratings and ran counter to every other network's strategy of airing reruns. Burning the remaining episodes off in this way seems to clearly indicate that Fox was ready to be out of the *Arrested Development* business.

The way the Fox network handled the series—both in terms of stifling the series' growth and failing to support the show via a strong advertising campaign—has led many to speculate that the network was in fact hoping that the series would do poorly in order to justify its cancellation. It is difficult to determine if the lack of support caused the low ratings, or if the low ratings caused the network to be less supportive, but regardless, *Arrested Development* finished the 2005–2006 season at #123 in the Nielsen Ratings, coming in just behind the Pamela Anderson-fronted sitcom *Stacked* (2005–2006) and WWE's *Friday Night Smackdown!* (1999–present), providing all the justification Fox needed for ending the series ("Nielsen Ratings"). But what many fans and critics would argue is that while ratings (and thus the bottom line) are obviously the primary factor in determining a show's continuation, engendering goodwill from the viewers may also pay off in the long run. As NPR columnist Linda Holmes wrote of NBC's decision to preserve struggling shows such as *Chuck* (2007–2012) and *Friday Night Lights* (2006–2011), it sometimes makes more sense for a network to keep underperforming-but-beloved shows in their lineups, as it buys them "a tiny, tiny measure of goodwill" from viewers. *Scrubs* (2001–2010) and *Cougar Town* (2009–2015) creator Bill Lawrence seems to agree with this assessment, further adding that having a "loyal, cultish audience" makes a show more appealing and valuable to the networks (Schneider). And Lawrence has some significant experience in this area: both of his shows were picked up by other networks after their original networks cancelled them (*Scrubs* was picked up by ABC after NBC cancelled it; *Cougar Town* was picked up by TBS after ABC cancelled it). What these examples illustrate—along with *Arrested Development*'s transition to Netflix—is that low ratings may not be as terminal for shows as they once were. There appears to have been more life left in *Arrested Development* than Fox realized, and as television increasingly expands to new platforms and digital programming gains wider acceptance, a well-liked show may be just what networks need to break through the clutter of the overwhelming amount of programming available. In the end, though, regardless of the reasons why Fox cancelled *Arrested Development*, it is safe to argue that the show has managed to find its place among the pantheon of exceptional shows, overcoming a reluctant audience, self-imposed hurdles, and an obstinate network to achieve the feat.

Works Cited

Donaghy, James. "*Arrested Development*: the Defining Sitcom of Our Times." *The Guardian*. 4 Oct. 2011. Web. 7 May 2014. http://www.theguardian.com/tv-and-radio/tvandradio blog/2011/oct/04/arrested-development-defining-sitcom.

Drucker, Michael. "*Arrested Development*—Season Three: The Critically-Acclaimed but Ratings-Deficient Show Comes to a Close with This Season Three Set." IGN.com. 11 Aug. 2006. Web. 9 May 2014. http://www.ign.com/articles/2006/08/11/arrested-development-season-three.

Evans, Bradford. "Mitch Hurwitz Explains Why 'Arrested Development' Didn't Jump to Showtime When Fox Canceled It in 2006." SplitSider.com. 10 Jan. 2013. Web. 2 Aug. 2013. http://splitsider.com/2013/01/mitch-hurwitz-explains-why-arrested-development-didnt-jump-to-showtime-when-fox-canceled-it-in-2006/.

Franich, Darren. "Do You HATE a TV Show That Other People Love?" *Entertainment Weekly*. 30 Nov. 2010. Web. 13 May 2014. http://popwatch.ew.com/2010/11/30/hate-tv-show-people-love-glee/.

_____, et al. "25 Best Cult TV Shows From the Past 25 Years." *Entertainment Weekly* 3 Aug. 2012: 36–43. Print.

Gitlin, Todd. "Prime Time Ideology: The Hegemonic Process in Television Entertainment." *Social Problems* 26.3 (1979): 251–266. Print.

Goldblatt, Henry. "The Mother of all Good-Byes." *Entertainment Weekly* 6 Sep. 2013: 26–37. Print.

Goodman, Tim. "Latest Fox Comedy 'Arrested Development' is So Funny It's Doomed." *SFGate*. 31 Oct. 2003. Web. 5 May 2014. http://www.sfgate.com/entertainment/article/Latest-Fox-comedy-Arrested-Development-is-so-2569032.php#page-1.

Greene, Andy. "*Arrested Development* Creator Mitch Hurwitz on His Two-Year Odyssey to Revive the Show." *Rolling Stone*. 20 May 2013. Web. 2 Aug. 2013. http://www.rollingstone.com/movies/news/arrested-development-creator-mitch-hurwitz-on-his-two-year-odyssey-to-revive-the-show-20130520.

Heisler, Steve. "Interview: Mitch Hurwitz." *The A.V. Club*. 5 Oct. 2010. Web. 1 Sep. 2013. http://www.avclub.com/articles/mitch-hurwitz,45886/.

Hills, Matt. *Fan Culture*. New York: Routledge, 2002.

Holmes, Linda. "Farewell to an Unlikely Hero: Why 'Chuck' Packed Such a Potent Punch." *NPR.org*. 27 Jan. 2012. Web. 13 May 2014. http://www.npr.org/blogs/monkeysee/2012/01/27/145986575/farewell-to-an-unlikely-hero-why-chuck-packed-such-a-potent-punch?sc=tw.

Johnson, Steven. *Everything Bad Is Good for You*. New York, Riverhead Books: 2005. Print.

Kurtz, Howard. "His Night in the Sun." *The Washington Post*. 8 Nov. 2005. Web. 6 May 2014. http://www.washingtonpost.com/wp-dyn/content/article/2005/11/07/AR2005110701686.html.

Martin, Brett. *Difficult Men: Behind the Scenes of a Creative Revolution*. New York: Penguin: 2013. Print.

"Nielsen Ratings for the 2005–06 Season." TV.com. 28 May 2006. Web. 13 May 2014. http://www.tv.com/shows/alias/forums/nielsen-ratings-for-2005-06-season-90-2534-252664/.

Robinson, Tasha. "Interview: Mitchell Hurwitz." *The A.V. Club*. 9 Feb. 2005. Web. 1 Sept. 2013. http://www.avclub.com/articles/mitchell-hurwitz,13913/.

Schneider, Michael. "With So Many on the Bubble, Can Smart Comedies Survive?" TVGuide.com. 1 Mar. 2012. Web. 14 May 2014. http://www.tvguide.com/News/Smart-Comedies-Survive-1044281.aspx.

Schramm, Wilbur. "How Communication Works." *The Process and Effects of Communication*. Ed. Wilbur Schramm. Urbana: University of Illinois Press, 1954. 3–26. Print.

Snierson, Dan. "The Moment of Bluth." *Entertainment Weekly* 1257. (2013). 26–34. Print.

"Chalk one up for the Internet: It Has Killed *Arrested Development*"

The Series' Revival, Binge Watching and Fan/Critic Antagonism

MICHAEL GRAVES

Airing from 2003 to 2006, *Arrested Development*'s run on Fox preceded both the advent of Twitter and Netflix's streaming service, technologies enabling viewers to, alternately, discuss and "binge-watch" television series. Yet, these technologies are now inextricably linked to the series, since *Arrested Development*'s revival on Netflix was made possible, at least in part, by a vocal audience of cult fans and television critics who lobbied for the series' return on social media platforms such as Twitter. Given Twitter's role in the revival of *Arrested Development*, it is not surprising that fans and television critics took to the social media platform in the days following the launch of the fourth season on May 26, 2013. What is surprising, however, is the debate that was spurred regarding this new approach to content dissemination. The practice of binge watching (viewing many episodes in rapid succession) factored heavily into this debate, with the disparate groups arguing for the "correct" way to watch and evaluate the fourth season, all fifteen episodes of which were immediately made available through Netflix's streaming service. For instance, the "all-at-once possibility of online streaming" led *The New York Times*' Mike Hale to proclaim, "Chalk one up for the Internet: it has killed *Arrested Development*," a sentiment that drew the ire of Netflix chief content officer Ted

Sarandos (Hale). Hence, while new distribution channels provide additional outlets for cult television series and social media platforms offer the lure of participatory communication between all invested parties, these technologies also cultivate factional animosity. By focusing on the revival of *Arrested Development* as well as the debate stemming from the release of the series' fourth season on Netflix, we can see the power of cult audiences, the ways in which shifting distribution strategies foster new reception practices, and the discourses surrounding the return of the series.

The Revival of Arrested Development

Centering on the comedic travails of the dysfunctional Bluth family, the Fox sitcom *Arrested Development* premiered on November 2, 2003. Given the pedigree associated with the series' production company Imagine TV and the bidding war over the pilot that ensued between Fox and NBC, *Arrested Development* seemed poised for commercial success (Lotz). Yet, despite being lauded by critics and garnering six Emmys and one Golden Globe over its three-year run, the series struggled with low ratings. In fact, following the announcement of *Arrested Development's* first Emmy nominations in 2004, Hurwitz quipped, "An Emmy would be nice, but I'd settle for an audience" (Posner). However, this audience never materialized, and the sitcom finished its first season ranking as the 120th most watched program as well as the 88th most popular show among the desirable 18–49 demographic (ibid.). *Arrested Development* continued to underperform throughout its second and third seasons, and Fox ultimately canceled the series after the season three finale "Development Arrested" (3:13). In the wake of the series' cancellation, Showtime approached Hurwitz about bringing *Arrested Development* to the cable network. While suggesting that the series may return in an alternative form, Hurwitz declined to move *Arrested Development* to Showtime, noting "If there's a way to continue this in a form that's not weekly episodic series television, I'd be up for it" (Snierson). The alternative to weekly episodic television appeared to be a feature film, a strategy suggested by Ron Howard (playing himself) in the season three finale ("Development Arrested" 3:13). Although this "maybe a movie" approach seemed to many to be a long shot at the time, it was hardly unheard of since the similarly beloved-but-low-rated Fox series *Firefly* (2002) had recently found a second life via its motion picture follow-up, *Serenity* (2005).

It was the Internet—not a feature film—that would provide the alternative form suggested by Hurwitz. Writing after *Arrested Development's* cancellation, television scholar Amanda Lotz noted that the emergence of iTunes' content distribution could, in fact, open up alternative distribution channels for similarly beloved but canceled television series. In the years following *Arrested Development*'s cancellation, streaming services, such as Netflix, Hulu, and Amazon Instant Video, also began challenging the linear model of television programming by offering on-demand content. In a paper posted on the company's investor relation webpage in April 2013, Netflix CEO Reed Hastings argued that the linear model—even when coupled with DVRs—restricts audiences to watching programs at preordained times. As such, Hastings proclaimed, "The linear TV channel model is ripe for replacement" (Hastings). In the company's bid to supplant this linear programming model, Netflix released full seasons of their original television series *Hemlock Grove*, *Orange is the New Black*, and *House of Cards* simultaneously in 2012 and 2013, thereby providing audiences with greater control over their television viewing. Hence, the increasing availability of non-linear programming made possible through digital distribution is characteristic of what Chuck Tryon identifies as an emerging "on-demand culture" (1–2). In fact, *Arrested Development*'s popularity continued to grow in the years following the series' cancellation as individuals discovered the series on DVD and through online streaming services, formats that facilitated an appreciation of the sitcom's densely structured narrative, rapid-fire joke delivery, and subtle in-jokes.

Arrested Development's already impressive reputation also continued to improve in the years following its cancellation. *Time* magazine regarded the series as one of the hundred best television shows of all time (Poniewozik, "All-Time"), and *Entertainment Weekly* proclaimed, "Once in the history of time comes a sitcom like *Arrested Development*" (Goldblatt). Coupled with this near-universal critical acclaim, a vocal, cult audience championed *Arrested Development* after Fox's cancellation. Fans sent artificial bananas—a reference to the Bluth family's frozen banana stand—to Fox's offices in a failed bid to have the series renewed (Barton 165). In addition, two *Arrested Development* fans produced *The Arrested Development Documentary Project*, a film that concludes with individuals pondering the sitcom's possible return to television. Such proselytizing by what Will Leitch regards as "the most persistent cult in popular culture" kept *Arrested Development* current in the popular culture imagination.

These efforts did not go unnoticed, and after a seven-year absence, *Arrested Development* returned for a fourth season on Netflix on May 26, 2013. Linking *Arrested Development*'s prestigious critical reputation, Netflix's non-linear programming model, and the sitcom's expanding fan base, Sarandos announced the series' revival in a press release, noting *"Arrested Development* is now widely viewed as one of the top TV comedies of all time and Mitch Hurwitz is bringing it to Netflix in a brand new way, crafted for the on-demand generation that has come to discover the show in the years since it last appeared on TV" ("Netflix to Launch New Season"). Moreover, as a gesture of gratitude for their steadfast adoration and outreach, Hurwitz penned a handwritten letter to *Arrested Development* fans and posted it on the show's Facebook page (May 26, 2013), thanking them for helping to bring about the series' revival and proclaiming that *Arrested Development* "is yours now." However, whereas a similar effort to revive the canceled cult television series *Veronica Mars* (2004–2007) through a crowdfunded movie was described by *Los Angeles Times* television critic Robert Lloyd as "a way paved with love," *Arrested Development*'s fourth season was received with significant acrimony. Although the simultaneous release of all fifteen episodes of the series' fourth season on Netflix should have marked a time for celebration by *Arrested Development*'s fans and critics—two groups united in their adoration of the sitcom—quite the opposite occurred. These factions used Twitter to engage in an often-heated discourse centering on the evaluation of the series' fourth season, with the practice of binge-watching factoring heavily into this discourse.

Binge-watching

Although used within discourses of television fandom since the late 1990s, "binge-watching" entered the mainstream lexicon in 2013, making Oxford Dictionaries' "Word of the Year Shortlist" ("Oxford Dictionaries Word of the Year 2013"). Defined as "to watch multiple episodes of a television program in rapid succession, typically by means of DVDs or digital streaming," the practice of binge-watching became more commonplace with the advent of online streaming services (ibid.). For instance, a 2013 survey conducted by Harris Interactive on behalf of Netflix found that 61 percent of those surveyed regularly binge-watched (Danner). The Harris Interactive study also offered a more robust definition of binge-watching, with 73 percent of survey respondents defining a binge as viewing "between 2–6 episodes of the same TV show in one sitting" (Stenovec).

Despite findings by Harris Interactive indicating viewers' overwhelmingly "positive feelings" toward viewing multiple episodes in quick succession, a negative association with binging content persists (ibid.). *The Atlantic*'s Nolan Feeney, for example, crafted a definition of binge-watching, linking the consumption of multiple episodes with feelings of guilt. For Feeney, binge-watching is "to watch at least four episodes of a television program, typically a drama in one sitting... through an on-demand service or DVDs, often at the expense of other perceived responsibilities in a way that can cause guilt." Grant McCracken, a cultural anthropologist who worked with Harris Interactive on the study, opposes this negative perception of binge-watching. "Binge-watching is not reckless or indulgent," McCracken argues, "It's a smart and even contemplative way to watch certain kinds of TV. Good TV especially" (Stetler, "Netflix Finds Plenty of Binge Watching"). Robert J. Thompson similarly links binge-watching with "quality TV," a style of contemporary American television programming characterized by literary and cinematic aspirations, narrative complexity, and serialized mythologies (Thompson xix). Thompson maintains that "the optimal way to watch *Breaking Bad, The Wire, Homeland,* or *Dexter* is the same way you'd read a novel—and you wouldn't read one chapter of *Moby Dick* per week" (Herbert). Hence, watching multiple episodes in quick succession effectively enables the viewer to draw connections between episodes and comprehend the nuances present in complex series.

In an effort to avoid the negative connotations associated with binge-drinking and binge-eating, some scholars and industry professionals use the term "marathon" in place of "binge-watching." Todd Yellin, Netflix Vice President of Discovery and Personalization, prefers describing a multiple-episode viewing sessions using this term as it "sounds more celebratory" than binge-watching (Jurgensen). Given that Netflix is inextricably linked with the viewing practice, the privileging of the lesser-used "marathon" over "binge-watching" is expected. Highlighting the company's embrace of binge-watching, Netflix's Sarandos notes, "Our own original series are created for multi-episodic viewing, linking up the content with new norms of viewer control for the first time" (Danner). Coupled with Netflix's simultaneous release strategy, the company's "Post-Play" feature further encourages the consumption of multiple episodes by both minimizing the credits at the conclusion of an episode and presenting viewers with the option to immediately watch the series' next episode. If a viewer does not select the next episode within the allotted time, Post-Play automatically plays the following episode. Hence, Netflix is engineering a "marathon" viewing experience—one facilitated by the company's delivery system and technologies—characterized by the consumption of multiple episodes.

The widespread prevalence of binge-watching is transforming television for producers as well. As John Jurgensen of the *Wall Street Journal* observes, the practice disrupts revenue streams tied to advertising and syndicated reruns

(Jurgensen). Phil King, president of programming and sports at CTV, Canada's largest privately owned network, fears the erosion of advertising revenues as the practice of binge-watching becomes more prevalent: "You only have so many hours in the day. And if you are watching commercial-free binge viewing you may not be watching the linear feed" (Wong). Yet, while the practice may weaken the traditional economic model, the binge-watching of a series' past seasons can also potentially lead to increased ratings for new seasons. For instance, the ratings for the premiere of the first of *Breaking Bad*'s (2008–2013) final eight episodes more than doubled the previous season's premiere (Wallenstein, "Netflix Flexes"). Given that the ratings for returning series often track in the opposite direction, *Breaking Bad*'s record-breaking premiere was something of an anomaly. Illustrating *Breaking Bad*'s aberrant ratings surge, *Time*'s Poniewozik likened a five-year-old television series receiving its highest ratings yet to an elderly runner posting his best marathon time ("'Breaking' Record"). Poniewozik proclaimed, "It may be too sweeping a statement to say this never happens, but: *this never happens*" (ibid.). *Variety*'s Andrew Wallenstein credited the availability of *Breaking Bad*'s past seasons on Netflix as the dominant factor affecting the series' atypical ratings resurgence ("Netflix Flexes"). *Breaking Bad* creator Vince Gilligan also attributed the longevity of his series to the advent of streaming services and the emergence of the "cultural creation of binge-watching" (Watercutter).

Binge-watching is also transforming the practice of television writing. In addition to crafting strong cliffhangers at the commercial breaks and conclusion of individual episodes, television writers now approach the creation of episodes and seasons with an awareness of audiences watching the series "in a giant inhalation," as *Breaking Bad*'s Gilligan notes (Jurgensen). This awareness on the part of television producers fosters a type of serialized storytelling that can be appreciated when viewed in multi-episode binges. Andrew Lenchewski, a producer of the USA Network series *Royal Pains* (2009–present), maintains, "Without question, the binging trend has put pressure on many shows to favor serialized story lines" (Gay). Thus, binge-watching fosters what Gilligan terms a "hyper-serialized" approach to television writing characterized by a longer form, complex serialized storytelling that can be appreciated when viewed in multi-episode binges (Jurgensen). However, binge-watching is not without its detractors, those who regard the practice as eroding television's structural integrity. *Slate*'s Jim Pagels, for instance, views binge-watching as a "pandemic" plaguing television, one that actually undermines the integrity of individual episodes and diminishes the power of cliffhangers, thereby fundamentally weakening "one of the defining features of television as a medium," the interplay between an episode's narrative arc and a season-long narrative arc.

It was into this shifting media landscape that *Arrested Development*'s fourth season premiered on Netflix. Prior to the release of season four, Hurwitz ruminated on the advent of streaming services and binge-watching. While observing that "this is a new media where you get to see all the episodes at once" (Stelter, "Bananas, Anyone?"), Hurwitz suggested that binge-watching also has its drawbacks. "A moment of reflection can be helpful when watching someone's creative work," Hurwitz noted, "I will get to the end of *Mad Men* and be forced to come up with my own English-major conclusions about what happened" (Jurgensen). Despite this reservation, Hurwitz crafted the series' fourth season with binging in mind, in a way that actually lent credence to Pagels' critique of producing television for an audience of binge-watchers. Instead of crafting narrative arcs for each individual episode, Hurwitz noted, "We're sort of driving into the next episode rather than wrapping things up" (ibid.). Hurwitz's approach to storytelling was influenced by Netflix's unique delivery system, admitting, "it's not the same kind of storytelling I think I would have told" had the episodes been released through another distributor (Topel). Hence, the fourth season of *Arrested Development* was the first of its kind, a season of television created specifically for binge-watching. Given the uniqueness of Hurwitz's approach, it is not surprising that *Arrested Development*'s fans and critics disagreed on the "correct" way to view the sitcom's fourth season.

The Fan/Critic Antagonism

All fifteen episodes of *Arrested Development*'s fourth season were made available at 3:01 a.m. Eastern time on May 26, 2013. As Netflix did not release any of the season's episodes in advance, television critics rushed to screen episodes of the fourth season in an effort to publish reviews appearing the following day (Stetler). *The New York Times*' Mike Hale was one such critic. Hale's review of the fourth season began "Chalk one up for the Internet: It has killed *Arrested Development*." While acknowledging that he only had time to "binge" eight of the season's episodes before his deadline, Hale found fault with an overlapping narrative structure that depicted similar events from multiple characters' points of view. In place of the chronological structure at work in the series' first three seasons—one that featured the series' large ensemble cast—the show's fourth season focused each episode on a different member of the Bluth family. As the season progresses, the show depicts key scenes over and over again, from the perspective of the respective episode's featured character, thereby providing additional layers of insight. Hale maintained that the show's "overly complicated" narrative approach privileged story over humor, concluding his review with the rather scathing proclamation: "It's hard to imagine being anything but disappointed with this new rendition." Hale was not alone in his assessment, as the sitcom's fourth season failed to satisfy many critics' high expectations. *The Wall Street Journal*'s Nathan Rabin, for instance, opined that the series was "reduced to doing [a] shaky imitation of itself."

Netflix and those involved in the production of the fourth season attempted to quell the torrent of negative reviews, countering that critics were, in effect, watching the series' fourth season incorrectly. Shortly after Hale published his review, Sarandos questioned the merit of critics evaluating the new iteration of *Arrested Development* before watching all fifteen episodes:

> If you're a critic in New York and you set your alarm for 3 o'clock in the morning, and you wake up and watch a half-hour of television and write a review, which is like the equivalent of writing a review of the first 10 minutes of a movie, *you're probably not going to have a great experience* [Wallenstein, "Netflix Chief," emphasis added].

Will Arnett, who plays Gob Bluth, also weighed in on the critical backlash. Referring to Hale's review, Arnett noted, "I think that's irresponsible. I think that you need to watch all the episodes" (Lederman). Yet, while encouraging fans and critics to reserve judgment until they have seen the entire season, Arnett cautioned fans not to binge-watch:

> *I urge people to watch them slowly* and really absorb all the material that's coming at them—[because] it's a lot and there are a lot of loose ends and pieces that connect—and really watch all the episodes and take a minute and think about what they've just watched, because nobody's ever done anything like it before [Lederman, emphasis added].

Hence, the discourse surrounding the reception of *Arrested Development*'s fourth season centered on two opposing views: those who panned the season either did not binge-watch enough episodes or binged too many episodes.

In the days following the release of *Arrested Development*'s fourth season, the series' fans and critics continued this discourse on Twitter. While the critical reception was mixed, fan assessment of the fourth season was decidedly more positive. As such, Twitter became the terrain on which the quality of *Arrested Development*'s fourth season was contentiously negotiated. Fans dismissed unfavorable reviews, arguing that Netflix's unique distribution model necessitated a new set of critical criteria. That is, whereas Hale argued that the "all-at-once possibility of online streaming" brought about *Arrested Development*'s demise, fans countered that Netflix's release strategy and the binge-watching mode of reception it encourages birthed a new form of storytelling. Given the perceived newness of the show's approach to the fourth season, fans disagreed on the "proper" way to view the episodes. In their defense of the sit-com's fourth season, for example, fans paradoxically argued both for and against binge-watching, as the following tweets display:

> @**NancyPrager**: I thought it was great, in 3–4 [episode] blocks. Unique story-telling method. Critics who binged missed out! Now when is the movie? [28 May 2013].
>
> @**BrokeBoredLazy**: There's a reason they were released like this. The criteria for judging the [episodes] shouldn't be the same as a weekly serial [26 May 2013].

While @NancyPrager insists that binging anything more than four episodes detracts from the season's "unique storytelling" experience, @BrokeBoredLazy suggests that watching the episodes in a more traditional, non-binge manner runs counter to the Netflix's simultaneous release strategy. Although fans of *Arrested Development* disagreed on how the series' fourth season should be viewed, there was consensus that these episodes should be evaluated according to a new paradigm.

While fans deemed critics as steadfastly opposed to change, some critics acknowledged that a shift in the status quo was, in fact, needed. With that said, the advocated shift centered less on how best to watch a simultaneously released season of television and more on the discourse surrounding such seasons. Jeff Jensen, *Entertainment Weekly*'s television critic, addressed the debate surrounding *Arrested Development*'s fourth season in a series of tweets:

> @**EWDocJensen**: I think we in media are still figuring out how to carry out a conversation with readers re: content dumps like AD4 and [House of Cards] [28 May 2013].
>
> @**EWDocJensen**: We would gain more by worrying about creating new models of conversation for new models of content delivery [28 May 2013].

Instead of binging and reviewing an entire season in one day, Jensen argued for an alternate, more delayed mode of reception and criticism, such as:

> @**EWDocJensen**: Waiting a week or longer to review. Or reviewing an [episode] a day [28 May 2013].

While conceptualizing a manner of discourse that might nullify the strong feelings evident in the days following the release of *Arrested Development*'s fourth season, Jensen still clings to a mode of conversation more aligned with a linear model of television. In other words, Jensen attempts to sidestep the thorny issues associated with watching, evaluating, and discussing a concur-rently distributed series by ignoring Netflix's non-linear release strategy. *Time*'s

Poniewozik concurred with Jensen and observed that the prior models of discourse tend to break down when the content discussed is a simultaneously released season of television:

> @**Poniewozik**: *Part of it, I think, is accepting you can't have the same kind of conversation as before—maybe more akin to discussing a book* [28 May 2013].

In addition to a problematic vagueness related to how a discussion of a novel differs from that of a television season, Poniewozik interestingly uses the same analogy previously offered by Thompson. Yet, whereas Thompson maintains that one reads a novel and watches a television season in one sitting, Poniewozik's assertion runs counter to that notion (Herbert). Nonetheless, Poniewozik appears hopeful that an alternate mode of discourse is possible, one in which simultaneously released content is reviewed and discussed over a prolonged period, as opposed to the currently dominant practice of binging and discussing content within a small time frame.

Other critics were less optimistic about the potential of shifting forms of discourse to alleviate the tension between disparate groups. For *Entertainment Weekly*'s Mark Harris, for instance, the antagonism was an unavoidable consequence of Netflix's release strategy. In the following exchange, Harris and a fan negotiate the ability to binge-watch an entire season with the value of doing so:

> @**MarkHarrisNYC**: *I would not enjoy the final seasons of Breaking Bad or Mad Men as much if AMC dumped all the [episodes] on me at once and said here, happy eating* [28 May 2013].
>
> @**RyanOneil**: *I'm not sure how your series of tweets isn't summed up, "I can't help myself"* [28 May 2013].
>
> @**MarkHarrisNYC**: *This isn't about being "forced" to binge. It's about how many people reshape their viewing habits to fit a [company's] delivery system* [28 May 2013].
>
> @**RyanOneil**: *The delivery system allows one to view how one wants, so those that are reshaping are doing so out of choice* [28 May 2013].
>
> @**MarkHarrisNYC**: *A choice heavily encouraged by social media and "I'm first!" culture that is often at the expense of the show & of viewer pleasure* [28 May 2013].

Hence, the lure of contributing to the social media conversation as well as the perceived power of being among the first to do so become the dominant factors privileging binge-watching. Nonetheless, Harris views the coupling of Netflix's distribution strategy with the prevalence of social media as detracting from one's viewing experience. In this way, the debate between fans and critics can be seen as a symptom of the "culture of complaint" fostered by social media— and not binge-watching itself (Rowe, Ruddock, and Hutchins 298–299).

Fans shared Harris' sentiment, arguing that the newness of the binged content was the cause of enflamed tensions on all sides of the divide. These fans believed that the optimal binge-watching condition occurred well after the release of the content and was therefore isolated from the ensuing social media conversation:

> @**KarenValby**: The great pleasure of a binge comes when undertaken alone, months or years away from chatter of crowd response [28 May 2013].
> @**Blankmon**: Binge-watching makes sense for a latecomer, but not sure why it would be good for fresh material [28 May 2013].

Thus, binge-watching does not inherently foster animosity; rather, the practice concentrates the conversation in the days immediately following the content's release, thereby magnifying the dissatisfaction and disdain arising on social media platforms. As produces, fans, and critics negotiate how best to implement, watch, and discuss simultaneous content releases, binge-watching will undoubtedly play a crucial role.

Conclusion

The release of *Arrested Development*'s fourth season on Netflix should have been a time for celebration among the sitcom's fans and critics, as both of these disparate groups championed the series during and after its run on Fox. The series' lofty reputation as well as the efforts of fans to keep *Arrested Development* in the zeitgeist factored significantly into Netflix's decision to revive the beloved series. And while backlash surrounding a heavily hyped media property is nothing new, what is unique about *Arrested Development*'s return is the ways in which the practice of binge-watching figured into the debate over the quality of the show itself. As exemplified by *Arrested Development*'s fourth season, Netflix's simultaneous release strategy encouraged binge-watching, which in turn, fostered a heated debate as the groups negotiate the "correct" way to view and discuss content distributed through a new delivery system. While new distribution channels provide additional outlets for cult television series and social media platforms offer the lure of participatory communication, these technologies will also likely continue to cultivate factional animosity.

Works Cited

Barton, Kristin M. "Chuck Versus the Advertiser: How Fan Activism and Footlong Subway Sandwiches Saved a Television Series." *Fan CULTure: Essays on Participatory Fandom in the 21st Century*. Eds. Kristin M. Barton and Jonathan Malcolm Lampley. Jefferson, NC: McFarland, 2014. 159–172. Print.

Danner, Meredith. "Netflix Survey Says 61 Percent of People Polled 'Binge-Watch' TV Regularly." Examiner.com. 15 Dec. 2013. Web. 17 Apr. 2014. http://www.examiner.com/article/netflix-survey-says-61-of-people-polled-binge-watch-tv-regularly.

Feeney, Nolan. "When, Exactly, Does Watching a Lot of Netflix Become a 'Binge'?" *The Atlantic*. 18 Feb. 2014. Web. 17 Apr. 2014. http://www.theatlantic.com/entertainment/archive/2014/02/when-exactly-does-watching-a-lot-of-netflix-become-a-binge/283844/.

Gay, Verne. "How Will Binge Watching Change TV?" *Newsday*. 3 Jul. 2013. Web. 17 Apr. 2014. http://www.newsday.com/entertainment/tv/how-will-binge-watching-change-tv-1.5619328.

Goldblatt, Henry. "Arrested Development." *Entertainment Weekly*. 14 Apr. 2005. Web. 16 Apr. 2014. http://www.ew.com/ew/article/0,,1046374,00.html.

Hale, Mike. "A Family Streamed Back to Life." *The New York Times*. 26 May 2013. Web. 17. Apr. 2014. http://www.nytimes.com/2013/05/27/arts/television/arrested-development-on-netflixcom.html?_r=0.

Hastings, Reed. "Netflix Long Term View." *Netflix*. 22 Jan. 2014. Web. 17 Apr. 2014. http://ir.netflix.com/long-term-view.cfm.

Herbert, Geoff. "'Arrested Development': Why Binge-Watching and Netflix 'Cheating' Aren't All Bad." Syracuse.com. 24 May 2013. Web. 17 Apr. 2014. http://www.syracuse.com/entertainment/index.ssf/2013/05/arrested_development_binge_watching_netflix_cheating.html.

Jurgensen, John. "Binge Viewing: TV's Lost Weekends." *The Wall Street Journal*. 13 Jul. 2012. Web. 17 Apr. 2014. http://online.wsj.com/news/articles/SB10001424052702303740704577521300806686174.

Lederman, Marsha. "What Will Arnett Thinks of the Negative Reviews for Arrested Development." *The Globe and Mail*. 14 Jun. 2013. Web. 17 Apr. 2014. http://www.theglobeandmail.com/arts/television/what-will-arnett-thinks-of-the-negative-reviews-for-arrested-development/article12568600/.

Leitch, Will. "The Persistent Cult of *Arrested Development*." *Vulture*. 12 May 2013. Web. 17 Apr. 2014. http://www.vulture.com/2013/05/arrested-developments-persistent-cult.html.

Lloyd, Robert. "'Veronica Mars' Lovers Kick Start New Path to Film in Hollywood." *Los Angeles Times*. 14 Mar. 2013. Web. 17 Apr. 2014. http://articles.latimes.com/2013/mar/14/entertainment/la-et-st-critics-notebook-veronica-mars-kickstarter-20130314.

Lotz, Amanda. *The Television Will Be Revolutionized*. New York: New York UP, 2007. Print.

"Netflix to Launch New Season of Arrested Development on May 26." *PR Newswire*. 4 Apr. 2013. Web. 17 Apr. 2014. http://www.prnewswire.com/news-releases/netflix-to-launch-new-season-of-arrested-development-on-may-26–201409981.html.

"Oxford Dictionaries Word of the Year 2013." *Oxford Dictionaries*. 19 Nov. 2013. Web. 17 Apr. 2014. http://blog.oxforddictionaries.com/press-releases/oxford-dictionaries-word-of-the-year-2013/.

Pagels, Jim. "Stop Binge-Watching TV." *Slate*. 9 Jul. 2012. Web. 17 Apr. 2014. http://www.slate.com/blogs/browbeat/2012/07/09/binge_watching_tv_why_you_need_to_stop_.html.

Poniewozik, James. "All-Time 100 TV Shows." *Time*. 5 Sep. 2007. Web. 17 Apr. 2014. http://entertainment.time.com/2007/09/06/the-100-best-tv-shows-of-all-time/.

_____. "'Breaking' Record: What Boosted Walter White's Ratings?" *Time*. 13 Aug. 2013. Web. 17 Apr. 2014. http://entertainment.time.com/2013/08/13/breaking-record-what-boosted-walter-whites-ratings/.

Posner, Ari. "Can This Man Save the Sitcom?" *The New York Times*. 1 Aug. 2004. Web. 17 Apr. 2014. http://www.nytimes.com/2004/08/01/arts/television-can-this-man-save-the-sitcom.html.

Rabin, Nathan. "'Arrested Development' Fourth Season Premiere: An Early Assessment." *The Wall Street Journal*. 26 May 2013. Web. 17 Apr. 2014. http://blogs.wsj.com/speakeasy/2013/05/26/arrested-development-season-four-episode-one-an-early-assessment/.

Rowe, David, Andy Ruddock, and Brett Hutchins. "Cultures of Complaint: Online Fan Message Boards and Networked Digital Media Sport Communities." *Convergence: The International Journal of Research into New Media Technologies* 16.3 (2010): 298–315. Print.

Snierson, Dan. "'Development' Hell." *Entertainment Weekly.* 31 Mar. 2006. Web. 17 Apr. 2014. http://www.ew.com/ew/article/0,,1178690,00.html.

Stelter, Brian. "Bananas, Anyone? The Bluths Are Back." *The New York Times.* 23 May 2013. Web. 17 Apr. 2014. http://www.nytimes.com/2013/05/26/business/media/arrested-dev elopment-returns-on-netflix.html.

_____. "Netflix finds plenty of binge watching, but little guilt." *CNN Money.* 13 Dec. 2013. Web. 27 Jan. 2015. http://money.cnn.com/2013/12/13/technology/netflix-binge/.

Stenovec, Timothy. "Don't Feel Bad, Everyone Binge-Watches Netflix, Says Netflix." *The Huffington Post.* 13 Dec. 2013. Web. 17 Apr. 2014. http://www.huffingtonpost.com/2013/12/13/binge-watching-netflix_n_4441059.html.

Thompson, Robert J. "Preface." *Quality TV: Contemporary American Television and Beyond.* Eds. Janet McCabe and Kim Akass. New York: I.B. Tauris, 2007. xvii-xx. Print.

Tryon, Chuck. *On-Demand Culture: Digital Delivery and the Future of Movies.* New Brunswick: Rutgers UP, 2013. Print.

Wallenstein, Andrew. "Netflix Chief Rips New York Times Over Negative 'Arrested Development' Review." *Variety.* 30 May 2013. Web. 17 Apr. 2014. http://variety.com/2013/digital/news/netflix-chief-rips-new-york-times-over-negative-arrested-development-review-1200489764/

_____. "Netflix Flexes New Muscle with 'Breaking Bad' Ratings Boom." *Variety.* 12 Aug. 2013. Web. 17 Apr. 2014. http://variety.com/2013/digital/news/netflix-flexes-new-muscle-with-breaking-bad-ratings-boom-1200577029/.

Watercutter, Angela. "*Breaking Bad* Creator Vince Gilligan on Why Binge-Watching Saved His Show." *Wired.* 4 Jun. 2013. Web. 17 Apr. 2014. http://www.wired.com/2013/06/break ing-bad-season-5-dvd/.

Wong, Tony. "Binge-Watching: The Rise of All-You-Can-Eat TV." *The Star.* 27 Dec. 2013. Web. 17 Apr. 2014. http://www.thestar.com/entertainment/television/2013/12/27/binge watching_the_rise_of_allyoucaneat_tv.html.

Appendix: Episode Guide

In putting this book together, it became apparent early on that there were some discrepancies regarding the order in which *Arrested Development*'s episodes were meant to be viewed. The problem arose from Fox's decision to air some of the episodes out of their intended order, causing confusion for a number of viewers. Subsequently, ancillary content distributors—specifically Netflix's streaming service—have retained Fox's original non-sequential order, causing even further confusion for viewers who have since watched the series primarily or exclusively on those platforms. To alleviate confusion and clarify the episode structure used throughout this book, below is the established order of episodes (as presented on the DVDs).

Season 1

	Episode Title	Original Air Date
1	"Pilot"	November 2, 2003
2	"Top Banana"	November 9, 2003
3	"Bringing Up Buster"	November 16, 2003
4	"Key Decisions"	November 23, 2003
5	"Visiting Ours"	December 7, 2003
6	"Charity Drive"	November 30, 2003
7	"My Mother, the Car"	December 21, 2003
8	"In God We Trust"	December 14, 2003
9	"Storming the Castle"	January 4, 2004
10	"Pier Pressure"	January 11, 2004
11	"Public Relations"	January 25, 2004
12	"Marta Complex"	February 8, 2004
13	"Beef Consommé"	February 15, 2004
14	"Shock and Aww"	March 7, 2004
15	"Staff Infection"	March 14, 2004
16	"Missing Kitty"	March 28, 2004
17	"Altar Egos"	March 17, 2004
18	"Justice Is Blind"	March 21, 2004
19	"Best Man for the Gob"	April 4, 2004
20	"Whistler's Mother"	April 11, 2004
21	"Not Without My Daughter"	April 25, 2004
22	"Let 'Em Eat Cake"	June 6, 2004

Season 2

	Episode Title	Original Air Date
1	"The One Where Michael Leaves"	November 7, 2004
2	"The One Where They Build a House"	November 14, 2004
3	"¡Amigos!"	November 21, 2004
4	"Good Grief"	December 5, 2004
5	"Sad Sack"	December 12, 200)
6	"Afternoon Delight"	December 19, 2004
7	"Switch Hitter"	January 16, 2005
8	"Queen for a Day"	January 23, 2005
9	"Burning Love"	January 30, 2005
10	"Ready, Aim, Marry Me"	February 13, 2005
11	"Out on a Limb"	March 6, 2005
12	"Hand to God"	March 6, 2005
13	"Motherboy XXX"	March 13, 2005
14	"The Immaculate Election"	March 20, 2005
15	"Sword of Destiny"	March 27, 2005
16	"Meat the Veals"	April 3, 2005
17	"Spring Breakout"	April 10, 2005
18	"Righteous Brothers"	April 17, 2005

Season 3

1	"The Cabin Show"	September 19, 2005
2	"For British Eyes Only"	September 26, 2005
3	"Forget-Me-Now"	October 3, 2005
4	"Notapusy"	November 7, 2005
5	"Mr. F"	November 7, 2005
6	"The Ocean Walker"	December 5, 2005
7	"Prison Break-In"	December 12, 2005
8	"Making a Stand"	December 19, 2005
9	"S.O.B.s"	January 2, 2006
10	"Fakin' It"	February 10, 2006
11	"Family Ties"	February 10, 2006
12	"Exit Strategy"	February 10, 2006
13	"Development Arrested"	February 10, 2006

Season 4

1	"Flight of the Phoenix"	May 26, 2013
2	"Borderline Personalities"	May 26, 2013
3	"Indian Takers"	May 26, 2013
4	"The B. Team"	May 26, 2013
5	"A New Start"	May 26, 2013
6	"Double Crossers"	May 26, 2013
7	"Colony Collapse"	May 26, 2013
8	"Red Hairing"	May 26, 2013
9	"Smashed"	May 26, 2013
10	"Queen B."	May 26, 2013
11	"A New Attitude"	May 26, 2013
12	"Señoritis"	May 26, 2013
13	"It Gets Better"	May 26, 2013
14	"Off the Hook"	May 26, 2013
15	"Blockheads"	May 26, 2013

About the Contributors

Kristin M. **Barton** received a Ph.D. from Florida State University and is an associate professor and chair of the Department of Communication at Dalton State College. His articles have appeared in the *Journal of Broadcasting & Electronic Media*, *Journal of Popular Television*, and *Communication Quarterly*, and he contributed essays to *Joss Whedon: The Complete Companion* (2012) and *Investigating* Heroes (2011). He wrote *The Big Damn Firefly & Serenity Trivia Book* (2012) and co-edited *Fan CULTure: Essays on Participatory Fandom in the 21st Century* (2013).

Edwin **Demper** is an instructor at Hunter College. He originally hails from the Netherlands, but has been based in New York City since 2007. He is completing his doctoral dissertation, which deals with the connections between literary modernism, aviation, and fascism. His research interests include transatlantic modernism, Caribbean literature, and literary theory.

Kristin N. **Denslow** is a doctoral candidate in English at the University of Florida and a lecturer in composition at the University of Wisconsin–Green Bay. Her dissertation studies the afterlives of Shakespeare's *Hamlet* in film, television, and media. Her research interests include Shakespeare and adaptation, early modern theater, and the intersection of adaptation studies, writing studies, and digital humanities.

Kristin M. **Distel** is a doctoral student at Ohio University, where she is researching modernist and postmodernist adaptations of eighteenth-century ideologies. She is the author of published or forthcoming articles and essays on a diverse range of topics, including the work of Toni Morrison, Edgar Allan Poe, Natasha Trethewey and Larry Levis, Phillis Wheatley and Mather Byles, and Theodore Roethke.

Jonah **Ford** studies the interdisciplinary relationship between culture, philosophy and theology, looking closely at the stories we tell and how we tell them. Drawing on the insights of philosophy of religion and cultural studies, he explores how these fields deepen our understanding of music, movies, and television. Much of his previous work has looked at inherited religious themes, motifs, characters, and concepts as they appear variously in popular culture.

Dustin **Freeley** is an independent writer and scholar who has been a lecturer in the English departments of Hunter College, the College of New Rochelle, and Berkeley College, where he taught various courses in film, literature, composition, research writing, critical analysis, speech, and persuasive communication. He is a member of the Online Film Critics Society, a contributing writer at NextProjection.com, and the co-founder and lead writer at MoviesAboutGladiators.com. He has previously published essays on *Breaking Bad* and *The Shining*.

Matthew **Gannon** received an M.A. from the University of Chicago. He is the co-founder of *The Vonnegut Review*, an online project dedicated to reviewing the novels of Kurt Vonnegut and revitalizing discussions of contemporary literature. His interests in comparative literature include Marxism, psychoanalysis, and critical theory. His graduate research employed Walter Benjamin's theoretical perspectives to examine Chicago's World's Fairs and Museum of Science and Industry. His work has appeared in the *Los Angeles Review of Books*, *Jacobin Magazine*, and *Salon*.

Patrick Alasdair **Gill** is a lecturer in the English literature and culture section of the Department of English and Linguistics at Johannes Gutenberg University Mainz in Germany, where he also received a Ph.D. His most recent work examines the history and theory of poetic ambiguity, with particular reference to the poetry of Dylan Thomas. He has published essays on twentieth-century poetry, contemporary drama, and British and American television culture and has been a visiting lecturer at the University of Edinburgh and Jagiellonian University, Krakow.

Michael **Graves** is an assistant professor in the Department of Communication and Sociology at the University of Central Missouri, and he spends his summers teaching for Duke University's Talent Identification Program. His research focuses primarily on the media industry's use of transmedia storytelling and participatory strategies to engage with audiences.

Elizabeth **Lowry** received a Ph.D. in rhetoric and composition from Arizona State University, where she lectures upon the same. Her research interests include nineteenth century feminism, historiography, sustainability, public spheres theory, material culture, and women's autobiographies. Her published work appears in the *Rhetoric Review*, *Aries*, *Word and Text*, and in edited collections.

Bethany Yates **Poston** teaches humanities in Plano, Texas. She holds a bachelor's degree in psychology from the University of Texas at Dallas, an M.A. in British and American literature from Texas Tech, and a Ph.D. in nineteenth century American gothic fiction from Texas Tech.

Crisman **Richards** produces and hosts *The Crisman Show,* a weekly radio show and web series documenting revolution through conversation, storytelling, and music. She has been producing live variety shows since 2003, most recently serving on staff at SF Sketchfest, the largest comedy festival in the United States. She and her husband, Graham, run a production company in the San Francisco Bay Area.

James **Rocha** is an assistant professor of philosophy and religious studies and women and gender studies at Louisiana State University. He has published on numerous topics, including philosophy of race, ethics, feminist philosophy, political philosophy, and philosophy and popular culture. He is working on a manuscript on the ethics of hooking up.

Navid **Sabet** is a Ph.D. candidate at the University of Canberra, Australia, where he teaches cultural studies and creative writing. He is a member of the Centre for Creative and Cultural Research at the University of Canberra, and is interested in the intersections of creative expression and other areas of academic inquiry, including cultural studies and human geography, as well as the ways in which the arts can explore issues like identity, empowerment, and disadvantage.

Joseph S. **Walker** received a doctorate in contemporary American literature from Purdue University and has written on authors such as Don DeLillo, Charles Portis and Paul Auster. His recent work has examined popular culture and television in essays on programs including *The Sopranos, Mystery Science Theater 3000, Veronica Mars,* and *Community*. He is also a member of the Mystery Writers of America, and his fiction has appeared in *Alfred Hitchcock's Mystery Magazine* and a number of other journals and anthologies.

Index